Cases in Retailing

Cases in Retailing

Operational Perspectives

Edited by Cathy Hart, Malcolm Kirkup, Diane Preston, Mohammed Rafiq, Paul Walley

BLACKWELL *Business*

First published 1997

Reprinted 1999

Blackwell Publishers Ltd
108 Cowley Road
Oxford OX4 1JF, UK

Blackwell Publishers Inc
350 Main Street
Malden, Massachusetts 02148, USA

British Library Cataloguing in Publication Data
A CIP catalogue record for this book is available from the British Library

Library of Congress Cataloging in Publication Data
Cases in retailing : operational perspectives / edited by Cathy Hart ...
[et al.].
    p. cm.
    Includes bibliographical references and index.
    ISBN 0–631–20173–4 (alk. paper)
    1. Retail trade—Great Britain—Management—Case studies.
  I. Hart, Cathy.
  HF5429.6.G7C37   1997
  658.8'7'00941—dc20   96–24660
                                  CIP

Typeset in 11/13 Plantin by Photoprint, Torquay, Devon
Printed and bound in Great Britain by MPG Books Ltd, Bodmin, Cornwall

This book is printed on acid-free paper

Contents

PART III Operations and Customer Service

PART IV Human Resource Management

Case Editors and Contributors

Editors

Cathy Hart, Sainsbury Retail Fellow, Loughborough University Business School, Ashby Road, Loughborough, Leicestershire LE11 3TU

Malcolm Kirkup, C&A Retail Fellow and Programme Director for the Retail Management Degree, Loughborough University Business School, Ashby Road, Loughborough, Leicestershire LE11 3TU

Dr Diane Preston, Lecturer in Human Resource Management, Loughborough University Business School, Ashby Road, Loughborough, Leicestershire LE11 3TU

Dr Mohammed Rafiq, Lecturer in Retailing, Loughborough University Business School, Ashby Road, Loughborough, Leicestershire LE11 3TU

Paul Walley, Lecturer in Operations Management, Warwick Business School, University of Warwick, Coventry CV4 7AL

Contributors

Professor Joshua Bamfield, Head of the School of Business, Nene College of Higher Education, Northampton NN2 7AL

James Bell, Lecturer in Retail Management, Department of Management Studies, University of Surrey, Guildford GU2 5XH

Dr David Bennison, Senior Lecturer, Department of Retailing and Marketing, The Manchester Metropolitan University, Aytoun Street, Manchester M1 3GH

Melanie Chetwood, Senior Lecturer, Department of Retailing and Marketing, The Manchester Metropolitan University, Aytoun Street, Manchester M1 3GH

Professor Gary Davies, Post Office Counters Ltd Professor of Retailing, Manchester Business School, Booth Street West, Manchester M15 6PD

John Davison, Supply Chain Specialist, Retail and Distribution Business, IBM (UK) Ltd, 76 Upper Ground, London SE1 9PZ

Tim Denison, Senior Consultant, Cranfield Marketing Planning Centre, Cranfield School of Management, Cranfield, Bedford MK43 OAL

Dr John Fernie, Director of the Institute for Retail Studies, University of Stirling, Stirling FK9 4LA

Daniel Ganly, Senior Lecturer in Retail Management, Bournemouth University, Poole, Dorset BH12 5BB

Keith Laity, Senior Lecturer, Department of Retailing and Marketing, The Manchester Metropolitan University, Aytoun Street, Manchester M1 3GH

Linda Moirano, Lecturer in Retail Management, Bournemouth University, Poole, Dorset BH12 5BB

John Pal, Senior Lecturer, Department of Retailing and Marketing, The Manchester Metropolitan University, Aytoun Street, Machester M1 3GH

Mike Pretious, Lecturer in Retailing and Marketing, School of Management, University of Abertay, Dundee, Old College, Bell Street, Dundee DD1 1HG

Sue Scouler-Davison, Retail Training and Development Controller, Safeway Stores plc, 6 Millington Road, Hayes, Middlesex UB3 4AY

Alison Smith, Director, Professional Programmes and Management Development, Management Development Centre, Loughborough University Business School, Rutland Hall, Ashby Road, Loughborough, Leicestershire LE11 3TU

Professor Leigh Sparks, Professor of Retail Studies and Dean of the Faculty of Management, University of Stirling, Stirling FK9 4LA

Stuart West, Partner, Stanford Consulting Network, Visiting Fellow, Oxford Brookes University Business School, Wheatley, Oxfordshire OX33 1HX

Maureen Whitehead, Senior Lecturer, Department of Retailing and Marketing, The Manchester Metropolitan University, Aytoun Street, Manchester M1 3GH

Foreword

I am delighted, as Director General of the British Retail Consortium (BRC), to have the opportunity to welcome the publication of these case studies, which give an up-to-date and realistic insight into current retail operations.

The BRC, as the organization which represents 90 per cent of all UK retailers, is concerned with both the present situation and the future trends and issues prevalent within the industry. Retailing has always been a provocative and vibrant industry, but now, alongside all other areas of economic activity, retailers have to manage increasingly rapid technological and organizational change, as well as increased customer demands.

Future retail managers will be required to develop the business against this increasingly complicated backdrop. The market place will demand that managers understand and recognize emergent trends and can address issues in a timely and appropriate manner. Some of these issues and trends will include: the impact of technology; the growth of consumer power; the requirement for product innovation; the demands of growth and sustainability which will be placed on retail planners; environmental issues; and the need to develop a flexible and adaptive workforce which can operate the extended shopping hours demanded by customers.

Retailers have always been great users of technology. The information revolution has been harnessed successfully by retailers, as can be seen by the increasingly sophisticated EFTPoS and EPoS systems employed in stores. Stock control, ordering and the entire distribution and the logistics part of the supply chain is dominated by the use of advanced technology. Increasingly, the data collected via EPoS systems are used to analyse and then interpret buying trends. These are then used to plan and develop specific segmentation and targeting policies by the marketers as well as customer loyalty schemes and promotions.

The growth of consumer power requires retailers to be both aware of and responsive to changing demands. Legislation on labelling and guarantees is an on-going requirement. More long-term issues are those around areas of sourcing: do suppliers use appropriate materials and working practices? Consumers also require that products which were formerly considered exotic or seasonal are now universally available.

Five to ten years ago, a retailer's decision was more or less confined to whether to operate in the High Street or out of town. However, future retail managers will be required to work in a much more complicated arena, where High Street redevelopment, large regional centres and out of town locations will all have their part to play.

Finally, retail is a people business: currently the industry employs 2.4 million people. Managing diversity will be the heart of retail managers' responsibilities, with different people, working different hours, satisfying a raft of different needs. The competitive advantage of a business will increasingly be delivered by its people. Companies wishing to maximize this differential will need managers with not only the technical skills of selling and merchandising but also the people skills to get the best out of their staff. Only well managed and motivated staff will deliver the high level of customer service necessary to make the business successful.

An examination of these issues demonstrates quite clearly the reasons why the BRC believes it is essential to attract high-calibre graduates to secure the continued success of British retailing. The retail environment is a dynamic and challenging environment and the case studies in this book reflect this. They are live issues and are intended to stimulate debate. The greatest benefit from this book will be derived by challenging and questioning both the situations and the solutions, a process which mirrors the problem solving and analytical skills required of retail managers.

James May
Director General of the British Retail Consortium

Preface

The 1980s were a period of rapid change for British retailing, seeing a major shift in focus from the High Street to out of town shopping, the emergence of a more sophisticated and demanding shopper and the general intensification of competition as many sectors reached maturity. The 1990s have turned out to be no less turbulent for retailers, witnessing the emergence of new retail formats and ever changing customer needs, behaviour and demographics. In addition, developments in information technology continue to have a dramatic impact on retail operations and management, and even threaten the existence of certain forms of retailing.

The major retail multiples have recognized that to cope with these dynamics, remain competitive and continue to grow, they need a higher calibre and more professional retail manager. For many retailers, store management teams are now responsible not only for recruiting and managing labour, customer service, stock ordering, replenishment and merchandising, but also for the marketing of their stores. Individual stores need the flexibility to respond dynamically to the needs of the local market, while still offering the same quality and reassurance of the company brand image. Head office functions have also developed to keep pace with the external environment and internal structural changes within the organization. The centralized marketing function has become more focused on customer loyalty and the retention of existing customers, as well as trying to attract new customers. The buying function has recognized the importance of supplier relationships in sustaining quality supplies. Retailing logistics has evolved from a distribution function into a competitive tool for reducing customer response times. All of these developments create additional challenges and opportunities for retail managers to apply their skills and competencies in both centralized operational management and store management. Indeed, it requires a new breed of retail manager.

Attracting the right quality of graduates into retail management has not been easy. 'Retail companies need the best and most talented graduates, people with personality, drive, imagination and the energy to succeed',[1] but often students do not perceive retailing as an attractive profession, citing long hours and low pay as reasons for this view. However, for those who can meet the challenge, today's retailing offers graduates a wide variety of opportunities, excellent remuneration, early responsibility and the potential for relatively rapid promotion. With growing demand for well qualified graduates, many retail multiples found that they shared a common problem of trying to promote retailing as an exciting career before they could attract graduates to apply to their company. Realizing that more effective results could be achieved through synergy, 12 employers who recruited graduates formed the Consortium of Retail Training Companies (CORTCO) in 1987. The CORTCO associate members now include Tesco, Safeway, Kingfisher, Marks and Spencer, CWS, John Lewis, Boots and Sainsbury's. The consortium is dedicated to raising the awareness of retailing as a career and, ultimately, to change the image of retailing. The CORTCO concept required member organizations to set aside their normal competitive rivalry and work together in pursuit of this common goal.

Initially, CORTCO targeted graduates, careers officers and the careers service to improve the awareness of retail careers. This was then extended to include higher education institutions and the teachers of business studies. Common projects were identified which would support a collective approach. At its heart was the provision of training, education and work experience opportunities for undergraduates. A further objective was to educate the careers advisors in higher education about the intellectual challenge of retail store management. This involved careers fairs and conferences for the advisors.

An important early objective was to raise the quality and quantity of retail teaching material in higher education in order to increase both the students' and the lecturers' insight into these companies.

The particular vehicle chosen was the case study method and, in January 1988, the first two-day case study conference was held at Stanford Hall, near Loughborough. Participants included career officers, academics from higher education institutions and retail managers. Further successful conferences followed but, by 1993, it was felt that the cases needed to cover a wider topic range and reach a wider audience; distribution and dissemination of the case study material had been previously limited to the conference delegates.

Coinciding with the growth of graduate opportunities in retailing, the number of retail degrees and retail modules on business degrees has flourished. There are now at least 12 institutions offering undergraduate retail degrees, and many more offering retailing as a specialism in non-retail specific degrees, plus others offering post-graduate courses. Despite this growth and the dynamics of the industry, many lecturers have found themselves in the situation of having limited retail teaching material to draw upon. The vast majority of the textbooks are still US based and somewhat inappropriate to the UK retailing context and the needs of British students. Case studies were developed from the lecturers' own previous management experience, and through partnerships with specific retailers, but often they could not offer the variety of examples required to give the students the breadth of experience across different retail sectors. Lecturers have sought to address this deficiency by pooling their case material. However, much of the material developed so far has been written from a strategic management point of view and is not appropriate for many types of retailing courses. Hence, it has become increasingly evident that in order to develop the right calibre of future retail managers, lecturers need to offer a better insight into retail practice and, more specifically, middle management problem solving.

In 1993, following discussions between CORTCO and Loughborough University Business School, a new way of disseminating case material was agreed. Loughborough University was already involved in a case project with Sainsbury's, and an extension of this model was proposed to include the other CORTCO associate companies and lecturers from other institutions. During the following two years, eight CORTCO companies teamed up with 22 lecturers, resulting in the collection of case studies that appears in this book. There were two main objectives behind the development of this text. The first objective was to develop cases with 'a middle management focus, in order to present the typical problem solving issues likely to be faced by a graduate within their first five years of their career in a retail organisation'.[2] The second objective was to achieve a more operational focus rather than strategic focus for these cases.

The CORTCO associates see the purpose of this collection of cases as a window to the retail world, as 'a means of enabling students to have access to real life retailing issues and to then work through a problem that real managers have to solve.'[3] It is an ideal opportunity for students to see the mechanics of many retail functions. It is also aimed at anyone interested in how major UK retail companies operate, not just undergraduates and postgraduates, but also managers wishing to develop their careers in retailing.

The outcome from the project has been two-fold. First, it has established a greater working relationship between the industry and higher education, which can only benefit the future graduates and their respective retail employers. Second, what started as synergy between retailers has led to a greater synergy between academic institutions as different groups of lecturers realize that by sharing case teaching material, they improve the overall standard of retail teaching and employability of retail graduates within UK institutions.

While these case studies fill a gap, as the project progressed it became increasingly evident that there was a need to formalize this cooperative framework to fulfil the continuing need for good retail teaching material. The model of academics and industry working together has formed the foundation for a new retail discipline network, which is to be established in 1996. This project, jointly initiated by Manchester Metropolitan University, Loughborough University Business School and Glasgow Caledonian University, will be funded by the Department for Employment and Education and CORTCO. We hope that other academic colleagues and retailers will actively participate in the new network and contribute to the development of the next wave of retailing case studies.

Notes

1 Extract from the CORTCO rationale, 1993.
2 Neil Clark, Chairperson of CORTCO, 1994.
3 Hilary Woodland, Chairperson of CORTCO, 1996.

The Cases

All the cases in this book are based on leading UK retailers in a number of major retailing sectors dealing with major current issues. They are designed to reflect real management situations that trainee managers and store managers are likely to face. However, in a number of situations the cases are based on a composite of two or more organizations and are designed to reflect the fact that the situation illustrated is common to a number of retailing organizations. In other cases, the names of the organizations and/or the data have been disguised for reasons of commercial sensitivity. Although the cases reflect real situations, they are not designed to illustrate effective or ineffective management of situations by organizations but have been written for the purposes of classroom discussion.

The cases are designed to reinforce concepts and techniques acquired through reading and lectures by requiring the students to apply them to real situations. In addition, cases are intended to develop the analytical reasoning and problem solving skills of students. This may be done by either working through the cases individually or working in groups. Many of the cases include a set of questions to test the understanding of the situation by the students and to guide students in the solving of the case. Suggestions for further reading to encourage students to explore aspects of the case in more depth are included where appropriate.

In a number of cases, the students have incomplete information: this is deliberate and designed to reflect the fact that in most situations managers do not have all the information they want in order to make a decision. In these instances, students, like managers, have to make reasonable assumptions in order to arrive at decisions. The cases are of varying lengths and complexity reflecting the different amounts of time available for classroom sessions.

The cases are designed for intermediate to advanced courses in retailing. They are particularly suitable for courses on store operations, merchandising, retail marketing, buying, human resources management and logistics. The cases have been organized into four sections in order to reflect the major teaching themes of the cases. However, a number of themes are covered in several different cases and sections of the book, reflecting the cross-functional nature of many managerial problems. Below is a short summary of the purpose and content of each of the cases.

Case 1, 'Effective in-store sales promotion at Safeway', deals with the role of in-store sales promotion in the overall marketing strategy of a grocery superstore. Generally, retail sales promotions are used to generate short-term increase in sales, and are not necessarily consistent with the retailer's overall brand image. The case highlights the conflict between short-term and long-term promotion objectives, given that a store manager's performance is largely assessed on sales achieved.

Case 2, 'Store layout and merchandising in fashion retailing', examines the type of problem faced by many multiple fashion retailers in designing the layout for a new store, and particularly in attempting to maximize financial performance from limited selling space. The case requires students to juggle with a host of market, competitive, demographic, financial space and consumer behaviour considerations in designing a layout solution, and students will appreciate the complexity and trade-offs required in such situations. Considerable financial detail is provided to enable students to undertake data analysis and to appreciate the importance of financial information for merchandise and space allocation decisions. The case enables students to 'create' their own visual solution to the store layout problem and, in so doing, appreciate the creative aspects of store layout and merchandising in a realistic and stimulating way.

It is generally recognized that retailing is a local business. Case 3, 'Store merchandising in an area of urban regeneration: the Safeway store at Crewe', highlights the problems and opportunities associated with opening a grocery superstore in an area that has suffered a decline in its traditional sources of employment and is undergoing economic change and restructuring. The case raises the question as to how far merchandising policies should deviate from the 'national norm' for similar stores.

Case 4, 'The operational implications of locational decision-making: a case study of the Belfast Co-operative', examines certain location decisions facing the Belfast Co-operative in 1990–1. The case enables students to consider the implications of trading in an unusual and sensitive operating environment – which presents unique trading conditions, legislative background and cultural nuances. The case is presented in three stages and moves the reader through different scales of analysis: from the wide sectoral shape of the Northern Ireland grocery market, to the Co-op's position in that market, and its subsequent assessment, development and successful operation of a new superstore. Students have the opportunity to examine the implications of trading in Northern Ireland, to undertake a site assessment and to consider the implications of a particular location for merchandising, staffing, local marketing and network planning.

Customer loyalty has become a central concern in retailing over the past couple of years and in particular in the intensely competitive grocery sector. Case 5, 'Developing customer loyalty: the Saver Card experience', examines the issues that concerned Sainsbury's when it was developing its Saver Card loyalty scheme. The case deals with issues of which customers should be targeted, the levels of incentives offered, database marketing, strategic versus tactical use of loyalty cards and the choices facing Sainsbury's in differentiating its scheme from that of its main rivals.

In recent years the major grocery retailers have been significantly expanding their interests in petrol retailing. Case 6, 'The development of petrol retailing at Tesco', provides an insight into how Tesco developed this aspect of its business between 1990 and 1995. The case examines the decision making process of the manager at Tesco appointed to review and then operationalize a new petrol buying strategy. The case considers how Tesco wished to change the way it interacted with its supply chain, to improve the security of petrol supplies and to enhance the profitability of petrol retailing. Students have the opportunity to examine supplier choice and negotiation issues, and to understand the ways in which petrol retailing differs from the retailing of other products, the reasoning behind changes in buying policy and the main operational issues involved in implementing such changes.

Case 7, 'Scottish Co-op's meat purchasing and supply', examines some of the changes introduced in meat purchasing procedures by the Scottish Co-op. The changes were introduced to improve profitability and include new specification systems and the centralizing of ordering and distribution. The case provides a practical illustration of the problems involved in the previous meat purchasing practices and a detailed account of the new systems. Students have the opportunity to understand the nature of leakage, the benefits of controlling leakage, the benefits of tightly controlled buying procedures and good relationships with suppliers.

Time has become a critical commodity for retailing logistics in the 1990s. Lead times and service levels throughout the supply chain are critical factors in achieving the highest levels of customer service through product availability and quality. To achieve these objectives at a minimum cost involves efficient and effective management of the warehouse or distribution centre. Case 8, 'Warehouse management systems at Tesco', illustrates how warehouse management systems can contribute to minimizing lead time. Students are introduced to a number of operational problems which are likely to emerge from the implementation of these systems, and are required to consider the components of lead time, impact of mispicking, distribution and warehousing productivity concepts.

One of the primary tasks of any retailer is the effective and efficient management of inventory. Most retailers use sophisticated computer systems to perform high volumes of stock record transactions, to monitor and control stock levels. Case 9, 'Managing Stock Management III in Safeway stores', describes the inventory management system at Safeway, to evaluate the basic principles which the system rests on. Issues such as forecasting and demand, data integrity, wastage control and stock availability are discussed from the store management perspective.

The move to centralized distribution over the past decade has provided numerous benefits for many multiple food retailers. However, the development of centralized networks utilizing composite distribution has been limited by factors such as store growth, acquisition and government planning restrictions. Case 10, 'Retail logistics: the case of Tesco stores', discusses the operational issues which Tesco logistics has had to address in the aftermath of its takeover of the Scottish multiple grocery, Wm Low. The case then introduces another factor into the distribution network: the Metro operation. Students have the opportunity to evaluate the impact of

the Metro concept on Tesco's logistical support to stores, to assess
the operational options open to Tesco and to evaluate the human
resource management implications of changes in the distribution
network.

Case 11, 'Health care provision at Boots the Chemist' considers
the external and internal changes impacting on Boots the Chemist
during the 1990s and how this led to changes in the retail strategy
regarding the provision of health care products and services. Students are encouraged to identify the barriers and constraints that
may restrict local decision making, not least the tight legislative
framework within which Boots has to operate for key products in
this area.

In the current competitive climate, the importance of customer
service is being recognized as vital in retaining customers. Case 12
introduces Post Office Counters Limited as an unusual example of
retailing, encompassing a huge network of largely independent
businesses. The case examines the critical issue of queuing, specifically focusing on queue management, customer perceptions and
staffing. Students are given the opportunity to examine the queuing
problem from different perspectives and to recommend alternative
solutions.

Store security remains an important issue for all retail companies.
Retailers have tried a variety of ways to deter or prevent theft of
articles from stores. However, each method of deterrence or prevention has certain costs and different levels of effectiveness. Case 13,
'Developing a security strategy at Metro '99, describes the attempts
of one retailer (name disguised) to implement electronic article
surveillance (EAS), or tagging, into its stores. The case looks at the
effectiveness of EAS, some of the alternative choices of security
systems and the implementation issues involved in its introduction.

As retailers search for more ways of evaluating branch performance and monitoring customer behaviour, Case 14, 'Electronic
customer counting and tracking systems in fashion retailing', introduces a new technology designed to complement the type of
information collected by EPoS systems. Interest in infra-red electronic customer counting and tracking (ECCaT) systems is growing
fast, and, through the case, students can appreciate some of the
questions and potential difficulties of using the technology, but also
the many potential applications presented by ECCaT systems as an
additional management tool. The case can also be used to debate

the merits of different technologies currently available for customer counting and tracking. Extensive data are provided and the case lends itself ideally to spreadsheet analysis; the basic ratios and calculations necessary can provide students with good practice in basic arithmetic, numerical reasoning and presentation of data in a retailing context.

New store development is an immense and continuing investment for most multiple retailers, and Case 15, 'Managing a store relocation project: Marks and Spencer in Kendal', presents a relatively unusual example of new store development combining both a relocation and the redevelopment of an existing supermarket site. Considerable detail is presented to enable students to understand both the construction and commercial aspects of store development activities within a major multiple retail organization. Students can understand the role of a store manager in a new store opening project, and to appreciate the importance of teamwork, communication, coordination and effective organization and planning for the success of such a project. The case is ideal for introducing students to the concepts and techniques of 'project management'. The detailed review of commercial and construction activities enables students to apply key project analysis and planning tools and to learn through application.

Case 16, 'CORTCO management competencies for graduate recruits to the retail industry', provides an introduction to the concept of management competencies and how they may be used with particular reference to the retailing industry. Recent work carried out by CORTCO has been based on establishing which management competencies are important for a retail manager; a list of CORTCO competencies is included in the case. For undergraduates who may be considering a career in retailing, the case provides a background on the notion of competence, an understanding of the arguments for and against the competence approach and guidance on how to identify personal competencies and to demonstrate these to prospective employers.

One of the most difficult skills for a graduate manager to develop is that of human resource management. When faced with managing up to 400 staff, the role of the supermarket manager has to encompass leading and motivating a team, while simultaneously managing the commercial aspects of the business. Measuring manager performance in human resource skills is less defined than measuring financial performance.

Case 17, 'A tale of two store managers: performance measurement at Sainsbury's', examines retail performance measurement on two different levels: the store manager and the retail store. It illustrates these issues in relation to the scenario of a new superstore opening, and explores the factors involved in evaluating and choosing a new branch manager.

Case 18, 'The public relations side of recruitment and selection', suggests that recruitment and selection in both retailing and other industries needs to be considered in a wider context. That is, the process is effectively an advertisement for the recruiting company and all applicants, whether successful or not, are existing or potential future customers. The case outlines the main stages of a typical graduate recruitment exercise using the example of Sainsbury's. More importantly, however, and particularly through the activity ideas, it encourages students to think through and plan the public relations side of the process.

Acknowledgements

We would like to acknowledge the contribution of all the companies, the individual retail managers and the team of case writers who have been involved in helping to bring about this collection of cases. Particular thanks must go to Hilary Woodland and Annette Thomas, who have been a driving force throughout the project.

PART I

Marketing and Merchandising Management

1

Effective In-store Sales Promotion at Safeway

Melanie Chetwood

The Manchester Metropolitan University

Introduction

UK food retailers are facing increasing competitive pressures owing to the growth of food discounters in the UK, including the expansion of foreign firms such as Aldi and Netto, and to the prospect of approaching saturation of the UK food retail market, as fewer and fewer of the population find themselves outside reasonable driving time of a major food superstore.

These pressures are forcing food retailers to become more competitive in their offers and have resulted in a greater emphasis on all elements of the marketing mix for the major operators. Thus, in terms of *product*, new product development continues apace, with the emphasis placed on high value-added items and own brands in order to maintain margins. In terms of *place*, increasing attention is being paid by the major operators to the location of their stores and to the design, layout and facilities offered by their outlets. With regard to *price*, the superstore operators have all brought down prices on their basic ranges, in order better to compete with the discounters, and are paying closer attention to this element of the marketing. Finally, in terms of *promotion*, advertising and sales promotions are being used to create and reinforce the retail brands of each of the major operators.

Some of the information in this case study has been changed in order to highlight particular issues for discussion.

This case study deals with one of the marketing tools most commonly used by food retailers, in-store sales promotion.

The Project

As a newly appointed marketing manager for Safeway, your first project is to evaluate Safeway's use of in-store sales promotion at Safeway, X, a representative Safeway store of 29,800 square feet sales area, carrying approximately 15,000 lines, located in Cheshire. Your predecessor in this job had already started work on this project and you have been given a file containing the work completed to date. You have been given one week in which to complete the work and make your recommendations to your manager.

The File

The file you have been given contains five documents. Those documents which are in italics are hand-written and appear to be notes made by your predecessor. The information in the file is as follows.

Document 1: extract from Safeway's mission statement

We are committed to creating an enduring food retail business. We aim to be a leader in our industry . . .

Food expertise and customer service are key to our reputation as a quality, caring company.

We take pride in imaginatively anticipating and responding to the national, regional and local needs of our customers. We will provide them with a significantly wider choice of high-quality products and excellent value, in an attractive and convenient shopping environment.

Document 2: trade area information for Safeway, X

Safeway, X, is a 29,800 square feet store, located on the southern edge of a moderately sized industrial town in Cheshire. Details on the demographic profile of the trade area of the store are given below.

Within the immediate catchment area of the store, which consists mainly of the southern part of the town, the demographic profile of the population is as shown in table 1.1.

Table 1.1

	Immediate catchment (%)	GB average (%)
Owner occupied households	44	56
No car households	58	40
2 + car households	6	15
Social class I	1	5
Social class II	5	19
Social class IIIN	6	9
Social class IIIM	37	26

Within the wider catchment area of the store, which includes the rural areas surrounding the town, the demographic profile of the population is as shown in table 1.2.

Table 1.2

	Wider catchment (%)	GB average (%)
Owner occupied households	76	56
No car households	25	40
2 + car households	24	15
Social class I	7	5
Social class II	27	19
Social class IIIN	3	9
Social class IIIM	22	26

Unemployment for the catchment area is slightly below the national average.

Competition

Competition within the trade area of the store consists of a 46,000 square feet Asda, located in the town centre, and a 46,000 square feet Co-op, also located in the town centre. Both of these stores opened in the late 1970s, but the Asda has recently been refitted.

Document 3: excerpt from the minutes of the marketing strategy meeting of 10 March 1994

Present: A. Allen
          B. Bates
          C. Crane
          D. Davies

6.3 A stated that he felt that sales promotions were primarily a tool for creating an increase in demand, for instance by encouraging trial of a new product or increased usage of an existing product, and did not necessarily have to play a part in the overall marketing strategy of the company.

6.4 B disagreed, saying that sales promotions should be an integral part of the company's marketing strategy and that in his view, they should translate the favourable attitudes towards brands or products created by advertising, into actual purchase. Sales promotions would therefore be less effective, he felt, if they were not integrated with the company's overall marketing objectives, and indeed, could actually undermine the brand or product on promotion.

6.5 A argued that successful retailing was about increasing sales and that sales promotions were an effective way of achieving increased sales in the short term.

6.6 B responded by saying that sales promotions might be more effective at increasing sales in the longer term, if they were used as part of the overall marketing strategy.

6.7 A commented that retailers were always concerned with current sales, and that as stores were generally measured on sales achieved, sales promotions were inevitably one of the tools used to achieve immediate increases in sales.

6.8 C then raised the issue of whether sales promotions could be used to increase store traffic and draw additional trade from a wider catchment area around the store, or whether the objective should be to increase sales from existing customers.

6.8 D suggested that discussion of this matter should be postponed until after the completion of the evaluation of sales promotion planned for Safeway, X, and this was agreed.

Document 4: advantages and disadvantages of different types of sales promotions

Reduced Price Packs.

Advantages: Wide appeal of money off. Can be implemented quickly. Effective for small and large brands, because no economies of scale.

Disadvantages: Not distinctive.

Bonus Packs (extra product given away at no extra cost).

Advantages: Costs less than equivalent reduced price pack. Forces consumer to use up more product. Can accustom consumer to buying a larger size.

Disadvantages: May be expensive to produce larger pack if not a standard size.

Free Sample Packs (free sample of one brand given away with purchase of another brand).

Advantages: Inexpensive way of sampling a product. Promotes both brands. Can be aimed at specific consumers, e.g. car-owners via windscreen wash.

Disadvantages: Uncontrolled way of sampling – same purchasers may end up with a number of samples.

Free Gift Packs (free item attached to pack, e.g. icing nozzle with icing sugar).

Advantages: More effective at attracting new purchasers. If set-building, can attract new purchasers and hold them. Distinctive.

Disadvantages: Limited number of affordable high-appeal items available. Better for large brands because of economies of scale.

Coupon on Next Purchase (brand carries coupon giving money off next purchase of brand).

Advantages: Can increase frequency of purchase among existing users. Can retain loyalty of existing users.

Disadvantages: Lack of immediacy. Appeals mainly to existing users.

In-store Demonstrations (samples of product given away in store, recipe demonstrations).

Advantages: Can attract new purchasers. Educates consumer in use of product.

Disadvantages: Expensive.

Document 5: commonly used sales promotions in Safeway

1   'Linksave': this is where if one product is bought, another product is given away free, e.g. buy a pack of six tomatoes and get a cucumber free.

2   'Multisave': this is where if two of the same product is bought, a third is given away free.

3   Standard on-shelf price reduction: this is where a product is reduced by a certain amount for a limited period.

4   Standard off-shelf price reduction: this is where a product is reduced by a certain amount for a limited period and given an off-shelf display, e.g. a plinth or basket in the aisle, to highlight the promotion.

5   End-display price reductions: this is where a product is reduced for a limited time and is put on an end-display, which again highlights the promotion.

6   In-store sampling and demonstrations.

The major promotions offering price reductions are generally supported by full-page advertisements in the national press in such papers as the *The Daily Mail* and *Today*, during the week in which the promotion is being held.

The Project

SALES PROMOTIONS AT SAFEWAY, X

A typical number of sales promotions under way at any time in a typical Safeway store would be approximately 300. Sales promotions are usually carried out for a period of two weeks, with approximately 100 changing each week. Sales promotions may be either wholly supplier funded, a joint promotion between Safeway and the supplier, or funded solely by Safeway. The following are examples of sales promotions under way in Safeway, X, for a two-week period in July and August 1994, when you take up your new position.

• *Promotion 1*: A 'Linksave' promotion offering a free pack of Jacob's Flintstones biscuits (price 39p) with a purchase of 80

Tetley Tea Bags in a Flintstones packet (price £1.55). This promotion is off-shelf on a plinth facing the main entrance of the store.

- *Promotion 2*: A 'Multisave' promotion offering three Soreen malt loaves (45p each) for the price of two.

- *Promotion 3*: An off-shelf promotion offering a pack of 15 Coca-Cola cans for the price of 12 (£3.15). This promotion is displayed on a plinth at the end of the fresh produce aisle.

- *Promotion 4*: An off-shelf promotion offering a price reduction on nectarines from £1.25 per punnet to 89p per punnet. This promotion is on a plinth in the middle of the fresh produce aisle.

- *Promotion 5*: An on-shelf promotion offering a price reduction on PG Tips Instant Tea from £2.39 to £1.95.

- *Promotion 6*: An on-shelf promotion offering a coupon worth 50p off the next purchase of Safeway own brand washing powder.

- *Promotion 7*: A recipe card (one of various recipe cards displayed throughout the store), showing a recipe for summer pudding, displayed alongside the summer fruits, e.g. strawberries, raspberries.

- *Promotion 8*: A stamps promotion offering a stamp for every £10 spent at the store, which can be collected and used to obtain reduced prices on pieces of a Royal Doulton Tea Service, e.g. a set of two plates (retail price £9) can be obtained for 15 stamps plus £2.49. Four different designs are available for collection and are also available for purchase at the normal retail price within the store. The promotion is advertised by a large poster displayed at the entrance to the store. This promotion commenced in April 1994 and will finish in October 1994.

- *Promotion 9*: An in-store demonstration of Italian cheeses, with a demonstrator offering tasting and recipe ideas.

RESULTS OF SALES PROMOTIONS AT SAFEWAY, X

Your analysis of the sales promotions reveals the results shown in table 1.3, based on the week's sales immediately prior to the promotions and the two weeks sales during the promotion.

Table 1.3 Analysis of sales of items on promotion

Promotion	Week 1 (pre-promotion)	Week 2 (during promotion)	Week 3 (during promotion)	Promotion cost per unit*	Pre-promotion gross margin (%)
	Units sold				
Promotion 1 (Tetley tea/ Jacobs biscuits)	25	235	205	30p	20
Promotion 2 (malt loaves)	105	226	165	16p	25
Promotion 3 (Coca-Cola)	7	60	54	58p	20
Promotion 4 (nectarines)	900	1880	1447	25p	30
Promotion 5 (PG Instant Tea)	5	3	2	35p	20
Promotion 6 (washing powder)	145	163	157	38p	25
Promotion 7 (strawberries)	600	900	850	5p per leaflet (1500 leaflets)	30
Promotion 8 (Italian cheeses)	32	56	48	£300 per week	30

Notes:
1 * Excludes distribution and overheads.
2 Costs and margins are not actual Safeway figures.
3 Promotion 8 (Royal Doulton) has been running for 20 weeks, and will end in another six weeks. During the first five or six weeks of the promotion, sales of the Royal Doulton products amounted to between £500 and £1500. Since then, sales of the products have been running at £6000 to £7000 each week.
4 Promotions 1, 2 and 5 are jointly funded by the manufacturers and Safeway, 50 per cent each.

The Tasks

1   Evaluate the sales promotions described in the case and make recommendations for future implementation of sales promotions at Safeway, X. Your evaluation should include an assessment of what you believe the objectives of each promotion to be and should include consideration of the following:

● overall marketing strategy;
● local marketing;

- retail branding;

- display and ordering issues.

2   You have been given only one week to complete this task. If you had been given more time, what further research might you wish to carry out, and how would it help you to make your evaluation and recommendations?

3   In addition, you have been asked to devise in-store sales promotions for four of the following products for Safeway, X. Include your objectives and your methodology for evaluating the success of your objectives.

- fresh peaches;

- Safeway own label christmas crackers;

- wholemeal flour;

- Safeway own label champagne;

- anti-freeze;

- a new type of oven cleaner.

4   Finally, you are asked to comment on the advantages and disadvantages of a centralized sales promotion strategy.

Further Reading

Davidson, H. (1987) *Offensive Marketing*, chapter 11. Harmondsworth: Penguin.

Weller, E. (1992) The place to sell is in the store. *Progressive Grocer*, 71 (11).

Wilson, R., Gilligan, C. and Pearson, D. (1993) *Strategic Marketing Management*, chapter 13. Oxford: Butterworth-Heinemann.

2

Store Layout and Merchandising in Fashion Retailing

Malcolm Kirkup and Linda Moirano

Loughborough University Business School and Bournemouth University

Introduction

The situation described in this case study took place in August 1995. Stephen Thomas had just been appointed to his new role. At the age of 29 he was the youngest of nine area managers ever appointed by Ace Menswear. He had an excellent, albeit brief, retail track record. After graduation he worked for three years as a department sales manager in menswear with a national department store, before moving to a chain of specialist menswear stores in 1990. Stephen spent two years as manager of two small branches in London, followed by three years as manager of one of the company's largest stores in the Lakeside Shopping Centre, Thurrock. He had managed the Thurrock store since it had opened, and turnover and profit growth had outstripped most other stores in the company's chain of 200 outlets. Ace Menswear's Retail Operations Director had been impressed at Stephen's interview by his maturity and interpersonal skills, and particularly by his enthusiasm for fashion and commercial awareness.

An extensive induction programme was organized for Stephen, and he enjoyed a structured and comprehensive introduction to all

This case study has been developed from information provided by a number of fashion retailers, but the specific data and names have been disguised to preserve confidentiality. The information and the tasks suggested, while realistic, have also been simplified in order to ensure that students of retail management can focus on specific learning objectives.

the key departments in Ace Menswear's head office. A week was spent on the road with an existing area manager, followed by sessions in the departments of store operations, finance, human resources, display, marketing, estates and buying and merchandising. Ace Menswear believed strongly that area managers should have a significant input into the way their stores were merchandised, in terms of layout and also (within limits) the choice of products that were stocked in particular branches. Stephen's experience in this area was relatively limited, and the Retail Operations Director therefore suggested that his induction should include a specific store-merchandising project.

An ideal project had arisen soon after Stephen's arrival. The company had recently completed negotiations to acquire a new store with an opening date in late September 1995. His specific task was to put forward recommendations on an appropriate product package for the new store, and to plan the layout (including space allocation for each product group, and positioning of displays and key fixtures), making appropriate use of marketing and financial information. He was also asked to assess the likely profitability of his recommendations.

Making full use of the contacts he had made at head office during his induction programme, Stephen assembled a mass of information, some of which is discussed below and some presented in the exhibits.

Market Positioning

The Marketing Department provided a useful starting point to understand the company's overall strategy and market positioning. The company's 120 retail outlets sold fashion clothing targeted at men aged 15–35, although some stores (space permitting) also sold boyswear targeting 10–14 year olds. A recent consumer research study, commissioned by Ace Menswear's Marketing Department, suggested that the company's customers tended to be price-conscious but also sought good quality clothing that would last. They regarded themselves as fashionable, but were not obsessed with chasing the latest styles or fads. The research study suggested that 45 per cent of Ace Menswear's customers were women, buying for their husbands or their sons.

The consumer research also suggested that Ace Menswear had a good reputation for its 'casual' ranges of clothing – particularly jeans, knitwear and sweatshirts. Ace Menswear was also popular for 'boyswear', and was one of the few specialist clothing multiples in the UK to target the 10–14 age group. In some stores Ace Menswear sold suits, footwear and/or sportswear, although the research study suggested that the company presented a confused image, and was often referred to as a 'jack of all trades'. Stephen learned that the company was trying to rectify this problem by focusing on fewer product ranges, taking into account local competition and market characteristics.

The majority of the company's stores had an area of around 3000 square feet, although high occupancy costs (rent, rates and service charges) in many prime locations had led them to consider opening a number of smaller 2000 square feet stores. The location of stores tended to focus in the south of England, although they had a number of branches in the midlands and the north-west.

In 1994 the company had around a 1.5 per cent share of the menswear market in the UK. Their main multiple competitors included Marks and Spencer, Burton, Top Man, Debenhams, Fosters, C&A, BHS, River Island and Littlewoods. A merchandise audit conducted by the company in 1994 found that Ace Menswear had lower prices than Marks and Spencer, River Island, BHS, Top Man, Burton and Debenhams, but slightly higher prices compared to Fosters, C&A and Littlewoods.

The New Store and Location

The location analyst within the marketing department provided Stephen with details of the new store, local competition and a demographic profile of the town. The new store was of 2000 square feet net sales area on two floors (1500 square feet ground and 500 square feet on a mezzanine), with changing rooms on the ground floor and staff/stock facilities on the mezzanine (see figure 2.1). The store frontage was floor-to-ceiling glass. Rent and service charges for the unit amounted to £70,000 per annum, and the company was budgeting for a total sales turnover of £500,000 for the first year of trading. Wage costs were budgeted at 8 per cent of turnover, rates at 4 per cent, heat, light, distribution and other costs at 3 per cent, and depreciation of fixtures and fittings at 4 per cent. The company expected to make a branch profit (before head office costs) of £65,000 in the first year.

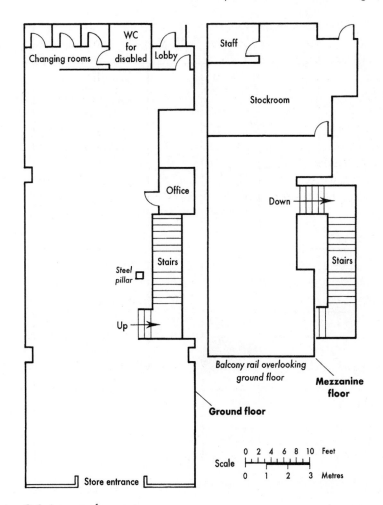

Figure 2.1 Layout of new store.

The store was located within an enclosed shopping centre in a major town, and occupied a terraced site. The store was adjacent to Olympus Sports and Next. The shopping centre was anchored by Marks and Spencer and Debenhams, and also featured a large C&A store and WH Smith. Figure 2.2 shows the layout of the centre, and also highlights the net selling areas (in square feet) allocated to menswear by each of Ace Menswear's main clothing competitors.

The town itself had a catchment population of around 175,000, and Stephen had been advised that it had a more affluent profile than most other towns which featured in the company's portfolio (see table 2.1).

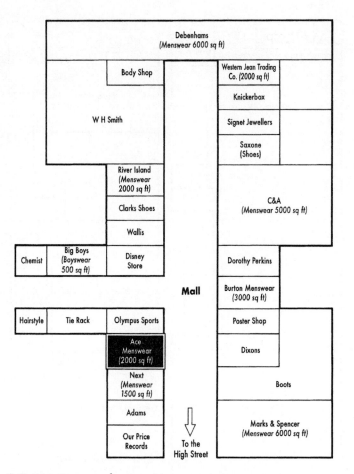

Figure 2.2 Location map for Ace Menswear's new store.

Merchandise Range and Display Considerations

Following discussions with buyers, merchandisers, the market research manager and the display department, Stephen Thomas assembled the table shown in exhibit 2.1. This table helped, first, to summarize the core ranges stocked by most Ace Menswear stores, and additional ranges stocked by some of the larger outlets in the store portfolio. Stephen had been advised that any of these ranges could be stocked in the new store, provided adequate space was available. Some core ranges could be excluded if they were felt to be performing poorly or if more appropriate products were available

Table 2.1 Demographic profile of the town

	Catchment population	Percentage of catchment population	GB average %
Population			
Males	84,023	48.1	48.4
Females	90,548	51.9	51.6
Age structure (years)			
0–9 years	24,440	14.0	13.7
10–14	12,219	7.0	6.3
15–19	13,267	7.6	7.0
20–24	14,489	8.3	8.0
25–34	26,709	15.3	15.9
35–44	24,439	14.0	14.2
45 +	59,005	33.8	34.9
Occupations			
Higher professional/managerial	3993	8.5	6.7
Intermediate professional/ managerial	16,492	35.2	30.4
Non-manual occupations	7358	15.7	13.5
Semi-skilled occupations	9716	20.7	26.4
Skilled manual occupations	5873	12.5	13.6
Unskilled occupations	1686	3.6	4.7

and considered necessary given the market and competitive environment.

The table helped, second, to show the typical display space allocated to each of the products for a 3000 square feet Ace Menswear store. To ensure that the basic options and adequate consumer choice were provided, and to help minimize the 'jack of all trades' image, Stephen was advised that there was a 'minimum' amount of display space required for each product range. He was also advised to be cautious about trying to expand too greatly the display space allocated to a particular product line, because there was a limit to the number of additional options and variety that could be sourced for the season. For each range there would also be a 'maximum' display space – this would enable the complete variety of options to be displayed, but beyond this the store would simply be repeating lines. The maximum display space for core ranges was

Exhibit 2.1 Product range: autumn/winter 1995–6

1	2	3	4	5	6
Product Descriptions *Core Ranges Stocked by most Ace Stores	Approx national consumer spend A/W 1994/5 £m	A/W sales growth between 1994 and 95 in Ace Store %	A/W sales 1994/5 (typical 3000 sq ft store) £	Markdown value A/W 1994/5 (typical 3000 sq ft store) £	Shrinkage value A/W 1994/5 (typical 3000 sq ft store) £
FORMAL					
Trousers*	340	5%	19259	1541	96
Jackets*	90	6%	14302	1144	72
Blazers			5363		
Melton Jackets			8939		
Shirts*	370	1%	24010	1921	240
Shirts			18620		
Dress Shirts			5390		
Suits	330	8%	29738	2379	149
CASUAL					
Jeans*	380	8%	72378	8685	2171
Levi/Lee/Wrangler			46322		
Ace Jeans			26056		
Denim Shirts/Jackets*	50	6%	13217	1586	198
Branded denim shirts			3833		
Ace denim shirts			2776		
Branded denim jackets			4097		
Ace denim jackets			2511		
Knitted Shirts/Sweats*	200	2%	33986	5098	340
Shirts polo/roll neck			19372		
Sweatshirts			14614		
Jogging Trousers*	70	–14%	11329	1133	113
Casual Trousers*	230	8%	23129	2775	116
Knitwear*	190	5%	17937	2691	269
Levi knitwear			4305		
Ace knitwear			13632		
Casual Overshirts	55	18%	11140	1671	167
Casual Woven Shirts*	180	6%	19070	2288	286
Sportswear	870	2%	26056	3908	391
Tracksuits			12507		
Shirts			4169		
Trainers			9380		

Exhibit 2.1 Product range: autumn/winter 1995–6 (continued)

7	8	9	10	11	12
Retained gross margin A/W 1994/5 (typical 3000 sq ft store) %	Av stock value A/W 94/5 (typical 3000 sq ft store) £	Price points 1995/6 Minimum and Maximum £	Staff costs value for A/W 1994/5 (typical 3000 sq ft store) £	Typical display space allocated in Ace stores 2500–3000 sq ft (standard display units)	Minimum display space to offer main lines in each category (standard display units)
44.9	3209	£19.99–£34.99	2268	3.0	1.0
43.7	2648	£36.99–£79.99 £36.99–£79.99 £36.99–£79.99	1728	2.25	1.0
44.1	3637	£8.99–£24.99 £8.99–£19.99 £19.99–£24.99	1764	3.5	1.5
46.4	8260	£99.99–£119.99	3402	4.5	2.0
45.3	11135	£19.99–£44.99 £29.99–£44.99 £19.99	4410	10.0	2.0
48.8	1915	£19.99–£44.99 £29.95–£44.99 £19.99–£24.99 £39.99–£49.99 £34.99	882	2.0	2.0
50.0	4997	£9.99–£12.99 £9.99–£12.99 £12.99–£19.99	2205	5.0	2.0
48.3	2517	£14.99–£19.99	882	2.0	0.5
45.7	3854	£17.99–£24.99	1418	3.5	1.0
48.0	2562	£17.99–£49.99 £24.99–£49.99 £17.99–£34.99	1323	3.0	1.0
46.1	1485	£14.99–£24.99	819	1.5	1.0
43.4	2724	£12.99–£24.99	1323	3.0	1.0
44.8	3831	£8.99–£49.99 £29.99–£39.99 £8.99–£14.99 £19.99–£49.99	2511	4.5	2.0

Exhibit 2.1 Product range: autumn/winter 1995–6 (continued)

1	2	3	4	5	6
Product Descriptions *Core Ranges Stocked by most Ace Stores	Approx national consumer spend A/W 1994/5 £m	A/W sales growth between 1994 and 95 in Ace Store %	A/W sales 1994/5 (typical 3000 sq ft store) £	Markdown value A/W 1994/5 (typical 3000 sq ft store) £	Shrinkage value A/W 1994/5 (typical 3000 sq ft store) £
OUTERWEAR					
Casual Jackets/Anoraks	150	2%	18503	2220	93
Premium Jackets/Leather	95	7%	14476	2171	72
Premium Trench Coats	30	–6%	7364	1105	37
UNDERWEAR	270	5%	6923	346	69
Briefs			1454		
Boxer shorts			3462		
Socks			2007		
ACCESSORIES	100	10%	5240	629	262
Ties			3720		
Belts			1520		
FOOTWEAR			8308	748	25
Shoes	250	–3%	3905		
Boots	300	–3%	4403		
DISCOUNT			17980	899	270
Swearshirts	20	4%	9170		
Joggers	20	4%	8810		
BOYS					
Denim	50	11%	20203	2424	606
Denim jeans (Ace)			10708		
Denim shirts (Ace)			4849		
Denim jackets (Ace)			4646		
Clothing	30	16%	40406	6061	808
Sweatshirts			16971		
Tops			9697		
Jackets			8485		
Trousers			5253		
Footwear/Accessories	80	8%	9913	991	50
Trainers			4560		
Shoes			1883		
Boots			2875		
Accessories			595		
TOTALS	4750		464867	54414	6900

Exhibit 2.1 Product range: autumn/winter 1995–6 (continued)

7	8	9	10	11	12
Retained gross margin A/W 1994/5 (typical 3000 sq ft store) %	Av stock value A/W 94/5 (typical 3000 sq ft store) £	Price points 1995/6 Minimum and Maximum £	Staff costs value for A/W 1994/5 (typical 3000 sq ft store) £	Typical display space allocated in Ace stores 2500–3000 sq ft (standard display units)	Minimum display space to offer main lines in each category (standard display units)
49.7	6168	£49.99–£69.99	1890	3.0	1.0
51.5	4523	£99.99–£149.99	1575	2.5	1.5
51.5	3682	£89.99–£99.99	945	1.5	0.5
41.8	865	£1.99–£2.50 £1.99–£2.49 £2.99–£4.50 £1.99–£2.99	504	1.0	1.0
49.4	663	£5.99–£12.99 £5.99–£12.99 £5.99–£12.99	421	0.75	0.75
47.1	2026	£24.99–£54.99 £24.99–£44.95 £34.99–£54.99	1145	1.5	1.0
36.9	1997	£7.99 £7.99 £7.99	1292	3.0	1.5
55.3	2845	£16.99–£29.99 £16.99–£19.99 £16.99–£19.99 £29.99	1304	3.0	2.0
48.6	5460	£10.99–£69.99 £10.99–£16.99 £14.99–£29.99 £39.99–£69.99 £17.99–£29.99	2646	6.0	4.0
46.8	2202	£4.99–£39.99 £17.99–£49.99 £19.99–£34.99 £24.99–£44.95 £4.99–£9.99	1134	1.5	1.0
46.9	83205		37791	71.5	32.25

felt to be approximately three times the minimum, and for additional non-core ranges twice the minimum.

The display department also provided drawings of the types of floor equipment used by the company for displaying merchandise (see figure 2.3), together with a guideline on the relative size and display capacity of each piece of equipment, which varied significantly (see figure 2.4). The equipment included wall display units, large floor units, centre floor stands and units for small items (such as underwear, socks and accessories), and Stephen had been advised that the maximum display capacity of a 2000 square feet store was probably equivalent to around 50 standard display units. The relative size of cash and wrap facilities was also provided.

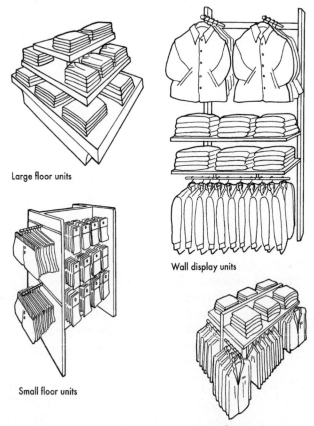

Large floor units

Wall display units

Small floor units

Centre floor stands

Figure 2.3 Sketches of available display equipment.

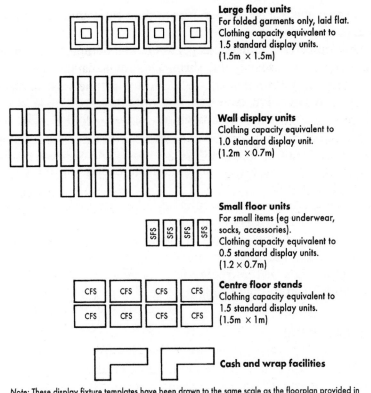

Large floor units
For folded garments only, laid flat.
Clothing capacity equivalent to
1.5 standard display units.
(1.5m × 1.5m)

Wall display units
Clothing capacity equivalent to
1.0 standard display unit.
(1.2m × 0.7m)

Small floor units
For small items (eg underwear,
socks, accessories).
Clothing capacity equivalent to
0.5 standard display units.
(1.2 × 0.7m)

Centre floor stands
Clothing capacity equivalent to
1.5 standard display units.
(1.5m × 1m)

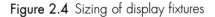

Cash and wrap facilities

Note: These display fixture templates have been drawn to the same scale as the floorplan provided in figure 2.1 and can therefore be cut out and overlaid directly on to the floorplan.

Figure 2.4 Sizing of display fixtures

Financial Information

The Finance Department provided a 'financial profile' of typical stores, although Stephen found that much of the information applied to typical performances in 3000 square feet stores because of the nature of the company's estate.

Exhibit 2.1 shows the financial information that Stephen was able to gather. As a total company, Ace Menswear in 1994 had a turnover in excess of £85 million, with a net profit before tax of around £5 million. Column 3 highlights the sales growth experienced in each product category between autumn/winter 1993–4 and autumn/winter 1994–5, and Stephen was advised that these should be considered against a like-for-like sales growth for the company as a whole of around + 5 per cent. Stephen was also advised that Ace stores often achieve 60–65 per cent of their total annual sales within the autumn/winter season.

From the merchandising department he obtained the value of reductions (mark-downs and shrinkage) for a typical 3000 square feet store in autumn/winter 1993–4, by product category. The personnel department provided him with the total staff costs for each branch for the autumn/winter season 1993–4. He talked to a store manager of a 3000 square feet branch to try to assign these costs to individual product groups. The manager produced some estimates to the best of his ability, and these are shown in column 10.

Stephen did not have time to review the entire range of products for the forthcoming season but felt it would help to know the upper and lower price points of the merchandise purchased by the buying department for the forthcoming season. This would provide him with a good idea of the trading level of Ace Menswear, and these prices are shown in column 9.

Case Questions

Read the information contained in the case study. You are to assume the role of Stephen Thomas, area manager for Ace Menswear, who has been asked to prepare a report which addresses the following tasks.

1   What product assortment would you recommend for the new store for the autumn/winter season 1995–6? You must provide detailed reasoning for your recommendations, and you must show that your recommendations are based on detailed analysis of the financial and marketing data provided in the case study.

2   Based on the product assortment you have chosen, design a layout for the new store, using the floorplan and display fixture templates provided. Your layout should include decisions on space allocation for each product group, appropriate positioning of displays and key fixtures, and appropriate choice of the number and type of display fixtures. *Your objective must be to design a solution which makes the best use of the space available in the store, exploits likely consumer shopping behaviour and seeks to maximize the financial performance of the store.* Your layout recommendations should be accompanied by detailed reasoning, and

you must show due regard for the principles of effective visual merchandising and store layout and an understanding of consumer behaviour.

3   Assess the likely implications of your recommendations for branch profitability, store operations and merchandising.

Further Reading

McGoldrick, P.J. (1990) *Retail Marketing*. New York: McGraw-Hill, chapter 5, pp. 145–54.

Mills, K.H. and Paul, J.E. (1988) *Applied Visual Merchandising*, 2nd edn. Englewood Cliffs, NJ: Prentice Hall.

Levy, M. and Barton, W.A. (1992) *Retailing Management*. Homewood, IL: Irwin, chapter 19, pp. 663–97.

Levy, M. and Weitz, B.A. (1995) *Retailing Management*, 2nd edn. Homewood, IL: Irwin, chapter 19, pp. 552–74.

Lusch, R.F., Dunne, P. and Gebhardt, R. (1993) *Retail Marketing*, Cincinatti, DH: South Western Publishing, chapter 12, pp. 402–43.

Stone, E. (1990) *Fashion Merchandising*. Columbus, OH: Glencoe.

Walters, D. and White, D. (1989) *Retail Marketing Management*. London: Macmillan Press, chapter 7, pp. 139–76.

3

Store Merchandising in an Area of Urban Regeneration: the Safeway Store at Crewe

Maureen Whitehead

The Manchester Metropolitan University

Stage 1: The UK Grocery Market Place

The UK grocery market has, throughout the 1980s and into the 1990s, seen increasing levels of industry concentration, as a handful of key players have grown from strong regional chains to positions of national prominence. At the same time, small-scale independents exist alongside large-scale organizations, frequently competing by offering high levels of personal service or stocking specialist product lines. As a result, the sector is made up of large-scale, fiercely competitive organizations jockeying for position as an industry leader at the top end of the market and a large number of independents and small chains whose activities are far more fragmented. Tesco, Sainsbury's, Gateway and Safeway dominate the top end of this market. At a regional rather than national level, different store groups dominate the various regions (see table 3.1).

Table 3.1 Regional strengths

Tesco	Anglia, London, Wales and West
Sainsbury's	Anglia, London, South East
Asda	Lancashire, Scotland and Tyne Tees
Safeway	Scotland, South East, London
Kwik Save	Lancashire, Wales, W. Midlands
Co-op	Anglia, South West, Scotland

Source: The British Shopper (1993).

Table 3.2 Demographic profile of major organizations' customers

Company	Social categories				
Tesco	AB	C1	C2		
Sainsbury's	AB	C1			
Asda		C1	C2		
Gateway			C2	D	
Safeway	AB	C1			
Kwik Save			C2	D	E
Co-op			C2	D	

Source: The British Shopper (1993).

These differences in market strength reflect the patterns of historical development of the companies. A further operating difference between the companies lies in their appeal to different target groups (see table 3.2).

Stage 2: Safeway, the Company

Stage 2 of the case focuses on Safeway's position in the UK grocery sector. In particular, attention is drawn to how the company has achieved this position and its current market strengths and weaknesses. This background is provided to enable the student to appreciate the structure of the company and consequently to improve case analysis.

Safeway forms part of the Argyll Group, one of the leading UK food retailers with annual sales of almost £6.0 billion, and over 69,500 employees (Argyll Group plc, 1994). The company also operates one other food retailer, Presto, a regional supermarket in the north-east of England and in Scotland. Currently, Safeway represents four-fifths of group sales. The company has grown to its present size through acquisition as opposed to organic growth, in contrast to its rivals Sainsbury's and Tesco, whose past growth has been largely generated from either internally generated revenue or a combination of revenue and rights issues.

The Argyll Group has three main strategic objectives:

1   To achieve sufficient scale to compete effectively in the national market.

2   To maximize the exploitation of scale economies.

3   To enhance competitiveness so as to secure a profitable position in consumer markets.

Although earnings and dividends per share grew at a compound annual rate of 16 per cent over the five-year period to 1993, in 1993 the competitive environment made this year-on-year progress more difficult. In particular, several leading competitors launched price initiatives. Asda, after struggling in the market place in the 1980s, has refocused its operation and returned to its price appeal which formed the basis of its success in the 1970s, reviving its slogan of 'The Asda price', and Tesco launched its value ranges of specially selected lines in simple packaging. This new level of increased price competition is believed to be a significant market trend that will continue in the future. The reason for this belief is the entrance of new competitors in the grocery distribution sector. These new entrants, in particular the German Aldi chain and the Danish Netto group, have chosen to focus their operations in the north-west, north-east and midlands regions. These discount groups offer a limited line of products at deeply discounted prices. Table 3.3 shows Safeway's year-on-year growth for 1990–4.

Table 3.3 Safeway year on year growth 1990–4

	1990	1991	1992	1993	1994
Sales area (square feet)					
20,000 and above	110	130	147	176	200
10,000–19,999	146	152	148	144	138
Under 10,000	35	28	27	25	27
New store openings	23	18	17	30	26
Av. store sales area (000 sq. ft)	18.7	19.4	20.0	20.7	21.2
Av. sales per store (£000 per week)	203.2	223.8	237.6	250.3	263.7
Sales per sq. ft per week (£)	11.2	11.76	12.29	12.56	12.68
Market share (per cent)	4.5	5.2	5.4	5.8	6.0

Source: Argyll Annual Report (1994).

MERCHANDISE ASSORTMENT

Safeway retails its own brand products as well as manufacturer brands. A typical Safeway store will carry 15,000 products. Over 80 per cent of these products are British sourced or produced. In addition to the merchandise ranges, there are extra services in the form of dry cleaning, post offices, pharmacy departments, bakery, coffee shops and delicatessen. The company sees future growth being created through greater enhancement of the Safeway brand itself. This will take place in part as a result of an improved market offering, achieved through greater attention to design, layout, merchandising and the development of its Safeway brand ranges. Quality and value for money is the cornerstone of the company's market offering and the merchandise ranges are developed to support this strategic positioning. The depth of the range and assortment of quality products creates this perception of quality and value. Collaboration with the company's French partner Casino, a member of the same buying group as Argyll, has assisted in the development of new ranges e.g. wine, expanding the variety of international wines. The company has also been active in developing a wider choice of regional products, both mainstream products and specialist products, e.g. Welsh cheese, dried ham from Dorset.

Stage 3: The Safeway Store at Crewe

Crewe is located 34 miles south of Manchester and has been an important railway and industrial town in Cheshire. Much of the town's housing stock is made up of small terraced houses, largely owner occupied, but not necessarily affluent (Crewe and Nantwich Borough Council, 1994). Unemployment in the Crewe travel to work area is below average for the north-west at 10.1 per cent, but above the Cheshire average of 7.7 per cent. The majority of the population of the Crewe area are located in the town of Crewe itself. As part of the area's economic development strategy, investments have taken place in attracting new companies to the area, in particular hi-tech and service organizations. These companies have established themselves within the Crewe Business Park.

Additional to the attraction of new industries to the area, plans are currently underway to develop a new retail park providing

148,000 square feet of retail space. Planning permission has also been granted for a new Sainsbury's store, which is due to open in 1995. These initiatives have been accompanied by an increase in the total population of the area since 1981, from 121,353 to 125,021, and a corresponding increase in available food spend from £1393 wk to £1435 wk.

SAFEWAY STORE DEVELOPMENT AT CREWE

The new store opening at Crewe provided the company with an opportunity to acquire a good site in a town with ageing super-market facilities. Although the demographics of the town itself were not ideal, in the wider Crewe area, comprising the more rural parts of the county, consumer demographics were more favourable to the Safeway market offering. At the time of opening, the new store competition in the area was from two other major groups, Asda and the Co-op. These two stores, although having a loyal customer base, were vulnerable to the opening of a new, more up-market offering, as they had both been developed in the late 1970s. The company anticipated that the majority of its customers would be attracted from within the town of Crewe itself and to the east and south of the site (Barnes, 1989).

MERCHANDISING POLICY

In-store merchandising is determined initially by space planners in the company's head office based on computerized information. Through electronic point of sale (EPoS) systems, trade sales and trade histories of products can be used to allocate footage to products. The flow of products remains uniform nationally and the Crewe store conforms to this nationally determined product flow. The plan is then sent from head office to store. High-volume, low-profit items are placed at the bottom of the shelving (e.g. baked beans), whereas high-profile, new products are placed at a level to catch the consumer's eye and are frequently placed next to a similar established line.

At store level, management works within the plan and decides on the facings within different commodity groups. Within the Crewe store, a typical week would see 20–30 product updates. The store manager is then responsible for implementing the plan and subsequent updates, within given productivity levels. As part of this process, visits take place to competitors' stores to look at specific commodity groups in order to assess whether the product is a good selling line. The Safeway Crewe store itself stocks from 13,000 to 15,000 lines and trades from 29,400 square feet of sales area.

Discussion Points

1 What are the major features of the UK grocery retailing market in the 1990s?

2 What changes are taking place both in the structure of the market and in consumer behaviour?

3 To what extent is grocery retailing a local as opposed to a national business?

4 What are the strengths and weaknesses of the Safeway market offering, *vis-à-vis* its competitors?

5 To what extent should regional variations in food consumption patterns influence in-store merchandising?

6 What are the advantages and disadvantages of centrally determined merchandise plans for store managers?

7 What are the opportunities and threats to the Crewe store of the area's plans to develop a retail park and Sainsbury's store? Should the company implement any merchandise changes to respond to these new developments?

References and Further Reading

Argyll Group plc (1994) Annual Report and Accounts.

Barnes, S. (1989) Safeway Location Report.

The British Shopper (1993) Oxford: Nielsen, in association with NTC Publications.

Collins, A. (1992) *Competitive Retail Marketing*. Maidenhead: McGraw-Hill.

Crewe and Nantwich Borough Council (1994) Economic Development Strategy. Crewe: CNBC.

Curham, A. (1974) The effects of merchandising and temporary promotional activities on the sales of fresh fruit and vegetables in supermarkets. *Journal of Marketing Research*, 9, August, 286–94.

Duke, R. (1991) Post saturation, competition in UK grocery retailing. *Journal of Marketing Management*, 7 (1), 63–75.

Grant, A. (1987) Supermarketing: is the market at saturation point? *Financial Times*, Retailing Conference, London, 17 June.

Henderson Crossthwaite, Institutional Brokers (1993) *Food Retail Perception and Reality.* London: Henderson Crossthwaite.

4

The Operational Implications of Locational Decision Making: a Case Study of the Belfast Co-operative

John Pal and David Bennison

The Manchester Metropolitan University

Stage 1: The Context – Grocery Retailing in Northern Ireland

INTRODUCTION

This case study introduces readers to the grocery retail sector in Northern Ireland as it existed in 1990. Since then there have been many shifts in the political arena that have changed the perception of many mainland based retailers. This case therefore highlights the situation as it existed in 1990 when the Belfast Co-operative was assessing its trading performance in Northern Ireland. In order to do that, this first stage of the case study will outline some of the salient environmental factors impacting on retailers.

THE RETAIL ENVIRONMENT

Northern Ireland has a population in excess of 1.5 million, with Belfast accounting for more than one-quarter of this. The well documented political unrest of the past 25 years has led to the destruction of parts of many town and city centres. For instance, in 1972 the Belfast Co-op had its largest department store razed to the

We would like to thank the Co-operative Wholesale Society for providing the data to undertake this study, and in particular Chris Mardell, Eddie Allan and Adrian Lorimer for their help and advice. We are also indebted to Carole Jamison for coordinating all the arrangements required to complete the case study.

ground, resulting in damage of more than £10 million. Belfast as a whole lost an estimated 25 per cent of its retail floor space in the period 1970–5 (Brown, 1985a, b). Between 1980 and 1990, twenty shopping centres totalling over two million square feet have opened (Brown, 1990).

This growth in shopping floor space has been attributed to a combination of the lessening of the IRA's commercial bombing campaign, central government investment in the transportation infrastructure, increased promotional campaigns of retailers and local authorities and the general increase in consumer expenditure (Brown, 1990).

The centre of Belfast, for instance, has been subject to different amounts of security cordons wrapping around it in an effort to prevent bombing campaigns. Cars were prohibited from entering parts of central Belfast. These cordons have now been removed but the searching of customers' bags on entering shopping centres and even individual shops is still present.

In 1989–90 many non-food multiples were trading in Northern Ireland and specifically in Belfast. Companies such as C&A, Marks and Spencer, the various trading formats of the Burton Group, MFI, B&Q, the main banks and building societies were all represented and had been for some time. In fact, the central area of Belfast is not unlike that of any mainland city in terms of retailer representation.

SPECIAL LEGISLATIVE MEASURES

While the Province is subject to the legislation applying to the rest of the UK, it displays some noticeable differences which have resulted in a different retail landscape. One extra legal provision of particular note is in place. The Fair Employment Practice Act of 1989 requires all employers to ensure that there is no discrimination on the grounds of a person's religion. Companies have to monitor this, are regularly audited by the Fair Employment Department and have to make annual returns and a three-year summary of the religious composition of the workforce. The legislation does not seek to ensure an even split (i.e. 50/50) of Protestant and Catholic but does set quotas and requires that all the necessary procedures have been taken in the recruitment and selection of staff, and that any subsequent promotions are done without any religious bias. Failure to implement the legislation can lead to heavy financial penalties, and individuals discriminated against on religious grounds can receive up to £30,000 compensation. Failure to submit a monitoring return can result in a fine of £2000 plus a further fine for every subsequent day the return is outstanding. This whole topic is dealt with in more detail elsewhere (e.g. Aiken, 1992; Rea and Eastwood, 1992).

THE GROCERY SECTOR

Market structure

For the period up to 1990 it was found that 'a recent investigation of the structure and profitability of the Northern Ireland food retailing sector carried out by the authors has revealed that market saturation within the region has already occurred' (McHugh et al., 1993, p. 33).

In 1989, 60 per cent of grocery retailing was accounted for by Northern Ireland based multiples; 7 per cent by GB based multiples e.g. Littlewoods, Marks and Spencer; 18 per cent by symbol/voluntary groups; 12 per cent by independents; and 3 per cent by the Co-operative Society. However, none of the major British grocers, such as Sainsbury, Tesco, Asda and Argyll, was represented in the Province at this time. Table 4.1 provides a contrast between the GB and Northern Ireland grocery markets.

Table 4.1 Concentration ratios in the grocery market, 1987

	Total (£ million)	Percentage of trade accounted for by the largest five grocers
Great Britain[a]	31,005	38.8
Northern Ireland[b]	900	75.0

[a] Business Monitor: Retailing, 1987.
[b] Northern Ireland Economic Council, 1990.

In 1989, three of the major Northern Irish based food multiples had profit margins of 9 (Wellworth), 6 (Stewarts) and 4 per cent (Crazy Prices).

Consumer spending

Incomes are up to 20 per cent lower than the UK average. While the total average weekly expenditure for Northern Ireland and the UK were broadly similar in 1988 at £199.68 and £196.44 respectively, there were some marked differences in levels of spend on specific categories (FES, 1988). One of the main differences was in the level of spend on food, with households in the Province spending 13 per cent more on that commodity than the average for the rest of the UK. Own label products are not a significant part of the grocery market.

The figures below show the variations in weekly food expenditure for Northern Ireland, indexed against the UK for 1989 (UK = 100).

Bread, cakes	159
Milk, cheese	116
Meat, bacon	119
Fish	93
Oils, fat	148
Sugar, sweeteners	147
Fruit	101
Vegetables	109
Confectionery	89
Hot beverages	77
Soft drinks	135

Figure 4.1 shows the position of Belfast relative to the mainland and some of the main ferry crossings.

Discussion Points

1 Using the information provided in stage 1, outline reasons why some mainland retailers may not have entered the Northern Ireland market.

2 What are the key features of the Northern Ireland grocery market?

3 Identify the main differences in grocery purchasing habits between the Northern Irish and UK customer.

4 What are the opportunities for retailers operating in the grocery market?

Figure 4.1 Some of the main ferry crossings between Britian and Ireland.

Stage 2: The Belfast Co-operative in 1990–1

INTRODUCTION

In 1990 the Co-op operated 23 stores, ranging in size from 700 to 8000 square feet. In contrast the average size of a new Sainsbury's superstore in 1990 was 32,320 square feet, and the average size of all their supermarkets was 22,110 square feet.

Of the Co-op's 23 stores, almost three-quarters were loss making. Half were located in 'neutral' areas, with the remainder evenly split between staunchly Catholic and Protestant areas.

The distribution charges made to the stores were artificially low and did not show the true cost of servicing them. The Belfast Co-op was managed as part of the Scottish region (i.e. from Glasgow), and was treated as a Scottish island.

The regional own label sales for all grocery retailers was running at about 6 per cent at this time, while the Co-op's 23 stores were achieving about 17 per cent own label sales. For the Co-op as a whole (i.e. Britain and Northern Ireland), the proportion of own label sales accounted for about a third of sales.

COMPETITION

In the Province as a whole Wellworth had 30 stores (with a total selling area of 317,000 square feet), while Stewarts had 29 stores and Crazy Prices had 12 (Retail Directory, 1991).

The Belfast area was seen as, generally, a saturated area with many of the best sites having been taken (McHugh *et al.*, 1993). There has been a general suburbanization of the population and associated retail facilities in much the same way as has occurred in Britain, and this has been exacerbated by the 'Troubles'. A number of suburban shopping centres, such as the Abbey Centre and the Park Centre, are anchored by major food multiples.

Discussion Points

1   What are the strengths and weaknesses of the Co-op's position at this time?

2   What are the options available to the Co-op?

Stage 3: The Yorkgate Proposal

Figure 4.2 shows the proposed location for a new Co-op food superstore of 50,000 square feet gross area. The map shows the likely catchment area, the competition and existing Co-op stores.

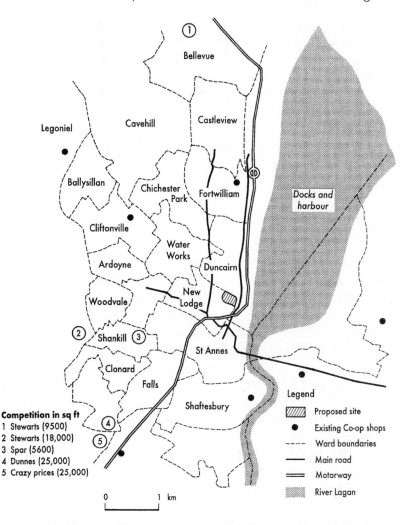

Figure 4.2 The catchment area, competition and existing nearby Co-op stores.

In the immediate vicinity of the site there is a marked absence of competition, with just corner shops and voluntary/symbol group stores. The Co-op itself has eight stores in the catchment. It is forecast that about 40 per cent of the store's turnover could be drawn from New Lodge, Duncairn and the northern part of the city centre, i.e. St. Anne's. These areas combined have about 28 per cent of households with access to a car. Table 4.2 shows some selected ward data for the immediate catchment.

Table 4.2 Ward data for immediate catchment of new superstore

Ward	Ward population	Roman Catholic	Protestant
New Lodge	6370	5479	249
Duncairn	4060	43	3021
Crumlin	3876	51	3030
Water Works	5760	4624	255
St Anne's	3983	729	2504
Chichester Park	5828	3310	1189
Fortwilliam	5113	1041	2914

Source: Northern Ireland Census, 1991. Crown copyright 1991. Published by permission of the Controller of HMSO.

It has been reported that the 'residential segregation of Roman Catholics and Protestants in Belfast is a long-standing feature of the geography of the city' and 'residential segregation is accompanied by activity segregation in that there was a failure of the two groups to interact positively with each other, even before the outbreak of the present Troubles' (Doherty, 1989, pp. 151–2).

The wider catchment has competition from a SuperSpar (5000 square feet) and a Stewarts store (9500 square feet), and Wellworth, Stewarts, Crazy Prices and Dunnes all have at least one store in excess of 18,000 square feet in the potential trading area of Yorkgate.

The cost of the superstore development is £8 million and it is intended to provide the anchor to a larger mixed retail/leisure proposal, including a multi-screen cinema and an integrated mall of 18 smaller shop units and a Co-op Concepts Furniture store. Parking for over 1300 cars is proposed. The site is a former tobacco factory, is surrounded to the north by densely populated housing in the New Lodge and Duncairn wards and, as figure 4.3 shows, abuts the two areas. One of the tower blocks in the New Lodge ward which overlooks the site houses an army observation point and soldiers are flown in by helicopter to man the post.

North Queen Street has featured quite often on the television news as buses have frequently been set ablaze on this road. The site is at the hub of arterial routes spreading to the residential suburbs of north-west Belfast (e.g. Ballysillan, Cavehill) and is alongside a motorway link to the east of the site serving the city centre and beyond.

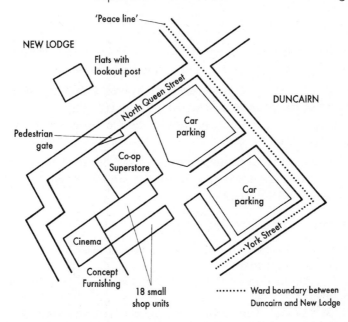

Figure 4.3 The site.

Factors to be taken into account when assessing edge of town and out of town retail proposals

(Summary of Regional Physical Development Strategy 1975–95, as cited in Northern Ireland Economic Council, 1990)

(i) The full effect of new proposals on existing town and suburban centres should be taken into account. For example, over-provision of shops on a large scale and the loss of trade by existing town and suburban centres could change the character of these centres, prejudice redevelopment, have serious economic, social and financial consequences, and distort the pattern of existing public transport services.

(ii) It may be advantageous to combine suburban shopping demand with social and welfare facilities in the form of a district centre.

(iii) The effect on the volume of traffic using roads in the vicinity of the proposed development site.

(iv) The effects on the less mobile sections of society who may be unable to make use of these stores – in particular the elderly and those without cars.

(v) The effects on the environmental amenity of proposals relating to greenfield sites.

Discussion Points

1 Analyse the site taking account of the characteristics of the immediate population and the competition.

2 Drawing on your knowledge from stages 1 and 2, the sensitive nature of the proposed location and the restrictions on new store development listed above, should the Co-op go ahead with this development?

3 What are the operational implications of the site in terms of merchandising, staffing, local marketing and impact on the rest of the Co-op's network?

References and Further Reading

Aiken, O. (1992) Why firms must show a lack of discrimination. *Personnel Management*, August, 54–5.

Brown, S. (1985a) Central Belfast's security segment: an urban phenomenon. *Area*, 17, 1–9.

Brown, S. (1985b) City centre commercial revitalisation: the Belfast experience. *The Planner*, 71 (5), 8–12.

Brown, S. (1990) Shopping centre development in Northern Ireland: a borderline case. *International Journal of Retail and Distribution Management*, 18 (1), 12–17.

Bennison, D. and Clarke, I. (1994) Network effectiveness: making locations work better. In P. McGoldrick (ed.), *Cases in Retail Management*. London: Pitman.

Bennison, D., Clarke, I. and Pal, J. (1995) Locational decision making in retailing: an exploratory framework for analysis. *International Review of Retail, Distribution and Consumer Research*, 5 (1), 1–20.

Davies, R. and Rogers, R. (1984) *Store Location and Store Assessment Research*. Chichester: Wiley.

Doherty, P. (1989) Ethnic segregation levels in the Belfast urban area. *Area*, 21 (2), 151–9.

McGoldrick, P. (1990) *Retail Marketing*. New York: McGraw-Hill.

McHugh, M., Greenan, K. and O'Rourke, B. (1993) Food retailers: stuck in the middle? *British Food Journal*, 95 (3), 32–7.

Northern Ireland Economic Council (1990) *Retailing in Northern Ireland*, Report 83, August. Belfast: NIEC.

Rea, D. and Eastwood, J. (1992) Legislating for Northern Ireland's fair employment problem. *International Journal of Manpower*, 13 (6–7), 31–40.

Retail Directory (1991), Newman Books Ltd, London.

Wrigley, N. (1988) *Store Choice, Store Location and Market Analysis*. London: Routledge.

5

Developing Customer Loyalty: the Saver Card Experience

Mohammed Rafiq

Loughborough University Business School

The whole of the grocery industry was taken by surprise when Tesco launched its Clubcard loyalty scheme nationally in February 1995. Tesco had been trialling the scheme since 1993 in a limited number of stores before launching it nationally. Until Clubcard's national launch, Sainsbury's had been using its own Saver Card loyalty scheme in 15 to 20 of its stores at any one time. Two months later Sainsbury's was operating the scheme in 50 of its stores and by July it was operating in 180 stores. Similarly, Safeway had been using its ABC customer reward card in 25 stores in February, but by April 1995 had extended it to 106 stores and was considering further expansion. Asda also began trialling its Club Card in different versions during this period, despite investing heavily in the Catalina system which provides customers with computer generated coupons at the checkout.

The Background

The rapid expansion of store numbers by the Big Five (Asda, Sainsbury's, Safeway, Tesco and Somerfield (formerly Gateway)) in the 1980s and 1990s, and growing car ownership, has given most

This case is intended for the purpose of classroom discussion rather than to illustrate an ideal or an indifferent handling of a business situation. The case study has been written with the kind cooperation of J. Sainsbury plc and information available from public sources.

shoppers a choice of two or more large supermarket stores within easy travelling distance. This has meant that most shoppers are not completely loyal to any one store and indeed there is evidence that they are becoming less loyal. The increasing concentration in the industry has also meant that it is becoming more and more difficult to increase market share, and any further increase is likely to be at the expense of the big players rather than small independents. The intensity of competition in the industry was further heightened by the onset of recession and the arrival of the European hard discounters in the early 1990s. Added to this, in real terms, household expenditure on food has remained static for the past six years. Hence, Sainsbury's and its rivals are putting increasing emphasis on customer loyalty in the face of intense competition in the sector.

Loyalty schemes *per se* are not new. They have been used by retailers for a long time. In fact, one of the original loyalty schemes, the trading stamp, originated in the USA in the late nineteenth century. Trading stamps are given by a retailer to customers (usually in proportion to expenditure) and can be redeemed for cash or goods. Each stamp is usually of low value and customers need to collect books of stamps to get a significant redemption. The idea behind such schemes is to get customers to spend a greater proportion of their expenditure in the store (rather than a competitor) and to frequent the store more often.

A trading stamp based loyalty scheme popular among UK retailers until the late 1970s was the Green Shield trading stamps scheme. This scheme collapsed in 1977 after Tesco withdrew from the scheme in its bid to reposition the store more up market. Some Co-operative societies still issue their own trading stamps. In the 1960s, when trading stamps first began to be widely used in the UK, Sainsbury's actively campaigned against them, arguing that the cost of the scheme would have to be passed on to the customer. However, Sainsbury's, like the other retailers, has not been averse to using other types of loyalty schemes. In fact, one of Sainsbury's recent successes was an air miles scheme, which involved collecting receipts to the value of a certain amount to qualify for discounted tickets to various destinations on British Airways flights.

What is new about the current loyalty schemes is that they are electronic rather than manual. While manual schemes are effective, they are relatively crude compared to the electronic schemes. Electronic promotional schemes consist of either electronically dispensed coupons or frequent shopper or loyalty clubs such as

Sainsbury's Saver Card. An example of the former is the Catalina system used by Asda stores. In this system, consumer purchases trigger the dispensing of coupons for the product bought, rival manufacturers' products or the store's own products. Asda is said to be using the system to increase the sales of its own label products.

The basic rationale behind club schemes is to increase profits by developing long-term relationships with customers, particularly loyal customers. An important underlying reason for targeting existing customers is that it is easier to sell more to existing customers than to recruit new ones. Loyal customers also tend to spend more than the average customer spend per visit. Hence, the loss of loyal customers can have a highly detrimental effect on store profitability.

An important requirement for the building of relationships with customers is a customer database. One of the features of the current wave of loyalty schemes is the building, as cheaply as possible, of a database of the store's customers, who can be encouraged to remain or become the store's most loyal customers. With electronic loyalty schemes it is also possible to gather data on the shopping habits of customers and to use this information to target specific groups of customers with incentives and offers. Unlike trading stamps and similar loyalty schemes, the new loyalty schemes can be branded by the retailers to reflect the store's image and values. One of the major problems with the Green Shield trading stamp scheme was that the same benefits were offered by all the retailers subscribing to the scheme.

An essential prerequisite of electronic loyalty schemes is the existence of an adequate information technology (IT) network. From an IT point of view, around the beginning of 1992 Sainsbury's was in a position where it could run an electronic loyalty scheme – that is to say, total networking of all branches, and central processing facilities that would run in application rather than off-line. Sainsbury's also knew that its major competitors were interested in loyalty schemes, which provided further impetus to the development of a scheme at Sainsbury's.

Designing the Saver Card Scheme

At the time when Sainsbury's was doing the design work there were quite a number of retailers who were running loyalty schemes based on plastic cards, but very often they depended on the customers receiving a statement at the end of every quarter (for example, the Spend and Save loyalty scheme which its sister company, Homebase, had been running since 1991). There were other schemes up and running (for instance, those run by petrol companies), where points are basically read on to a card and then at the redeeming location points read off the card. The design team felt, however, that such schemes did not give the customer the immediacy, the link or the attachment to the retailer that they thought could be achieved with a two-on-one scheme, i.e. points could be recorded and read off at the same time.

A working group consisting of marketing, retail and IT managers was set up to look into an electronically based loyalty scheme. The group took its brief from marketing colleagues, who sought to put the manual scheme into a format that would be as acceptable or more acceptable to the customer but run electronically. The aim behind the new scheme was to give the customer the immediacy of the paper and rubber stamp of a manual scheme, but without the customer having the hassle of carrying a piece of cardboard, so that customers would know at any one time when they shopped where they stood in relation to the earning and redemption of points. At the same time, an attempt was made to enhance the scheme by the use of the network system to give the customer something that looked better. In particular, Sainsbury's wanted to give customers something they felt that their competitors' schemes did not give, i.e. the immediacy of knowing how many points they had accumulated and their redemption value.

The immediacy of the scheme was greatly enhanced, in comparison to other schemes, by the simple expedient of pre-loading the card number on to the mainframe computer, making the card instantly usable. A customer could literally walk into a store, collect the card and go to the checkout and start collecting points instantly. Everyone using the Saver Card also receives on his or her till receipt a statement showing the opening balance, the number of points earned, the number of points redeemed and the redemption value of the points (see figure 5.1), thus giving the customer an immediate idea of the benefit of shopping at Sainsbury's. Redemption of the points is also quite simple and immediate: points previously collected can be redeemed against current purchases by telling the cashiers how many points to redeem as long as the value of the points redeemed does not exceed the total value of the transaction.

```
        J SAINSBURY PLC
        GREENCLOSE LANE
         LOUGHBOROUGH
           LE11 OAS
        TEL. NO.  01509 237724

                           £
          * FRENCH LAGER    3.79
          * ORANGE JUICE    1.99
          * LEMON TWIST     1.35
          BANANAS           0.95
          BRAN FLAKES 750G  1.89
          P/BAC PASTICCIO   1.69
          MAGAZINE AUGUST   1.00
          RADIO TIMES       0.68
          P/MUSH PASTICCIO  1.69
          AVOCADOS          0.42
        * PICK/MIX SINGL
            6 @  £0.19      1.14
        MULTIBUY
          BUY 6 SAVE 15P   -0.15
          * WILD RAIN GEL   2.49
          * F/STONE DRINK   0.65
          * F/STONE DRINK   0.65
          SPINACH           1.39
          AMERICAN P/SKNS   1.19
          MARMITE MUFFINS   0.67
          * WILD RAIN GEL   2.49
        MULTIBUY
          BUY 2 SAVE 125   -1.25
          * DOVE SP 2X100G  1.49
          * CAPUCCINO STKS  0.99
          JS CHSE/CHVE DIP  0.75
          * CLAIROL HSPRAY  1.69
          JS PAIN CHOC X4
          REDUCED PRICE     0.70
          JS BAGUETTE X3    0.89
          DESSERTS X6       1.09
          * THRMD T/PASTE   0.39
          CREOLE CHICKEN    1.29
          * STYLING CREAM   1.99


          33 ITEMS PURCHASED
        BALANCE DUE         35.99

        CASHBACK            40.00
          BALANCE DUE       75.99
        EFT                 75.99

        CASHBACK            40.00

        ********************************

        SAVERCARD NUMBER
          6341 7900 8376 6312

        SAVERCARD STATEMENT
                           PTS
          OPENING BALANCE   340
          POINTS REDEEMED     0
          POINTS EARNED      30

        NEW TOTAL           370

        CURRENT REDEMPTION
        VALUE FOR GOODS    £3.70

        ******************************

          MULTIBUY SAVING    1.40

        DATE: 27 JUL 95   TIME: 20:26
        LOC:  5  OP:  273  TRANS: 2405
           SAINSBURY'S
          EVERYONE'S FAVOURITE
             INGREDIENT
```

Figure 5.1 A till receipt showing a Saver Card statement.

As the idea behind the scheme is to reward loyal customers, the benefits of participating in the scheme were made variable, ranging from 0.75 to a maximum of 2.5 per cent of expenditure, as long as the customer spent more than the minimum required expenditure to qualify for points in any single transaction. For example, in the scheme that Sainsbury's operated at the Pepper Hill Store in Northfleet, in 1994 (see figure 5.2), a customer had to spend £20 before qualifying for any points and then received 10 points for every £20 spent thereafter. This contrasts with Tesco's Clubcard scheme, which awards shoppers 1 per cent incentive as long as a customer spends a minimum of £10 in a single transaction, and thereafter every £5 spent earns points. However, a customer has to spend a minimum of £250 in a quarter to earn the minimum award of £2.50 in vouchers. The Safeway scheme is the simplest of the three major stores, as it offers customers an incentive of 1 per cent of expenditure for every £1 spent in Safeway stores. For a more detailed comparison of the major loyalty schemes see table 5.1.

In order to make the rewards more appealing to shoppers and to lock them into Sainsbury's Saver Card scheme, there is a system of bonus points that customers earn when they accumulate a certain number of points. The system of bonuses means that the more points a customer earns the higher the bonuses, bonuses for which the customer does not have to buy goods. Bonus points are awarded when the customer reaches 200, 500, 1000, 1800 and 3200 points. The bonuses are, respectively, 100, 300, 600, 1200 and 3200 points, so that by the time a customer has accumulated 5000 points, 4000 are made up of bonuses (see figure 5.2). The system is designed to encourage shoppers not to redeem too quickly and to offer higher rewards to higher spenders.

With a loyalty scheme it is highly desirable to know who the customer is; hence, considerable effort is made to ensure that the customer filled in the registration form as this is not a prerequisite for using the Saver Card. Remarkably, 90 per cent of the customers filled in the form. It was fairly simple and included the name, address, postcode and the number of persons in the household plus level of income of the household (see figure 5.2). With this information Sainsbury's knows precisely who are participating in the scheme and where they come from. This is a major advantage of electronic loyalty schemes over manual ones, where the retailer had little idea who was participating.

REGISTRATION FORM

Please complete before using your Saver Card and post in one of the special boxes provided

Title └─┴─┴─┘ Initial(s) └─┴─┴─┘ Surname └─┴─┴─┴─┴─┴─┴─┴─┴─┴─┴─┴─┴─┴─┴─┴─┴─┴─┴─┴─┘

Address └─┴─┘

└─┴─┘

Town └─┴─┘

County └─┴─┴─┴─┴─┴─┴─┴─┴─┴─┴─┴─┴─┴─┴─┴─┴─┘ Postcode └─┴─┴─┴─┴─┴─┘

No. of persons in household └─┴─┘

If you do not wish to receive promotional details from
Sainsbury's, or other responsible organisations, please tick box ☐   Signature_____

Card No **63417900 0585 7256** ___ Expires **4 SEPT 1994** Only valid at **PEPPER HILL NORTHFLEET**

Your Card No. **6341 7900 0585 7256**   EXPIRES **4 SEPT 1994**   ONLY VALID AT   **PEPPER HILL NORTHFLEET**

The brand new way to save at Sainsbury's

Here's your very own Sainsbury's Saver Card. With it you earn Points which can save you up to £50 or more at this store until 4th September 1994 inclusive. To start, simply fill in the Registration Form and post it in one of the special boxes provided. Then sign your card and hand it to the cashier **before** you pay for your shopping.

How you earn Points

You earn 10 Points for every £20 you spend at the checkout*. So a £40 spend earns you 20 Points, a £60 spend earns you 30 Points, and so on. Your till receipt always shows the Points you've earned plus their value.

How you save money

Once you've earned Points, you can save money on future purchases in store. Just tell the cashier how much money you want to save and your bill will be adjusted accordingly†. But **don't use your Points too soon. It's much better to save them up, because then you'll be entitled to Bonus Points which mean even bigger savings!**

How you save even more money

By saving up your Points you earn **Bonus Points which lead to much bigger savings.**

Bonus Points are awarded when you reach 200; 500; 1,000; 1,800 and 3,200 Points - but only once at each level. Just look at the table and you'll see the more Points you save the bigger your Bonus gets. So by the time you reach 5,000 Points, 4,000 are made up of Bonus Points! After 5,000 Points, the cycle starts again. For instance, 5,200 Points give you 100 Bonus Points, making 5,300 Points: a £53 saving. It makes sense to go for the big Bonuses with a Sainsbury's Saver Card!

*Offer excludes Cashback and purchases of Gift Vouchers, Saving Stamps and from the Tobacco Kiosk, Coffee Shop and Petrol Station where applicable
†The value of Points redeemed in any single transaction cannot be higher than the value of that transaction
Points can be saved until Sunday 4th September 1994 inclusive
Points must be redeemed by Saturday 1st October 1994 inclusive
Saver Card customer enquiries 071 921 7075

SPEND*	POINTS SAVED	NEW BONUS POINTS	TOTAL POINTS	TOTAL VALUE
1 x £20	10	–	10	10p
20 x £20	200	100	300	£3
40 x £20	500	300	800	£8
60 x £20	1,000	600	1,600	£16
80 x £20	1,800	1,200	3,000	£30
100 x £20	3,200	1,800	5,000	£50

Figure 5.2 Part of a leaflet showing the Saver Card scheme operated at Sainsbury's Pepper Hill, Northfleet, store, 1994.

Another feature of the scheme is that it is centrally driven – that is, every transaction is on-line and is identified by the card to the centre on every occasion. This enables the managers at the centre to set the scheme earn and redeem levels at whatever level they wish

Table 5.1 Supermarket loyalty cards and what they offered, July 1995

Scheme	Operation	Reward	No. of stores	Direct mail
Sainsbury's Saver Card	Five points awarded for every £10 spent, double points in July and August 1995. Rewards on a sliding scale depending upon expenditure.	Discounts range from 0.5 to 2.5 per cent	180 out of 355 stores	No mailouts; discounts given at the till
Tesco Clubcard	The first £10 gives the shopper 2 points, every £5 spent thereafter gives 1 point. For 100 points you get £5 off. Minimum spend of over 60s and students set at £5.	Equivalent to 1 per cent discount	527 stores	Vouchers posted quarterly
Safeway Added Bonus Card	One point awarded for every £1 spent. 100 points give £1 in discounts. Also offers free tickets to various leisure attractions (Alton Towers etc.), one free child's ticket for every £50 spent.	Equivalent to 1 per cent discount	130 stores	No mailouts; discount given at the till
Asda Style Card	One point for every £1 spent redeemable against clothes and leisure goods in selected stores only.	Both give around 2.5 per cent return	On trial in 16 stores	No mailouts
Asda Club Card	Redeemable against anything in store, points vary from store to store.			

for any site, depending upon the marketing objectives. Indeed, the terms could be altered week to week in a given scheme, if management so wished. In fact, all the major parameters of the scheme are set at the centre, including the start time and finish time, the end of the earning period and the end of the redemption period. It also means that all of the administration of getting the scheme off the ground is lifted off the shoulders of store managers. All they have to do is hand out the cards, provide reasonable space to fill in the registration form and train the cashiers. So they do not have to do anything in setting up the scheme or administering it, which is all done at the centre.

Training

An average Sainsbury's superstore deals with around 25,000 customers a week; hence it is essential that the correct training is provided to employees coming into contact with customers using the Saver Card. This means training up to 300 cashiers and other staff for just one store. The training obviously involves familiarizing cashiers on how to add points to the Saver Card and how to redeem the points. Training is also given to ensure that customers present their card at the checkout. It is important that staff get customers to fill in the registration form, as this is voluntary in the Sainsbury's scheme. Customers, however, are also encouraged to fill in the registration form through the incentive of a prize draw (see figure 5.3). The training is carried out by the local store management.

Testing and Fine Tuning the Scheme

Sainsbury's found that in the initial stages of the schemes there was a fairly high level of interest, with around 60–70 per cent of customers taking the leaflets and listening to the explanation offered by staff. A proportion of customers then abandoned the scheme because the minimum level expenditure required to benefit from the scheme was too high for them. The vast majority of customers hung on to the card, and Sainsbury's found that very few customers redeemed their points, preferring instead to go for the bonuses. The regular customers obviously realized that the bonuses were worth having given that they are likely to continue shopping at that particular store.

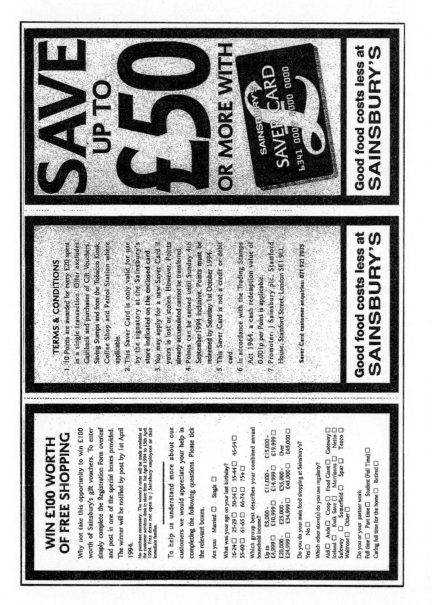

Figure 5.3 An excerpt from the Saver Card leaflet showing the use of a free prize draw.

In order to test customer reaction to different types of scheme, Sainsbury's also experimented with different levels of expenditure necessary to qualify for the rewards. For instance, in the scheme which Sainsbury's ran at its Pepper Hill store in Northfleet in 1994, a customer had to spend a minimum of £20 in a single transaction to qualify for the first level of rewards (see figure 5.2). In other stores where the loyalty scheme was tested there was no lower limit on expenditure: everything that a customer bought qualified, and with different bonuses, as well. In general, the reward levels in the initial schemes were more generous than schemes such as the Pepper Hill one. If a customer persevered and collected all the bonuses the rewards were quite significant. With profit margins as tight as they are in today's competitive environment, it is difficult to justify high rewards unless there is a high degree of certainty that a large amount of extra trade is generated and that the store will be able to hold on to it for a long time.

Sainsbury's also experimented with different lengths of period for the scheme. It found that interest in the schemes waned significantly after six months and that the optimum period was 13 to 15 weeks. This is the typical length of a Saver Card scheme, although for competitive and other reasons some schemes are considerably longer.

For example, in the Redhill (Surrey) store the Saver Card scheme began in late September/early October 1993 and it was designed to end in the first week of January. Customers had to spend £20 in a single transaction to start earning points. There was a fairly high level of interest, with some 60–70 per cent of the customers registering with the scheme. A proportion of the customers then abandoned it because of the £20 limit, as they just did not spend £20 in a single transaction. This did not worry Sainsbury's unduly, as the scheme was designed to attract the higher spending customers and to hold their weekly spending with Sainsbury's. Two things happened which had not been anticipated. Initially, the majority of customers redeemed their points after about six weeks. After that, however, the redemption rates decreased and, in fact, the closer it got to Christmas the lower the redemption rates got, with hardly anybody redeeming points during Christmas week. Sainsbury's had anticipated that the customers would redeem their points to fund Christmas shopping. Instead, the card holders threw in their Christmas spending as well to boost themselves up to the next level of bonuses and they all redeemed in January. The result was that, although there was an increase in sales during the Christmas period, there was also an increase in the payouts as a result of customers not redeeming their points at a time when consumer expenditure is traditionally high.

Targeting for Loyalty

Research suggests that there are basically three types of customers that a grocery retailer will attract: the 'loyals' (constituting roughly one third of shoppers), who do their main shop and spend the majority of their budget with their preferred store; the 'secondary shoppers' (constituting around 40 per cent of customers), who prefer one store for their main shop but regularly shop in another for the rest of their shopping; and the 'promiscuous shoppers' (around 15 per cent of customers), who are not loyal to any particular retailer and will frequently change where they do their main food shopping. The idea behind loyalty schemes is to move the shopper up the loyalty ladder; that is, from being a promiscuous shopper to becoming a habitual secondary shopper, and from there to a store loyal shopper.

The loyals typically spend 70 per cent or more of their grocery budget with their preferred store. The secondary shoppers will spend between 30 and 69 per cent of their budget at their preferred store and the rest will be divided between their second choice store and perhaps one or two stores. The promiscuous grocery shoppers will spend less than 30 per cent of their grocery budget in any one shop. The majority of multiple food retailers obtain over 50 per cent of their turnover from their most loyal customers. For the Big Five (Asda, Sainsbury's, Safeway, Tesco and Somerfield) the figure ranges from 55 per cent for Somerfield to 70 per cent for Sainsbury's.

Sainsbury's Saver Card scheme appears to be targeting the loyals and the secondary shoppers in the first instance. Promotions that require a spend of £20 or more to qualify for the first level of rewards are aimed very much at the present loyal and regular customer. Secondary customers are more likely to be spending less than £20 in any one visit, given that the average spend in Sainsbury's stores in 1994 was just under £23. The object of the Saver Card scheme is to make sure these customers keep coming regularly and, where possible, to encourage them to place more of their

grocery expenditure with Sainsbury's and not to go and be secondary shoppers somewhere else. To attract a significant number of
secondary shoppers the incentives have to be offered at lower levels
of expenditure, say £10 or less (see figure 5.4 for such a scheme), or

---

05/95

REGISTRATION FORM
Please complete in block capitals before using your Saver Card and post in one of the special boxes provided

Title _____ Initial(s) _____ Surname _____

Address _____

Town _____ County _____ Postcode _____

This information will not be passed on to other organisations. If you do not
wish to receive promotional details from Sainsbury's, please tick box ☐   Signature _____

May we take a moment of your time?
To help us improve our customer service would you please complete the brief questions below.

How many people are there in your household? |__|__|

Please indicate your age range
18-24 ☐ 25-34 ☐ 35-44 ☐ 45-54 ☐ 55-64 ☐ 65+ ☐
If you have any children in your household what ages are they?
Expecting ☐ 0-6mths ☐ 7mths-11mths ☐ 1-2yrs ☐
3-5yrs ☐ 6-10yrs ☐ 11-15yrs ☐
Do you have a dog?   Yes ☐ No ☐
Do you have a cat?   Yes ☐ No ☐
Do you have a car?   Yes ☐ No ☐

At which of the following stores do you do most of your grocery
shopping?
Sainsbury's ☐   Savacentre ☐   Asda ☐   Tesco ☐
Gateway ☐   Kwiksave ☐   Safeway ☐
Other (please specify) _____
Which other stores have you used in the last three months?
(Tick all that apply)
Sainsbury's ☐   Asda ☐   Gateway ☐   Kwiksave ☐
Tesco ☐   Other (please specify) _____

Card No **6341** **7900 8375 8426**   Points earned until **02 DEC 1995**   Points redeemed until **30 DEC 1995**

Your Card No.	**6341** **7900 8375 8426**	Points Earned Until	**02 DEC 1995**	Inclusive	Points Redeemed Until	**30 DEC 1995**	Inclusive

The new way to save at Sainsbury's

SAINSBURY'S
SAVER CARD
ONLY VALID AT
LOUGHBOROUGH
VALID UNTIL
02 DEC 95

Here's your very own Sainsbury's Saver Card. With it
you earn Points which can save you up to £50 at the
store(s) on the card until the date specified in the panel
above. To start, simply fill in the Registration Form and
post it in one of the special boxes provided. Then sign
your card and hand it to the cashier before you pay for
your shopping.

How you earn Points
You earn 5 Points for every £10 you spend at the checkout*. So a £40 spend earns you 20 Points, a £50 spend
earns you 25 Points, and so on. Your till receipt shows the
Points you've earned plus their value. Don't forget your
card. If you haven't got it, you can't earn points.

How you save money
Once you've earned Points, you can save money on future
purchases in store. Just tell the cashier how much money
you want to save and your bill will be adjusted accordingly †.
But don't use your Points too soon. It's much better to
save them up, because then you'll be entitled to Bonus
Points which mean even bigger savings!

How you save even more money
By saving up your Points you earn Bonus Points which
lead to much bigger savings.
Bonus Points are awarded when you reach 200; 500;
1,000; 1,800 and 3,200 Points – but only once at each
level. Just look at the table and you'll see the more Points
you save the bigger your Bonus gets. So by the time you
reach 5,000 Points, 4,000 are made up of Bonus Points! It
makes sense to go for the big Bonuses with a Sainsbury's
Saver Card!

*Offer excludes Cashback and purchases of Gift Vouchers, Saving Stamps,
National Lottery tickets and from the Coffee Shop, Shoppers' Restaurant,
Shoppers' Oasis and Petrol Station where applicable
†The value of Points redeemed in any single transaction cannot be higher than
the value of that transaction
Points can be earned and redeemed until the dates specified in the panel above
Saver Card customer enquiries 0171 921 7075 during office hours

SPEND*	POINTS SAVED	NEW BONUS POINTS	TOTAL POINTS	TOTAL VALUE
1 x £10	5	–	5	5p
40 x £10	200	100	300	£3
80 x £10	500	300	800	£8
120 x £10	1,000	600	1,600	£16
160 x £10	1,800	1,200	3,000	£30
200 x £10	3,200	1,800	5,000	£50

Figure 5.4 Part of a leaflet showing the Saver Card scheme operated at
Sainsbury's Loughborough store, 1995.

even allowing all expenditures to qualify for incentives. In the case of Saver Card, the system of rising bonuses may also encourage some secondary customers to put more of their secondary shopping with Sainsbury's, or indeed to spend more of their primary shopping with Sainsbury's. With most schemes Sainsbury's also attempts to attract new customers by advertising the scheme in the local papers. Sainsbury's own research shows that where it has run schemes of this style, there is a measurable increase in customer numbers.

There is some evidence emerging which suggests that loyalty schemes attract promiscuous customers rather than loyal ones. Indeed, those sceptical of the benefits of loyalty schemes argue that loyal customers would tend to shop at their preferred store irrespective of the loyalty rewards. They further point out that the major determinant in the choice of store in food shopping is still locational convenience, followed by price, product range and quality. Another criticism of loyalty schemes is that schemes that give the same reward to all customers do not discriminate between loyal and promiscuous shoppers and are, therefore, not different from a short-term sales promotion which does not necessarily build loyalty.

Incentivizing Card Holders

A major reason for launching loyalty schemes is the database of customers that the scheme enables the retailer to build. This database can then be used to target the shoppers with additional incentives to shop (such as money off coupons) and other marketing communications. In the early stages of development the use of such incentives was limited but Sainsbury's is actively examining this opportunity. This has become more urgent as both its main competitors, Tesco and Safeway, have been direct mailing their card holders with money-off coupons and other promotions to provide them with additional incentives to shop at their stores. These incentives are in addition to the loyalty rewards. Tesco also sent a Christmas magazine to its Clubcard members in November 1995.

One of the current weaknesses of the Saver Card is that, unlike Tesco's Clubcard and Safeway's ABC card, it has no data capture facility, which means that it does not record the individual items that a customer buys but only the total amount of the transaction. This means that customers cannot be targeted with promotions designed to exploit their buying habits. For instance, Clubcard's data capture facility allows Tesco to identify wine buyers and to target them with information about new wines, special promotions and price deals and so forth.

Strategic versus Tactical Use of Saver Card

From the beginning, Sainsbury's has regarded its loyalty scheme as a tactical rather than a strategic weapon and has used it largely in two types of stores. First, it is used where Sainsbury's has felt that there is a need to be competitively aggressive: a new store opening of a competitor, for example. On other occasions, Sainsbury's has introduced the Saver Card scheme into a store to invigorate shopper interest and to give store sales an uplift.

Although Sainsbury's has a good track record for store openings, sales expectations may not be met for a variety of reasons. For instance, Sainsbury's has encountered problems when opening branches in new trading areas, particularly in the north of England, Wales and one or two Scottish areas where the Sainsbury's name is not well known. While advertising helps in these cases, the Saver Card scheme may be introduced to provide an extra interest in order to build sales rapidly.

In terms of the competitor opening, one of the first stores to introduce the Saver Card scheme (the Bagshott Road, Woking, store) was chosen for that very reason. Sainsbury's main rival, Tesco, was opening just before Christmas within easy car striking distance. Tesco's new store opening was watched with interest, as it was known from previous experience to what degree there would be a dip in the sales of the Sainsbury's store: it does not matter how loyal customers are, if a new store opens there is a tendency for them to visit it out of curiosity. There was a slight dip in the sales of the Bagshott Road store, but in comparison with the downturn in sales that Sainsbury's had experienced in other competitor openings, it was nowhere near as pronounced and the trade returned to its former level within a couple of weeks. The Saver Card scheme had done its job.

In order to be an effective weapon against competitor openings, the introduction of the loyalty scheme has to be planned well ahead. This is not a great problem if a competitor is building a new store from scratch, as the lead times for such projects are fairly long.

However, if the competitor takes over an existing store and converts it to its own fascia, it may be difficult to react quickly. For example, even if Sainsbury's moved extremely quickly, it would take two or three weeks for store staff to be trained up and to set everything up on its mainframe computers. In addition, the production of the cards has a lead time of several weeks.

Assessing the Effectiveness of the Saver Card Scheme

In order to assess the effectiveness of the Saver Card scheme, a cost–benefit analysis needs to be undertaken. The costs of the Saver Card scheme can be divided into two: namely, set-up costs and the costs of the rewards that are offered to customers. The set-up costs include the cost of producing the loyalty cards, training employees and putting the names and addresses of the customers on a database (which is carried out by a third party for Sainsbury's). In addition, there are front-end computing costs associated with putting the cards on to the mainframe computer and, as the transactions come through, processing them at the top end. For a typical Sainsbury's store, it is estimated that the set up costs are in the range of £35,000 to £50,000 per store, depending on the level of take-up of the scheme. The costs of the rewards are determined by the structure of particular schemes but range from 0.5 to 2.5 per cent of sales during the period that the scheme operates. Assuming that any advertising costs are absorbed into the normal advertising budget, for a typical store the total costs for a scheme (including set-up costs and cost of incentives) running for 15 weeks range from an estimated £80,000 to £140,000. This amounts to between 1.0 and 1.5 per cent of sales. It is estimated that in order to break even this requires an uplift in store sales of 3–4 per cent.

Before the expansion in the number of stores operating the scheme, the vast majority of Saver Card schemes had been self-funding; that is, they generated enough extra sales to recover the costs. Of course, some schemes have been more successful than others, depending largely on the type of scheme that is being run. The Bagshott Road scheme mentioned above, for instance, was a fairly generous scheme, deliberately designed that way in order to make sure that it worked first time. Hence, it is not surprising to learn that it was a successful scheme. Others, where the bonuses were cut quite significantly, while they have not been as successful as the Bagshott Road scheme, are still seen as being worthwhile because they have been self-funding and generated more trade, as well as providing an extremely useful customer database that can be used for marketing purposes.

However, the success of a loyalty scheme is measured by the degree to which the scheme actually keeps customers loyal to the store even though the scheme has finished. Hence, Sainsbury's continues to monitor stores for some time after the scheme has closed to see whether sales levels achieved during the scheme are maintained or are tailing off. If sales levels revert back to the pre-scheme levels, then Sainsbury's needs to consider whether it should repeat the scheme.

Extensions and New Developments (Post February 1995)

Maintaining loyalty is not simply a function of what Sainsbury's does but also of what its competitors do. This was graphically illustrated by the national launch of the Clubcard. In the first three months after launching Clubcard, Tesco had managed to recruit five million customers to its scheme; that is, around one-quarter of UK households. It had also managed to take 0.6 per cent of Sainsbury's sales in areas where they were in direct competition. Such an aggressive move by its main rival made it imperative for Sainsbury's to reassess its Saver Card strategy. Hence, in July 1995 Sainsbury's extended the Saver Card scheme to 180 of its 355 stores. Shortly afterwards, it also announced that the Saver Card could be used at all participating stores instead of just at the issuing store. This was virtually forced upon Sainsbury's because Tesco's Clubcard could be used in any of its stores, but also made sense now that there were many more Sainsbury's stores where the Saver Card could be used. For competitive reasons Sainsbury's also reduced the initial qualifying expenditure to £10. At the same time Sainsbury's tried to seize back some of the initiative from its rivals by offering double points on purchases throughout July and August 1995 in all the 180 card issuing stores, thus providing a new twist to the seasonal price promotions that have become common over the past few years.

Despite these developments, as the busy Christmas trading season approached, one major question remained for Sainsbury's: should it completely abandon its selective approach and go for a national scheme like its main rival? And what form should it take?

Safeway, its other main competitor, had already announced that it was launching its scheme nationally in the autumn of 1995. Safeway hoped to tie in third parties in the leisure area to enhance its card offer. It had already negotiated a deal with Kays catalogue, where Safeway card holders would receive up to 40 per cent discounts on selected items in the jointly produced catalogue sent exclusively to Safeway's ABC card holders. Asda, on the other hand, appeared unlikely to roll out its scheme nationally, having been disappointed in the sales increases resulting from its experimental loyalty schemes. However, Sainsbury's is known to be looking at a number of different schemes to rival those of its competitors and give better rewards to loyal customers. In an interview with *Supermarketing*, in July 1995, David Sainsbury revealed some of the ideas behind any future scheme: 'We want to find something which gives better value to the customer, a product which really rewards loyalty. We would be looking to give bigger discount or other benefits.' He added: 'One of the things we might do is give greater benefits to the loyal shopper than one who just shops occasionally. If we can find a way of doing this we will launch such a product' (*Supermarketing*, 14 July 1995, p. 24).

In the early autumn of 1995 it looked as if a loyalty war was firmly on the cards!

Discussion Points

1   Why are so many leading retailers launching electronic loyalty schemes? Why is it that the discounters are not showing any interest in these schemes?

2   Compare the advantages and disadvantages of the following:

   (a)   trading stamp scheme;

   (b)   electronic coupon dispensers such as the Catalina system;

   (c)   electronic loyalty club cards.

3   What are the advantages/disadvantages of Sainsbury's Saver Card scheme to the customer compared with those of Tesco and Safeway?

4   How effective do you think the various schemes are in targeting loyal customers? Or are loyalty schemes glorified sales

promotions designed to increase short-term sales rather than developing long-term loyalty?

5 Should Sainsbury's abandon its selective scheme and follow Tesco's lead with a uniform national Saver Card? Justify your answer.

6 What features should a nationally launched Saver Card scheme incorporate so that it really rewards loyal Sainsbury's shoppers and is effective against the other loyalty cards in the market?

Further Reading

Anonymous (1993) Marketing guide 30: customer loyalty. *Marketing*, 23–6.

Anonymous (1995) Shoppers loyal despite schemes. *Marketing*, 2 March, 5.

Bidlake, S. (1993) Asda checks out Catalina system. *Marketing*, 14 October, 5.

Denison, T. and Knox, S. (1992) *Profiling the Promiscuous Shopper: a Report Examining and Evaluating Shopper Loyalty*. Crawley: AIR MILES Travel Promotions Ltd.

Dick, A.S. and Basu, K. (1994) Customer loyalty: toward an integrated conceptual framework. *Journal of the Academy of Marketing Science*, 22 (2), 99–113.

O Brien, L. and Jones, C. (1995) Do rewards really create loyalty? *Harvard Business Review*, 73 (3), 75–82.

PART II

Buyer–Supplier Relationships and Logistics

6

The Development of Petrol Retailing at Tesco

Mike Pretious

University of Abertay, Dundee

Introduction

Simon King made his way to his new desk at Tesco headquarters in Cheshunt at 8 a.m. on 1 June 1990, with a mixture of anticipation and apprehension. Simon had started his career at Tesco some four years previously as a graduate trainee, and had progressed rapidly within the chain. Only last week he had been the beef buyer: today he started a new job as petrol buying controller.

At the appointments board, Simon had talked of his successes in building relationships with suppliers in the meat trade, and had indicated that he was ready for a new challenge. Mike Frost, the director in charge of petrol retailing at Tesco, had told him that the new appointee would be in charge of refocusing the company's petrol business, a major part of which would involve changing the way that Tesco interacted with its supply chain in this product area.

Arriving at his office the following Monday, Simon sat down and opened the dossier that Mike had given him after he had accepted the job. He reached for his pen, and began to summarize the main issues.

The History of Petrol Retailing at Tesco

Tesco had begun selling petrol in the 1970s, opening its first petrol station adjacent to a new superstore in Rochdale. In the mid-1980s, petrol was being sold by Tesco at 12 locations across the UK. During the boom years of the later 1980s, concurrent with the 'race for space' by the grocery multiples, petrol stations were being opened by the chain at the rate of around 20 per year.

Operationally, Tesco in effect subcontracted the supply of petrol to its outlets to the major oil production companies, such as BP and Texaco. Before commencing to trade, Tesco invited tenders on a 'price per litre' basis from interested parties to supply each location on a five-year contract. The buying-in price of the petrol was not negotiated, but was based on a discount off the forecourt price of the company supplying it. Sites ordered their requirements from the successful bidder as necessary, and deliveries were made by tankers owned by the oil companies. After verification of the quantity of petrol received, invoices were paid at the agreed price by Tesco's administration centre in Cardiff.

By 1990 there were 100 Tesco petrol outlets, all adjacent to new out-of-town retail sites, and it had the largest petrol sales in the UK other than the retail divisions of the oil companies. This represented a 2 per cent share of the total market for petrol, and was worth approximately £300 million per annum in turnover.

The strategy adopted by Tesco with regard to its petrol business during this period was two-pronged. First, petrol represented a useful promotional tool: it was sold at discounted prices relative to those charged by the oil companies, incentivizing shoppers to visit Tesco locations in order to save money on an important item of their weekly expenditure. It was hoped that new customers for the core grocery business would thereby be gained, since Tesco would be perceived as offering value across the entire product range. Second, the petrol offer was an extension of the concept of 'one-stop shopping': it represented a convenient service to existing Tesco customers, who could refuel their vehicles at the same time as visiting the store. An important feature of this dual strategy was that while Tesco did not regard petrol solely as a 'loss-leader', its contribution to profitability would at best be marginal in comparison to the majority of merchandise sold by the chain.

Tesco, along with most of the other major grocery multiples, had recorded consistent year-on-year sales and profits growth during the 1980s. However, the end of the decade had brought economic recession, and with it competition to the company's core business from a variety of sources, particularly British and European discounters. With regard specifically to petrol retailing, the major oil companies were becoming increasingly concerned about the aggressive trading stance adopted by Tesco. Protecting the company's supply chain was becoming a major issue: what would happen if the oil companies no longer wanted to deal with a competitor?

The Background to 'Project Scorpio'

Simon King now felt that he understood the context in which he had been appointed. In this climate of uncertainty, all aspects of Tesco's trading strategy had to be carefully examined, and particular attention paid to areas of the business which appeared not to be maximizing profitability. As such, the company's approach to petrol retailing was under scrutiny.

Simon turned now to the outline of the project he was to work on, which Mike Frost had started to explain during his interview. Code named 'Project Scorpio', it had two main aims: first, to improve the security of petrol supply to Tesco; second, to enhance the profitability of Tesco's petrol retailing operations.

Simon considered these objectives carefully, and concluded that in order to achieve them, two separate but related aspects of the buying process would have to be tackled. To begin with, it was essential to find alternative sources to buy petrol from, who were not also Tesco's competitors at retail level. If he was successful in this aim, Tesco would gain greater control over its supply chain. The company might then be able to improve the payment terms under which it purchased, allowing it more strategic marketing alternatives.

Since Simon knew very little about the oil industry, the next day he called in a firm of consultants, Capitol Associates, to give him a briefing on where he might begin looking for new suppliers.

> You already know [said Capitol's Roger Harrison] that the major oil companies have vertically integrated organizational structures. Oil production, particularly refining, is most efficient as a continuous process. Thus, in order to sell what they produce, many oil companies have developed their own marketing channels. However, because demand for oil never exactly matches supply, companies often have to sell off part of their production to third parties, usually as futures contracts.[1] In many cases, these contracts are simply traded between various parties and are never exercised.

What you need to do, is to approach some of these traders with a view to them exercising their contracts instead of selling them on, and for them to physically supply Tesco with some of the oil they are committed to buy.

Roger later forwarded to Simon a list of six traders who had no UK marketing interests, and who might be prepared to do business in this way. Prices would be based on those of the Rotterdam spot market,[2] the detailed cost depending on the degree of involvement of Tesco in the distribution process of the petrol once it reached the UK.

Over the next few weeks, Simon made contact with the UK offices of these traders. At first, they were circumspect about dealing with Tesco, which was not a familiar company to them, but when Simon pointed out that he was prepared to offer them supply contracts for a year, coupled with a guaranteed trading profit, many became enthusiastic about the scheme. In particular, two of the larger traders, Vitol, based in Holland, and Mabanaft, based in Germany, indicated their readiness to participate.

At the same time as engaging in these preliminary negotiations with the oil traders, Simon was investigating the alternative buying and distribution arrangements that could be used. Three possibilities existed. *Package buying* involved the supplier delivering fuel to the forecourts, as was currently the case. *Terminal buying* required Tesco to organize road distribution from the point of collection at the oil terminal to the forecourt. *Ship buying* meant Tesco assuming responsibility for both distribution and storage facilities, and buying petrol by the ship.

Clearly, terminal buying and ship buying were more complicated than package buying. Each of these options would move Tesco further *upstream*, or closer to the refinery production process. However, the potential profit to Tesco would also be greater with each consecutive stage, as the company's independence from the oil companies would increase as it controlled more of the distribution chain. Discussions with Jim Duncan, the Tesco Logistics Director, confirmed that establishing a fleet of tankers in conjunction with one of Tesco's established road hauliers was feasible.

Simon also verified when each agreement with the major oil companies was coming to an end. While it would not take long for them to appreciate Tesco's new approach to petrol buying, it was important to maintain existing relationships, without jeopardizing established positions. He ascertained that most outlets were coming 'out of contract' during 1991 and 1992, giving him ample time to set up the new arrangements.

Operationalizing Project Scorpio

During the latter part of 1990 and the first few months of 1991, the invasion of Kuwait by Iraq caused petrol prices at the pumps to be raised by the major oil companies. Simon was instrumental in ensuring that Tesco was perceived by the public as offering 'the best deal around', with its own petrol prices always at a discount to those of the competition.

More than ever, the logic of Project Scorpio was inescapable: if Tesco could supply its outlets more efficiently, both consumers and the company would benefit, creating a 'virtuous circle' of increased profitability coupled with lower retail prices, in addition to guaranteeing the company's sources of supply.

Simon proposed to Mike Frost that the implementation of Project Scorpio should be in two stages. The first phase, *validation*, was to commence in the second half of 1991, and would last approximately a year. This would involve Tesco trialling each of the alternative buying arrangements, thereby gaining an understanding of the costs involved. The effect of each change on the UK supply situation, in particular the reactions of the major oil companies, would be monitored carefully. The second phase, *optimization*, would 'roll out' the most profitable petrol buying option on a national basis.

Mike agreed with Simon's proposals, and Project Scorpio went 'live' in August 1991, when Elf was terminated from seven sites and replaced with a 'package' deal.

Soon afterwards, the risks of dealing with the competition were underlined when a review involving six sites contracted to BP was concluded with the oil company indicating that it was not prepared to continue supplying petrol on the same terms as previously. This led to the first 'terminal' deal being struck with Mabanaft in November. Jim Duncan organized three tankers, to be leased from Wincanton Linkman, which would transport the petrol from the UK terminal where the petrol cargo was landed to the relevant locations.

March 1992 was a critical month for Project Scorpio. By now, Simon was ready to experiment with 'ship' buying. A deal was struck with Vitol to purchase a consignment of petrol 'on the water', in order to supply eight sites formerly contracted to Gulf. This involved negotiations with a further supplier, Webster's, the owner of the coastal terminal where the consignment would be delivered. Simon had been concerned about renting storage capacity, and needed reassurance from Rob Williams, the terminal manager:

> When an importer buys a consignment of oil, the quality is checked prior to delivery. It will only ever be stored in tanks which contain the same grade of product, but it is likely that the tank will be shared by other clients of the terminal. This is known technically as *co-mingling*. When your tankers collect petrol, we undertake to supply you with the same quality that was originally delivered, although it may not be from the same cargo of petrol that you actually bought.

Satisfied by Rob's explanation regarding the mechanics of petrol storage, Simon made arrangements for the ship to dock at Webster's terminal, and liaised with Jim Duncan to ensure that the necessary tankers would be available for onward distribution to the forecourts.

At the same time as organizing his first 'ship' purchase, Simon received the first sign of the effect Project Scorpio was having on Tesco's relationship with the major oil companies. Gulf, taken aback by the withdrawal of one of its supply contracts with the chain, wanted to discuss future terms. Simon arranged a meeting with Tony Dow, Gulf's Sales Director.

> Gulf greatly value the volume of business that Tesco have previously committed to us [Tony began] and we see now that you are capable of buying independently. I am therefore prepared to offer you the same terms for petrol bought from our UK oil refineries that you can get on the Rotterdam spot market, the advantage to you being that the costs of importation will be saved.

Graciously accepting the offer, Simon smiled to himself. He remembered the conversation he had had the previous year with Roger Harrison, regarding the need for the oil companies to maintain a continuous flow of products through their refineries in order to maximize efficiency. The benefit to Gulf, he thought, would be the mirror-image of the reason Tesco had initiated Project Scorpio: the oil company would have an assured market for much of the petrol produced by its UK operation, without having to export it at greater expense.

Project Scorpio: the Optimization Phase

In December 1992, Simon King sat down with Mike Frost to review the progress of Project Scorpio. By now, almost all of Tesco's petrol supplies were being bought either from one of the independent oil traders or from one of the major oil companies' inland terminals, on similar terms to the Gulf agreement. Under the new buying arrangements, the total gross benefit to Tesco would be over £10 million in a full year. Simon summarized the position as follows:

Of the three buying arrangements utilizing independent traders, 'ship' buying, as expected, has proven to be the most profitable. Supply from inland terminals owned by the major oil companies is cheaper still. However, it is important to realize that this option would not have been open to Tesco without us demonstrating our ability to import petrol successfully. It is therefore recommended that in the 'optimization' stage of Project Scorpio, we phase out 'package' buying and 'terminal' buying from the independents, while continuing to utilize 'ship' buying to a limited extent, even though this will not maximize overall profitability.

There is a definite synergy in controlling both tankers and forecourts, as Tesco can thereby optimize distribution efficiencies, as it has in its mainstream grocery business. Maintaining a fleet of tankers is also beneficial in promoting the company's credibility as a petrol retailer to potential customers. In the 'optimization' phase of Project Scorpio, more opportunities should exist to reduce distribution costs through better scheduling.

The project overall has already been a success. Tesco has achieved its first objective of securing its sources of supply. By treating petrol as a product similar to any other, we now have a stronger negotiating position, particularly with regard to the major oil companies, who cannot now dictate their own terms. We can now be more flexible in our pricing policy, allowing us either to enhance margins or to discount more deeply in order to gain further market share. New systems, financed by the increasing profitability of the business, will help us maintain our competitive advantage, and should ensure that in the future, Tesco becomes as important a player in petrol retailing as it now is in grocery retailing.

Table 6.1 Comparison of petrol retailing at Tesco, 1990–5

	1990	1995
Value (£)	300 million	1.5 billion
Volume (tonnes)	580,000	2,300,000
Market share (per cent)	2	8
Number of petrol stations	110	230
Per gallon discount against major oil companies (pence)	2	20
Gross margin (per cent)	5	7
Number of suppliers	5	9

Source: Tesco plc figures.

Notes

1   Where a commitment to buy a certain quantity of a given commodity is made, to be exercised at a given future point in time.
2   A 'spot market' price is the going rate for immediate delivery of a commodity.

Further Reading

Baily, P., Farmer, D., Jessop, D. and Jones, D. (1994) *Purchasing Principles and Management*. London: Pitman.
Davies, G. (1992) The two ways in which retailers can be brands. *International Journal of Retail and Distribution Management*, 20 (2).
Dawson, J.A. and Shaw, S.A. (1990) The changing character of retailer–supplier relationships. In J. Fernie (ed.), *Retail Distribution Management*. London: Kogan Page.
Duke, R. (1991) Post-saturation competition in UK grocery retailing. *Journal of Marketing Management*, 7 (1).
The Economist (1993) Europe's discount dogfight. 8 May.
Gadde, L.-E. and Håkansson, H. (1993) *Professional Purchasing*. London: Routledge.
Halstead, R. (1995) Pile it high, pour it cheap. *Business Age*, April.
Hogarth-Scott, S. and Rice, S.P. (1994) The new food discounters: are they a threat to the major multiples? *International Journal of Retail and Distribution Management*, 22 (1).
Howe, W.S. (1991) *Retailing Management*. Basingstoke: Macmillan.
Saunders, M. (1994) *Strategic Purchasing and Supply Chain Management*. London: Pitman.
Treadgold, A.D. and Reynolds, J. (1989) *Retail Saturation: Examining the Evidence*. Harlow: Longman.
Wrigley, N. (1994) After the store wars: towards a new era of competition in UK food retailing? *Journal of Retailing and Consumer Services*, 1 (1).

7

Scottish Co-op's Meat Purchasing and Supply: Transferring Responsibility for Leakage and Improving Profits

Keith Laity

The Manchester Metropolitan University

Introduction

Meat is one of the few retail commodities which is essentially a different product when it is sold from what it was when bought.[1] For example, a retailer buys a carcase, but sells up to 36 different retail products derived from it: rib, steak, mince, sausage, kidney and so on. Garry Cronie, experienced and able Operations Manager for Scottish Co-op, knew this better than most. He also saw that this simple fact cloaked several classic retail problems: profit margin, leakage and volume turnover.

Until now, the system for costing meat products had been simple and apparently satisfactory. In fact, the problem was that it was *too* simple. Stores would buy meat products from a group of suppliers located geographically close to them, and would be billed for the meat at its wholesale value. Each store would then sell the various cuts at recommended retail prices. At the end of any given period, the result would be presented like this:

	£	£
Opening stock	10,000	
Purchases at wholesale	70,000	
		80,000
Closing stock		10,000
Goods used		70,000
Retail sales		100,000
Gross margin		30,000
Gross margin (per cent)		30

If the gross margin fell within the organization's standard mark-up guidelines or notional margin (as in the example above it did), this would be considered a satisfactory result. However, Garry realized, the simple sums were capable of covering a multitude of sins.

Leakage

Leakage arises from three basic causes: waste, shrinkage and theft. These of course can never be cut out altogether; 0.5 per cent was considered by Scottish Co-op an acceptable leakage level. However, with most products you can judge whether a store manager is keeping leakage in reasonable check by judging sales of each product against the *retail* value of the stock delivered – easy enough to discover. If the manager has been delivered £100 worth of tins of beans at retail price, the stock at the end of a period shows that £72 worth has gone, but the cash sales total £68, you can see that leakage has accounted for 5.5 per cent – an unacceptable level.

With meat, on the other hand, the store manager has received a load of meat charged at *wholesale* prices at £100; the sales total £133, and so apparently there has been no leakage at all, since the company's gross profit margin has been achieved. But what in fact has been sold? It may well be that the manager has concentrated on a few lines on which a high retail profit margin can be made, to the extent that – if only we knew what the individual products were – sales *should* have totalled £150. Leakage has accounted for an unacceptably high 11 per cent, perhaps through too frequent marking down of slow-moving stock, through waste or even through theft.

This, Garry reflected, was the last product area still to be charged and costed in this way, and it was unacceptable. A better way of accounting for meat and meat products would have to be found, which would make store managers more accountable for their performance, increase profit to the group and deliver other benefits too.

Increased Turnover

The kind of meat products a retail store sells will be a reflection of the kind of area it serves. Well-to-do areas will buy larger than average quantities of cuts such as steak, fillet, topside and leg of lamb. Poorer areas will buy more mince, stewing meat and sausages. Different ethnic populations will have a preference for lamb over pork, different levels of education or sophistication can result in above-average demand for offal, veal or 'healthy' meats. Success in retailing comes from knowing your catchment area and stocking the products the customer wants. However, this crude charging system discouraged any such enterprise. Store managers would not stock on the basis of what people wanted, if the margin on such cuts was low. The system encouraged them to order the high-margin cuts, so that even with high levels of shrinkage and even theft, they could still show a spuriously acceptable profit. If their store was in a relatively poor area, where the demand for high-margin product lines was low, and this resulted in their sales being less than might have been, it was no concern to them. The customers' requirements could go hang, if it led to their having to stock a large amount of low-margin products. This meant, of course, that the Scottish Co-op's overall turnover was being reduced from its optimum; and it had only its own costing system to blame.

The root of the problem, Cronie reasoned, lay in the bewildering variety of cuts that could potentially be produced. The primal product 'beef' (i.e. beef as a whole or part carcase, charged at a single overall price per pound) could generate any one of 36 different products: rump steak, mince, forerib, whatever. Lamb generated 22 different cuts, pork 20. But if you ordered a carcase you were stuck with everything that came from it – whether *all* those products would sell well in your store or not. Retail managers might refrain from ordering as many, say, forequarters of beef as they could have sold, if it meant their having to stock (and perhaps generate high levels of leakage on) all the products that came from that same part carcase.[2] And in any case, who was to say that *this* store's retail product was *exactly* the same as *that* store's? If they came from different sources, and had been prepared by different butchers, one store might receive cuts of a more acceptable shape and size than another; one supplier might provide a larger number of pieces from a carcase than another supplier from a similar animal, because the skill of one butcher was better than another's, or because one interpreted the cutting specification slightly differently.

If stores were to be charged according to a potential retail value (as with tins of beans), the product had to be clearly definable and produced according to an exact specification. Thus everyone would know what was being ordered, what was delivered and how much it represented in terms of both cost and potential sale prices.

The first stage was therefore to draw up new specifications. Rather than having to order by the carcase, or part carcase, store managers could then more closely order exactly what it was they wanted. Accordingly, Garry Cronie drew up new and tighter specifications for each of the three primal species, which would now produce 17 separate order-derivatives from beef, yielding the 36 retail end-products; seven from primal pork; and five from lamb.

The specifications were very detailed, comprising

- product description;
- source;
- cutting standard;
- trim standard;
- fat cover;
- weight range;
- packaging;
- case-end information;[3]
- a photograph of the finished product.

This would ensure that there was little room left for personal opinion as to what constituted what product, and stores could order products which they knew would sell, with confidence. Armed with such close specifications, each store could be invoiced for its order at a retail value; managers would then have to account for significant shortfalls in their cash sales. The new specifications were combined into a booklet, which was circulated to stores and suppliers alike. Now everyone knew what each item was, what it looked like, what it should weigh – most importantly, how it should be charged as an item prepared for *retail*.

Distribution Costs

Since so major a reorganization as this was taking place, it seemed sensible at the same time to look at distribution and sourcing. An overwhelming case could be made for setting up central purchasing and distribution systems.

Accordingly, an order and distribution system was set up, by virtue of which the meat requirements for a whole region would be sourced from any three suppliers[4] from a list of eight for each primal, in any one week. Orders from all the stores in the region would be aggregated, and the total order split into three. The three suppliers best able to fill these three demands at an acceptable price that week would be asked to do so, and the meat would be sent to the stores according to the amount each had requested. Thus any given store might have all its pork (say) requirements from one supplier; or it might have some from one and some from another. Either way, thanks to the new specifications, it would all look the same and have the same *retail* value.

Naturally, small differences would occur in the price charged by the suppliers; but these would be dealt with in aggregate by the central purchasing depot. Thus, one week's demand for a single product – for example, leg of pork (bone-in) – might be as shown in figure 7.1.

The central nature of the buying function resulted in some new distribution costs, since previously groups of stores had dealt with nearby suppliers. They were now having to be supplied from a central warehouse, which might source the product from more widely scattered producers; and so the meat might travel many more miles than previously in refrigerated lorries. Nevertheless, central buying meant that better terms could be obtained, since the size of

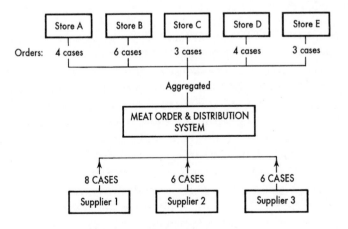

Figure 7.1 A week's demand for a single product.

order to any supplier was larger, and this offset any such increase in costs. Furthermore, there were savings to be had on administrative costs; on staff time spent on goods Inwards; and on telephone expense.

What is more, the improved scheme provided for a vendor rating system, which ensured optimum product quality; thus providing stores with a considerable competitive advantage.

In the example given in figure 7.1, slight differences in supplier prices would be evened out, and all stores in the group charged a common cost rate:

Supplier 1	8 cases × 45 lbs @ 70p per pound	£252.00
Supplier 2	6 cases × 45 lbs @ 68p per pound	£183.60
Supplier 3	6 cases × 45 lbs @ 71p per pound	£191.70
Total		£627.30
Stores supplied 20 cases × 45 lbs @ 70p per lb		£630.00

An adjustment between the central purchaser and Scottish Co-op of £2.70 would then need to be made. Each product would be treated similarly, some resulting in an adverse balance, some in a favourable balance. The overall balance could quickly and easily be settled.

Retail Profit

This only gets us as far as ensuring that all stores were charged the same cost price for the product (and of course the benefits, already mentioned, of regular specification, quality control and reduced administrative costs). Scottish Co-op now needed to establish what kind of profit margin any given meat product should carry.

Garry Cronie now instituted a major exercise whereby over 300 cutting tests were carried out, to calculate the retail sale value likely to attach to each different product. To ensure objectivity, it was essential that the tests – on each of the three primal species, and for each different product – were spread over several members of butchery staff, so that slight differences in skill levels were not concentrated on one particular species or product group.

Each test was designed to establish:

- the proportion of each retail cut within the primal;
- the total yield of saleable meat;
- the proportion lost in drip, fat, cutting etc.

Once they were completed, the results of all tests were grouped together and an average established for each primal purchase unit. These in turn gave the means to establish the actual retail value of all meat purchases, and hence a system by which retail charging could be applied to any store's purchases.

Even given the fact that red meat prices can vary considerably according to season (20 per cent above or below the year's average is by no means uncommon), the system could still be used effectively. The results established from the cutting tests were entered on to a spreadsheet; it was a simple matter to relate each to a given price for meat, and thus, when the wholesale price changed, to see at a glance what retail values would result.

The result of the exercise was to bring leakage firmly into view in the stores, without in any way weakening gross margin. Indeed, Garry Cronie reported, early indications were that gross profit on red meat had risen by 3 per cent; and poultry (brought under a similar central buying system) showed increased profits of 9 per cent.

These rises were offset to some extent by new distribution costs of 2.5 per cent and 7.25 per cent respectively. Nevertheless, now that leakage had become a visible issue, seeming to run at an average of about 2 per cent, management action could be taken and this might be expected to be reduced by half, thus effectively increasing gross margin by a further 1 per cent.

In addition, of course, the benefits would be felt by stores, suppliers and customers of

- better quality;
- more consistent product;
- a system which encouraged managers to stock the whole range of meat products;
- therefore, higher turnover.

Garry Cronie estimated that, based on a weekly total turnover (meat and poultry combined) for the group as a whole of £550,000, the financial out-turn would be considerable.

Given that poultry accounted for 40 per cent of turnover and meat for 60 per cent, the reader may wish to work out what the improvements yielded for the company. Bear in mind that, because of distribution costs, total cost of goods and carriage (previously estimated at £385,000 per week) would rise: poultry by 7.25 per cent and meat by 2.25 per cent. This would have to be set against the increase in profit. Add to this the likely improvement in leakage control – 1 per cent of turnover – and you should see how the project as a whole resulted in a sizeable total saving for Scottish Co-op.

Garry Cronie had every reason to feel very satisfied with his initiative. The whole CWS Retail group soon endorsed his satisfaction by adopting the system throughout its operations.

Background Information and Reading

The UK market for fresh meat is marked by several very particular features.

First, it is declining somewhat in *value*. The overall volume of meat sold remains fairly steady, and the sales totals increase year on year – but generally less than the rate of inflation. The Family Expenditure Survey[5] estimates that in 1993, the average British household spent £8.23 per week on meat and poultry, or 16.5 per cent of the total weekly shopping cost. This made it still the most expensive single category item in the average family's budget. Compared with 1980 prices, this figure showed a rise of 43 per cent, while the shopping basket cost as a whole showed a rise of 90 per cent. Therefore, it would seem true to say that the price of meat has reduced, in real terms, over the past 15 years or so in the UK. The retail market for all meats and meat products in 1994 was worth some £10.7 billion.

The Office of Population, Censuses and Surveys in 1993 suggested that the *consumption* of meat and meat products had declined from an average figure of 58.25 kg per head of population in 1980, to an average of 49.81 kg – a drop of 14.5 per cent.

This leads us on to the second feature of the market, that it exhibits several long-term *'internal'* trends:

- away from red meat towards white meat and poultry;
- away from fresh carcase meat towards processed meat;
- away from fatty cuts to leaner products.

There are numerous reasons for these trends.

There is a small but growing group of people who eat no meat at all; some because they believe this to be better for their health; others because they entertain a moral objection to the killing and eating of any living creature. A Gallup survey in 1993 reckoned that some 4.3 per cent of the population were *vegetarians* of one kind or another – which may not sound much, until one realizes that only a decade previously vegetarians accounted for less than 1 per cent of the population. The numbers may be small, but they are growing quickly enough to be significant and to have a marked effect on the meat market as a whole.

The *health consciousness* which is also growing in the UK accounts for some of the change in the nature of the market. Thirty-three per cent of those surveyed in 1994 for the National Health Survey[6] claimed to have cut down the amount of meat they were eating, or cut it out altogether – along with butter, sugar, fried foods, sweets and biscuits.

On the same subject, there have been a number of *health scares* associated with meat in the past decade. Concern has been voiced at:

- the use of veterinary drugs which may remain in the animal's body tissue and be consumed by humans;

- radioactive fall-out from the atmosphere, such as that which followed the Chernobyl incident;

- BSE (bovine spongiform encephalitis, or 'mad-cow disease');

- cruel or unpleasant slaughterhouse practice;

- the maltreatment of animals on farms or in transit.

Social changes also contribute. Traditionally, much of the cooking of hot meals in homes was done by the women of the household. The rising numbers of women in paid employment (46 per cent of all women in 1995) has meant that there is less time for women to cook; and though some men are taking over this function, there are many households where the result has been a decline in the amount of cooking done. Clearly, meat as one of the staples of the average diet will reduce when that diet begins to rely less on home cooking, and more on prepared foods, bought-in foods or eating out.

There has also been a change in the *kinds of meat cooked*, and the methods used; old housewifery skills, which could transform a piece of cheap, inferior meat, by slow cooking and the addition of vegetables and herbs, into a tasty dish, have largely been lost under the pressure of reduced availability of time and changes in food fashion.

Meanwhile, there has been a rapid increase in the numbers of microwave ovens and freezers in British homes. This has been accompanied by a sharp rise in demand for processed foods (pies, sausages, burgers), ready-cooked food and smaller cuts of meat, such as chops, cutlets and steaks, which require less preparation.

There have been other changes in the *pattern of eating* generally; for example, there has been a move away from formal patterns (all members of a family sitting down at a table to a meal of roast meat and hot vegetables) towards a much more informal pattern. Individuals often nowadays prepare food for themselves independent of other family members; shift-work causes problems in setting mealtimes when all can share; snacks are eaten in front of the television; eating out happens rather more frequently; and a new phenomenon has been noticed, particularly but not exclusively among the young, of 'grazing', or eating small amounts of food very often, rather than two or three large meals at set times. Such changes affect meat more than most kinds of food, since most foods are adaptable; meat, by its nature, needs quite a lot of time in preparation and cooking, and is not often used unless there are several people to share it; neither is it particularly well adapted to being eaten 'on the move'.

Demographic changes are also important. 'Family' meals are unlikely to happen where there is no family, and in the UK we have seen a rapid rise in the number of people living in modes other than the traditional nuclear family group. Indeed, it is estimated[7] that, by 1998, 62 per cent of all British households will consist of only one or two persons.

There are marked variations across the UK in the kinds of meat eaten, varying both by prosperity and by region. Better-off people are more likely to buy lamb joints. In the 1970s and early 1980s, when British membership of the Common Market was demanding major adjustments in sourcing and pricing of food supplies, cheap imports of mutton and lamb from the Commonwealth (especially New Zealand and Australia) as well as European countries brought the retail price down and it was a very popular and frequent purchase. The world market has now settled somewhat; 'set-aside'

Table 7.1 Meat consumed by region

	Per cent of national average consumption of beef	Per cent of national average consumption of lamb	Per cent of national average consumption of pork	Per cent of national average consumption of all kinds of meat
Scotland	119	48	81	95
Greater London	91	154	85	103
E. Anglia	110	100	151	116
N. Ireland	177	81	107	143

Source: BMRB/Mintel.

policies for agricultural land, and changes in farming methods have led to a buoyant world market for lamb, with a consequent sharp increase in price. Lamb is also perceived as a rather fatty meat. This is important not only because of the health concerns mentioned earlier, but also because consumers perceive the value of the joint as being the lean meat they can carve from it, while fat is regarded, along with bone, as waste. Because of this, lamb is eaten less in poorer areas of the country, but is still considered a delicacy by the more affluent.

Regionally, we can point to a number of salient points in the type and volume of meat which is consumed (see table 7.1). Some of these differences are doubtless owing to surviving tastes arising out of traditional regional farming practice; for example, the prevalence of beef cattle farming in Scotland, or of pig farming in the Eastern counties of England. Others may be due to demographic patterns; the relatively high numbers of affluent people in Greater London, for instance. Another factor may be the prevalence of certain recipes in a given area; for example, the Scots are great eaters of beef mince, with or without oatmeal.

The way meat is used and consumed is also subject to wide variation according to type, as table 7.2 shows. The very significant proportions of the total used in catering establishments echo a trend which has been visible for about a decade; that although at home we are, in general, eating less meat, we tend to make up for it to some extent when we eat out. A large majority of restaurant meals contain meat.

Table 7.2 Consumption of red meat in UK by end use, 1993, percentages by column

Type of use	Beef and veal	Lamb	Pork
Fresh, cooked in household	59	65	34
Processed, eaten in household	15	12	33
Fresh or processed, consumed in catering outlets	25	23	33

Source: Keynote.

Sources of Supply

Overall, the UK is nearly self-sufficient in meat. In 1993, 88 per cent of all meat used in the UK was home produced; and in addition, because of a good market for lamb, much of the UK's lamb production was exported.

The UK's consumption of meat by type, and its retail value, is shown in table 7.3, which gives the 1991 figures (the latest reliable estimates available at the time of writing). Such imports as the UK does make are usually to satisfy demand at a time when home produced meat is not available, being out of season – lamb, of course, being the type most frequently imported for this reason, usually from Australia and New Zealand. The other significant import is of bacon and ham products, where Scandinavia and the Netherlands are large suppliers.

Table 7.3 UK consumption of meat

	Per cent total meat consumption	Sales volume (thousand tonnes)	Retail value (£ million)
Poultry	28.2	622	1389
Beef and veal	21.4	472	2035
Bacon and ham	12.5	275	1025
Pork	10.9	239	845
Lamb	10.8	237	795
Other	16.2	357	870

Source: Euromonitor.

The Supply Structure

Before meat can become a retail product, the beast must be killed and the carcase cleaned and cut into sections. This is the work of the abattoir. Many large abattoirs are owned by vertically integrated meat companies such as Union International or Hillsdown Holdings. Others are owned by large, sometimes international, enterprises that have diverse interests, e.g. Berisfords, Northern Foods, Anglo Beef Processors, Sainsbury's, Swift and Borthwick. The remaining large abattoirs are owned by private companies (only a few of which operate more than one) together with a small number of farmer-owned cooperatives, and one or two that are owned by local authorities.

All of these plants, with one or two exceptions, operate as meat wholesalers. Moreover, many of these large plants will also have meat cutting and processing, vacuum packing and boxing facilities. Besides the wholesalers who have slaughtering facilities, there are others who wholesale meat but obtain their meat supplies from other abattoirs. Wholesalers trade carcases, primal cuts and more fully prepared or portion-controlled cuts of meat to their five broad categories of customer: retail butchers, supermarkets, meat product manufacturers, commercial and institutional caterers, and other wholesalers. The Meat and Livestock Commission describes the supply chain diagrammatically as in figure 7.2.

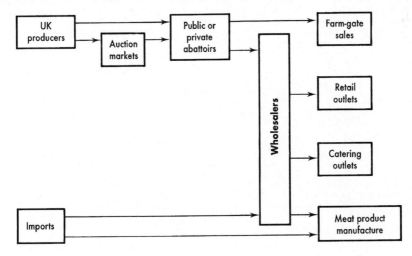

Figure 7.2 The meat product supply chain.

Among retail outlets, the sector which is experiencing most change is that of the small independent retail butcher. The growth of the supermarket chains and of freezer centres has taken away much of the market which was once exclusively theirs; by 1986 their share of the retail meat trade was down to only 36 per cent. However, by 1991 there had been something of a recovery; about 41 per cent of retail meat sales went through independent butchers. It may be that specialist butchers – kosher and halal among others – are reversing the trend. Certainly the older-established retail chains of butchers' shops are finding the going hard; Dewhurst closed 500 of its national chain of shops in the early 1990s. As usual, the two giants of retail, Sainsbury's and Tesco, have a large slice of the market; 25 per cent between them in 1991, according to figures from Euromonitor, with Gateway (now Somerfield), Asda and Safeway accounting for a further 13 per cent between them.

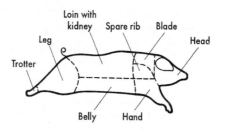

Figure 7.3 Origin of pork joints: side of pork showing main joints.

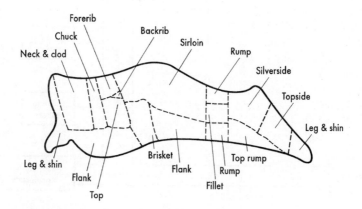

Figure 7.4 Cuts available from a side of beef.

Meat Cutting

Different parts of the carcase produce meat of differing types, which vary in quality, nutrition, and the kind of cooking required. A side of pork (one half of the beast, cut lengthways), for example, produces the main types of cut shown in figure 7.3. Figure 7.4 shows the cuts available from a side of beef.

Notes

1   See the background information at the end of this case for a fuller explanation of the way the meat market operates.
2   See the background information at the end of this case study for diagrams showing examples of typical cuts of meat.
3   Meat is delivered to stores in cases, and a paper or card label stuck on the end of the case gives details of the contents: type, size, weight, origin etc. Thus 'case-end information'.
4   See the background information at the end of this case study for an explanation of how the supply chain is organized in the UK.
5   Published by HMSO, 1993.
6   Jones Rhodes Associates, January 1994.
7   by the Office of Population, Censuses and Surveys.

Further Reading

Bowlby, S., Foord, J. and Tillsley, C. (1992) Changing consumption patterns: impacts on retailers and their suppliers. *International Review of Retail, Distribution and Consumer Research*, 2 (2), 141–9.

Dawson, J.A. and Shaw, S.A. (1989) The move to administered vertical marketing systems by British retailers. *European Journal of Marketing*, 23 (7), 42–52.

Forrester, R.A. (1987) Buying for profitability. *Retail and Distribution Management*, May/June.

Swindley, D.G. (1992) The role of the buyer in UK multiple retailing. *International Journal of Retail and Distribution Management*, 20 (2), 3–15.

8

Warehouse Management Systems at Tesco

James Bell and John Davison

University of Surrey and IBM

Competitive Advantage through the Distribution Mix: Implementing a Warehouse Management System

Traditionally, distribution and warehousing systems used by retailers have been viewed as a tactical imperative, literally delivering the goods, at minimal cost. Modern retailers, however, realize the advantages that can be derived from investment in such systems and view them as a trade-off between costs to the company and providing optimal service to the customer. As such, distribution and warehousing systems are an integral part of the companies' strategy and a major tool of competitive differentiation.

Recent gains have been made by restructuring distribution and warehousing channels on the back of streamlined product and information flows derived from EPoS and sales based ordering systems. Throughout the 1980s and 1990s companies such as Tesco invested in and restructured distribution and warehousing systems and achieved economies of scale in product movement, reduced lead times and reduced stockholding. The resulting high levels of service (measured by product availability to the customer) have added value to Tesco's product range and increased its competitive offer. In the increasingly competitive retail environment of the 1990s, further operational efficiencies have been and will continue to be sought in all parts of the distribution mix (warehousing, inventory management, transport and communication) in the search for competitive advantage in the retail market.

This case study examines the strategic development, planning and implementation of warehouse management systems (WMS) aimed at providing further operational efficiencies within Tesco distribution centres (DCs).

Welham Green: Ambient Grocery Distribution Centre

The Tesco distribution network includes nine regional composite centres, a bonded warehouse serving the whole country, three further national centres for slower moving lines and five regional ambient centres, of which the depot at Welham Green is one. This 15-acre site opened in 1987 and now employs over 400 people. Welham Green is managed directly by Tesco and currently handles a volume of approximately one million cases per week.

Since the site opened in 1987, Tesco has implemented a computerized WMS to manage the work patterns and physical flow of goods through the centre. Each movement of stock is treated as an assignment. Operators swipe assignment bar codes at the start and finish of each job. Under the previous paper based system, calculations and the recording of assignments were manual and time consuming. The computer system now allows bonuses for completing assignments within the standard time, to be paid on an individual basis.

Figure 8.1 shows the management structure at Welham Green.

Working practices are governed by union agreements which have evolved over time and, as a result, vary between distribution centres. Relations with the unions at Welham Green have been good.

Problems associated with implementing the new WMS at the centre fall into two categories: managing change; and difficulties with the technology itself. As the systems have been introduced and then developed, the management at the centre has faced a constant challenge in managing staff expectations.

Systems software was pre-tested, but not in a live environment. Consequently there were some errors which had an impact. For example, two fork lift trucks (FLTs) communicating with the system through radio frequency (RF) links and having the same address would cause the system to crash.

The benefits of the new systems include greater operating efficiency, reduced stockholding costs and much faster access to management reports.

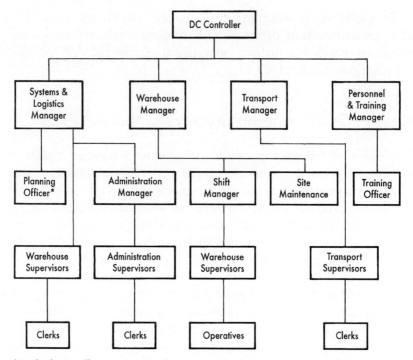

* It is the Planning Officer's primary role to forecast volumes on a daily, weekly and seasonal basis.

Figure 8.1 Tesco, Welham Green: management structure.

The Physical Flow: an Overview

The physical flow of goods through the centre is by FLT until the merchandise has reached the picking location, and by motorized picking trucks from there to the goods-out area. The flow is managed by three software systems: Denver, DCAMS and DCOTA. The role of these software packages is explained after this overview. Figure 8.2 illustrates the physical flow.

GOODS-IN

When the supplier's vehicle arrives at the depot to make a delivery, the order is cross-referenced with a receiving schedule from the stock control department. The vehicle is then given a time slot and directed to a delivery bay. Once the goods are received on to the Denver system, Denver allocates a location for the product to be put

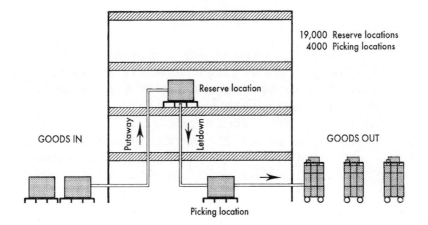

Figure 8.2 Tesco, Welham Green: the physical flow.

away into and generates a bar code for each pallet of merchandise. These labels are then attached to each pallet.

The introduction of goods-in scanning is seen as the next step in the development of the system and is currently in operation in the composite distribution centres.

PUTAWAY

Denver instructs a FLT to collect a pallet from the goods-in area. The system then informs the driver of the location that the product is to be put away into. The operator uses a hand-held gun to scan the bar code on the pallet as it is collected. The pallet is taken to a reserve location within the warehouse. There are 19,000 reserve pallet locations in the centre, each with its own address. To be efficient, the system identifies the nearest vacant reserve location to the product line's eventual picking location.

LETDOWNS

As the picking bays become empty, Denver generates letdowns. A FLT in the vicinity will be instructed to bring down new stock from its reserve location to refill the picking location. The system manages the rotation of stock. Clearing away empty pallets is an activity which is not yet controlled by the system.

The Denver system generates picking assignments based on store orders and transport planning requirements. These picking assignments go together to make up store deliveries. Assignments normally comprise various products loaded on to three cages. For each case required, a picking label is produced. This label is then attached to the case picked. The operator picks order quantities from bays at ground level. Completed assignments are then taken to the despatch bays ready for loading on to the Tesco distribution vehicle.

The Warehouse Management System

DENVER

The Denver programme underpins the computerised management of distribution and warehousing, not just in the Welham Green DC, but across Tesco's logistics infrastructure. It was originally bought as an off-the-shelf package and has, iteratively, been developed to match the specific needs of the company.

From sales recorded in stores, through EPoS terminals, orders are calculated, using a sales based ordering (SBO) system incorporating forecasting algorithms, and transmitted to suppliers using electronic data interchange (EDI). This triggers off the Denver system. Using orders and supplier confirmations, Denver begins tracking item movements through Tesco's supply chain. This overarching system then provides the backbone, on to which all other systems are integrated, for managing the throughput of products from order to delivery to the DC, from receipt to storage in warehouse and from order assembly and despatch to transportation to stores.

In Welham Green the system manages the million or so cases, covering some 18,000 product lines, passing through the centre each week. Welham Green has a total of 19,000 reserve pallet bays, 4000 picking bays and over 90 FLTs. The volume of data the system handles is thus substantial. The primary mechanism by which Denver initiates, coordinates and controls such large-scale item movement during the processes of delivery, receipt, storage, order assembly and order despatch is a schedule of activities referred to as the BOMB (build order maintenance).

DCAMS (DISTRIBUTION CENTRE ASSIGNMENT MONITORING SYSTEM)

DCAMS is the control system which specifically manages the processes of storage and order assembly for Denver following receipt of goods into the DC. Originally this was a bolt-on package and as such was live from day 1. DCAMS issues storage and order assembly work assignments based on the Denver data, monitoring work in progress through the swiping of bar codes assigned to particular aspects of each job. Finally, DCAMS, in turn, provides the necessary information for DCOTA to function.

DCOTA (DISTRIBUTION CENTRE ON-LINE TERMINAL APPLICATION)

The final tier of systems control is provided by yet another bolt-on package, DCOTA. It is the job of the DCOTA system to synchronize the activities of the FLTs in order to fulfil the storage and order assembly assignments generated by DCAMS. Each FLT has a terminal connected by radio to the system. DCOTA selects the driver for each job. Depending on the priorities of a given moment, a FLT can be exclusively on putaway as described above or on interleaving. When the FLT has deposited its putaway pallet in the reserve location, rather than returning empty directly to the goods-in area, it is instructed to work back towards goods-in, performing letdowns as it goes.

This interleaving is very much more efficient, as it reduces empty travel time for the FLTs. The DCAMS and DCOTA enhancements have generated efficiency savings of 12 per cent in warehouse hours.

Measuring Performance

The ultimate aim for the company is, of course, to get the right products to the right place at the right time and at the right cost. Currently, the Welham Green centre is meeting the target of 98.5 per cent service level of all orders delivered to stores with a lead-time of between 12 and 24 hours. The effective functioning of the above integrated systems is critical in achieving such service criteria. Using such systems allows the company to optimize the time allocated to and spent on the processes listed above.

It had previously not always been possible to achieve maximum efficiency within a DC because of a significant number of extraneous factors which may affect tasks affecting the various warehouse processes, some of which remained largely unmeasured. The introduction of DCAMS, however, has led to a 12.5 per cent reduction in hours attributed to 'non-measurable' activities. Bringing such activities within the scope of the system, of course, means that further productivity gains may be pursued. Similarly, DCOTA has resulted in a 20–25 per cent improvement in productivity in FLT operations.

These efficiency improvements should prove vital in further reducing waste and error in the Tesco supply chain and, as a result of optimising time spent on specific warehousing tasks and error correction, maximize sevice levels to the customer. This goal may be threatened by a number of operational issues, some of which may, at first sight, appear to be of a minor nature yet which, on further consideration, can have cumulative effects on the supply chain efficiency and, ultimately, on the company's competitive edge.

Warehouse Management Sytems: Operational Problems

The following are problems of varying significance encountered by the Tesco management team at Welham Green.

MISPICKS

Mispicks occur either through picker error or because merchandise in the picking location does not correspond with the system's data record. The current incidence of identified mispicks is 0.03 per cent.

This is, in itself, a low incidence of error. However, the effects of mispicking may be cumulative. For example, if stock is mispicked, unless this is detected by the warehouse or store (and stores do not, generally, carry out detailed recieving checks), the bookstock, or inventory holding figures, on which the computerized SBO system is based will be inaccurate for whichever products are affected. As the system's knowledge of store stocks is taken into account in the order generation process, any sales forecasts of the product(s) affected will be incorrect. Several order periods may elapse before the error is identified or 'smoothed out'.

PICKING LOCATIONS

Upon letdown, there may be some residual stock left in the picking location from the previous pallet. FLT operators on piece-rates are reluctant to move stock by hand.

SCAN GUNS

The FLT drivers carry hand-held scan guns with which to read the pallet bar codes. The bar codes in question are often too faint to be read properly. The back-up system is for the driver to key in the number manually. There is resistance to this because of the added time involved and the possibility of a greater incidence of errors. The scan guns in question cost over £700 each and frequently get damaged. They are repaired off-site and, including shipping time, this takes a week.

Future Developments

The continuing development of existing distribution systems is a another key consideration for Tesco. The case text makes reference to the next likely incremental step to be made. How should future developments be facilitated?

The Task

The above are operational problems, of varying significance, encountered by the Tesco management team at Welham Green. Your task is to outline how you would resolve each problem. In seeking a resolution to each, you are required to identify:

- any further information that you would need;

- who would need to be involved;

- a suitable process to resolve the problem.

You should also consider the extent to which these problems are related.

Acknowledgements

We would like to thank Barry Mills, David King, Don Stubley, Chris Carrington, Steve Cropley, Nick Thomson and Gloria Turpin for their assistance in compiling this case study.

9

Managing Stock Management III in Safeway Stores

John Davison and Susan Scouler-Davison

IBM and Safeway Stores plc

Introduction

In pursuit of the highest standards of customer service in terms of product availability and depth and breadth of product range, major retailers, particularly those in the food sector, have brought inventory management considerations to the forefront of modern retail management.

Inventory management is the mechanism by which the product and service criteria set out in the retailer's marketing mix are fulfilled. As such it is a core activity and can establish competitive advantage for the company. Without effective inventory management systems other activities and functions carried out within the company may, at best, fail to be optimized and, at worst, be rendered superfluous.

Effective inventory management ensures that the product is available when, where and in the quantities required by the customer. In recent years, most major retailers, particularly in the food sector, have introduced computerized inventory systems. These systems bring undoubted benefits through accurate data capture and the use of forecasting tools. They also, however, present a number of challenges to store based managers responsible for their efficient operation.

This case study examines the application of one of these systems, Safeway's sales based ordering (SBO) inventory management system, Stock Management III (SMIII).

An Overview of SMIII

Safeway Stores introduced the SBO system SMIII in the summer of 1992. It was fully implemented, for centrally distributed ambient product ranges including grocery, beers, wines and spirits and non-food departments, by the summer of 1993. Over the following year, fresh food departments, including produce, were added to the system.

The aim of SMIII was to improve the accuracy of the stock ordered for each store, leading to reductions in out of stocks and thereby sales maximization. Improvements have also been achieved in other ways, including reducing wastage, reducing backstocks and consistency in merchandising practices.

SMIII consists of a series of complex computer programs integrated with a number of Safeway computer systems. In practice, managing such a system calls for expert knowledge of the interaction between its components and operations requirements. The scope of this case study is to provide an outline of the general principles that the system rests on.

How Does SMIII Work?

In essence, SMIII works out the sales forecast for each product, then calculates the demand for each product using store inventory, and converts these quantities, via case rounding, to case quantities for ordering. This process relies on data input at several stages, at both store and head office level. The key stages and concepts involved in this process are listed below.

FORECAST

A sales forecast for every product is built up for each store through the capture of line-by-line sales information at the checkout. The sales forecast projects how much stock the store is likely to sell over the forthcoming order period(s).

THE DEMAND

When calculating the quantity of each line required, on a store by store basis, the system takes into account the following:

- how much stock the store already has;

- what space has been allocated to each product;

- the code life of the products;

- any outstanding deliveries;

- sales opportunities;

- business policies.

Using these parameters, the system will calculate the amount of stock needed for sales and the amount of stock needed to fill the shelf.

CASE ROUNDING

To convert the two figures, stock for sales and stock to fill the shelf, into cases for ordering, the system uses case rounding rules, as follows.

The system will always order sufficient stock to meet sales. The amount of shelf space for the product will be taken into account as the system decides whether to round up or down to a case multiple.

DATA CAPTURE AND INTEGRITY

The accuracy of the orders generated by SMIII will only be as good as the data it uses to make the order calculations.

SMIII obtains data from a number of sources and the efficient and effective operation of the system depends on each department or division getting its part in the process right. Departments in Safeway are responsible for entering product and item movement information into the system and processing stock as follows.

- Trading: ranging, space allocation, units per outer (UPO), data integrity.

- Supply chain: supply to depot, optimum lead times, data integrity.

- Distribution: delivery of right stock to store at right time.

- Store: replenishing shelves, scanning, accurate bookstocks.

All of these elements are important to the process of calculating store orders. If any one of them is omitted the process will fail. The two key aspects of SMIII that the above store disciplines affect are inventory and range.

INVENTORY

SMIII relies on accurate inventory data. Most product item movement (deliveries and sales) is captured through associated systems which update SMIII. SMIII is aware of stock being delivered to the store through the company's central distribution system and captures stock leaving the store through scanning at the checkouts recorded by the EPoS system.

However, the store is required to inform the SMIII system of stock that comes into the store through anything other than the normal distribution channels or leaves the store via any means other than through EPoS as customer sales. Examples of this include:

- spoilage (wastage);

- inter-store transfers;

- inter-departmental transfers (e.g. purchases for the staff restaurant);

- cross-picks (stock delivered but not ordered and vice versa);

- quality control (non-saleable damaged stock not offered for sale).

Stores will also undertake a bookstock check for any product that is out of stock or where stock levels of an individual product are exceptionally high or low. If the bookstock is inaccurate the store will inform the system, thus improving the accuracy of the next order.

RANGE

The SMIII system needs to know what products are within the store range and the amount of space provided to each. Stocking plans are determined by the trading division and are transmitted to store, where they are accepted into the store range. Stores are required to carry the full range of products within their plan size. Although

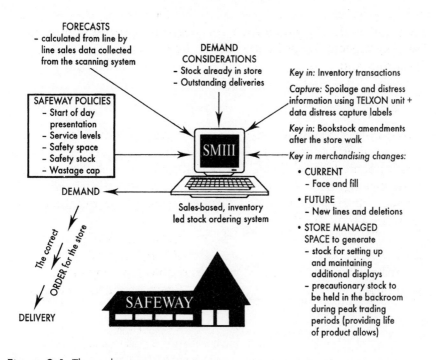

Figure 9.1 The order generation process.

stores are not allowed to delete products from the range, they are able to amend the amount of space, in terms of level of shelf-fill and numbers of facings, allotted to each line.

SMIII calculates an optimum quantity of stock to cover expected sales, safety stock levels (in case sales are greater than forecast) and stock levels required to maintain shelf presentation standards (although, for fresh food products, the system will only try and fill the shelf if it thinks that the product can be sold within its code life). For grocery and long-life products, if accurate 'fill and face' information is not correctly and expediently input into the system by the store, shelf presentation may be affected and, moreover, out of stocks or high backstocks may occur.

Figure 9.1 illustrates how the order generation process works.

Store Operations

There are a number of routines and disciplines required at store level to ensure that the orders generated accurately reflect the needs of the store so as to meet customer expectations.

One of the most important activities for the store is to maintain an accurate sales forecast for each product. Inaccurate sales forecasts will result in incorrect orders being generated. This could result in out of stocks, excessive backstock and/or unnecessary wastage. Maintaining the sales forecast is achieved indirectly through:

1   Accurately capturing sales through EPoS.

2   Replenishing shelves to maintain an in-stock position.

3   Merchandising products on the shelf in line with range plans, especially with regard to new lines and deleted products.

4   Accurately recording wastage information.

To achieve the above the store must:

1   Scan all products correctly so that sales data are recorded accurately.

2   Keep the back stockroom tidy with all stock visible and accessible. This will help when replenishing the shelves or counting stock.

3   Follow merchandising disciplines so that the layout of the shelf reflects the system's record of range and space. For example, if a product is merchandised on the shelf with half the capacity the system believes it has, then excessive backstock could result. The system will believe stock is needed to go on to the shelf when in fact it will be sitting in the back stockroom.

4   Follow shelf filling disciplines. Shelves must be stocked in a systematic and consistent manner so that stock levels can be clearly identified and products easily counted.

5   Perform daily out-of-stock checks to identify any products that are 'out-of-stock' where the system believes them to be 'in-stock'.

6   Where stock counts are required, carry them out accurately to ensure that errors in the store inventory are not committed.

The sales uplift expected from promotions will be managed by head office and store sales forecasts adjusted accordingly. However, for other occasions when significant local sales fluctuations are expected, action should be taken to change the forecast as required. Such changes will protect the underlying forecasts so that large fluctuations are treated as 'one-offs' and are not translated as trends by system algorithms.

The Scenario

It is a Friday in February, you are a Safeway store manager and you have just carried out a mid-morning inspection of your store. During the inspection you noted the following points.

Produce

- Presentation is poor within several commodity groups, e.g. root vegetables and loose apples.

- There is only one out of stock: cauliflower. This was due to a delivery shortage from the depot.

- The produce delivery was being worked and the shelves were in the process of being stocked.

- Product quality was generally good, although a number of grapefruit which were below standard were now being removed.

Grocery

- Promotional point of sale (PoS) was missing from an on-shelf promotion on the tea/coffee section.

- Loose stock was stacked behind other adjacent products on the soup section and appeared to have been there for several weeks.

- The back stockroom had been left tidy by the night team but was not laid out correctly, leading to a pallet of stock being inaccessible.

Frozen food

- Following the relaying of this section earlier in the week, the general level of presentation was poor although sales did not appear to be affected according to your EPoS sales read-out.

Deli

- Very good display.

Meat and dairy

- Presentation on fresh meat looked excellent.

- The quality of the meat was good, with code-life products able to last through the weekend.

- Ready meals presentation looked weak, although the adjacent fresh pasta lines had a full presentation, with additional back-stock to meet expected sales.

Front end

- Cashiers had not recognized the difference between two types of loose apples and had been recording sales incorrectly.

- There were no queues at the checkout.

The Task

Given the basic principles of SMIII, for each of the findings uncovered, identify what implications there are for the efficient working of the system and state what remedial action could be taken, in each instance, at store level to minimize disruption to the system. Table 9.1 can be used to record discussion points.

In a wider context, identify the sales and profitability implications of the above findings, paying particular attention to the following points:

- sales forecasting;
- sales maximization;
- wastage control;
- stockholding levels.

Table 9.1 Discussion point recording sheet

Problems identified	Causal factors	Implications for SBO	Immediate managerial action required

10

Retail Logistics: the Case of Tesco Stores

John Fernie and Leigh Sparks
University of Stirling

Introduction

Tesco is a leading innovator in retail logistics. This was not always the case and the transition from a supplier-driven to a Tesco controlled logistics system has occurred in a relatively short period of time. This case charts the development of logistics within the company as it shaped a growth strategy to challenge the market leader, Sainsbury's. In particular, the case discusses the operational issues which Tesco has had to address in the aftermath of its takeover of the Scottish multiple grocery, Wm Low.

Background

The transformation of Tesco from the era of 'pile it high, sell it cheap' has seen the number of stores decline, while the average size of store has risen dramatically (Figure 10.1). There have been large increases in turnover and pre-tax profit, and an enormous increase in the scale of the business between the 1960s and the late 1980s. The boost to turnover began in 1977, when the company through Operation Checkout stopped giving trading stamps and cut prices by 4 per cent but also started to move up-market.

The changes the customer sees are obviously focused at the store. However, behind the store revolution and the changing store port-folio (location, scale, type, age) lies a distribution transformation

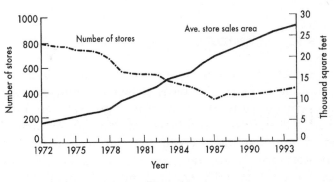

Note: 1993 and 1994 floorspace estimated.

Figure 10.1 Tesco plc: number of stores and average store sales area (UK food retailing).

without which the success of the 1980s could not have been achieved, and the base for the 1990s would be insufficient. It can be suggested that there have been three main phases in distribution strategy and operations. First, there was a period of primarily delivery direct to store. Second, there was a move to centralization and the refinement of the process of centralized distribution. Third, there has been the development of composite distribution.

The Tesco distribution system in the late 1970s in the wake of Operation Checkout almost came to a halt. The volume of goods being moved by Tesco proved too large to handle in the time scales required. Eighty per cent of all supplies were coming direct from manufacturers and there was a real danger that they were promoting cuts on lines that they couldn't deliver. At that time in its history, senior management realized that Tesco was as much in the business of distribution as of retailing.

Operation Checkout provided a short-term shock to the distribution system. There were major problems in handling the peak weeks and the increased volumes, but generally the company coped, albeit through running multi-shifts in the distribution centres. Having weathered the distribution effects of Operation Checkout, the company saw clearly that other changes to distribution would be needed as the 'new' business strategy took hold. In effect, by Operation Checkout and the move up-market that followed, Tesco was changing the mission, vision, strategy and culture of the company. This included distribution operations.

The Move to Centralization

The decision was taken to move away from direct delivery to stores to centralization in 1983. The basis of this decision was the realization of the critical nature of range control on the operations. Tesco always had delivered some products centrally, but the majority had come direct from manufacturers to stores. At its peak this reached a direct to store : warehouse ratio of 83 : 17. In addition to being inefficient for the store and operations and being unable to cope flexibly with increased volumes and quality, the system allowed almost no control or standardization of the retail outlets and of store managers. With direct to store delivery, managers were 'encouraged' to 'buy in' extra products on secondary lines to cover stock losses. The realization of the effects this was having on the business forced the decision to end buying-in and managers' deal books and allow the introduction of true stock results and range control. Centralization of control was established for the modern business. Tesco head office had to have this control if the company was to be transformed: centralized distribution was one plank in the control strategy.

Tesco adopted a centrally controlled distribution service delivering the vast majority of stores' needs, utilizing common handling systems, with deliveries having a maximum lead time of 48 hours. Seven key areas of this strategy can be identified. First, there was an extension and change to the existing fixed distribution facilities, including the building of new distribution centres. The location of these facilities was aimed at more closely matching distribution needs to the store location profile and to changes in this profile. Second, lead times improved. Improvements in technology allowed faster stock turn, allied to which was the scheduling of vehicles at all points in the channel. Third, common handling systems were used at the distribution centre and stores to handle stock replenishment more easily. Fourth, the demands of modern retailing required multi-shift working. Fifth, computer software modelled company decisions allowing the best use of all facilities. Sixth, dedicated (i.e. contract) distribution was used to meet high levels of performance. The standards required are set by Tesco and monitored by them. The contractors have to meet these specifications. Finally, new technology was used to maintain a strict inventory control.

In 1989 Tesco had 42 depots, of which 26 were temperature controlled. This in itself was a massive reduction from the plethora of small stock locations (including back-ups) found in the 1960s and 1970s, but was still capable of improvement. Fresh foods were basically handled through single-temperature, single-product depots. These were small, inefficient and only used for part of the day. Tesco had reviewed the service the network gave the stores and implemented improvements in all product areas in 1986 and 1987. This meant, for example, in the short life provisions network, that stores received more frequent deliveries from a rationalized number of depots (from eleven to six). Investment was made in the Dallas computer system (see chapter 8) in the frozen depots and accounting and budget changes allowed a more accurate idea of the cost of distribution.

The tactics in the late 1980s were to make as many improvements as possible in order to give the stores a better service. There were still some major shortcomings of the network. First, each product group had different ordering systems. Some were designed by the distribution contractor for their general use and were not sympathetic to Tesco needs. This complicated distribution. Second, with so many sites it was prohibitively expensive to have on-site Tesco quality control inspection at each location. This meant that the standards of quality desired could not be vigorously controlled at the point of distribution. Third, because only single product groups were handled, each store's delivery volume was low. Hence, it was not economic to deliver some products to all stores daily, so that consumers were not receiving fresh produce daily. Fourth, to maintain the best quality, some goods require a temperature controlled environment during delivery. As single products in warehouses they had to be carried on separate vehicles, which meant that a whole range of different vehicle types were needed to deliver the full range of products to each Tesco store. This added complication and congestion and was costly. Fifth, it was realized that the network would not cope with the growth Tesco forecast in the 1990s, especially in the area of chilled distribution, where new legislation to establish higher standards was to be introduced in the early 1990s. These factors combined to revise the changes necessary to meet emerging operational requirements.

Composite Distribution

The major change to the centralization strategy as presented above is that the company focused on the development of composite distribution. Composite distribution enables ambient, chilled, fresh and frozen products to be distributed through one system of multi-temperature warehouses and vehicles. Composite distribution uses specially designed vehicles with temperature controlled compartments to deliver any combination of these products. It aims to provide daily deliveries of products at the appropriate temperature so that the products reach the stores and customers at the peak of freshness. The insulated composite trailer can be sectioned into one, two or three chambers by means of moveable bulkheads. There is independent control for up to three temperature regimes. For example, frozen products at $-20\,°C$ can be carried with fresh meat at $0\,°C$ and bread and bananas at $+15\,°C$ without affecting product quality in any way. The size of each chamber can be varied to match the volume to be transported at each temperature. The composite distribution process was focused on eight distribution centres; seven of these were new purpose-built composite distribution centres, with the other an extension at Livingston in Scotland. Centralizing distribution of these products in this way has improved quality of product and service. These eight centres replaced 26 centres in the previous system.

The eight distribution centres each service approximately 50 stores in a single region of the country. The sites are all close to key motorway intersections or junctions. Of the eight composite distribution centres only two are run by Tesco. The remainder are operated by specialist distribution companies, with Wincanton Distribution running three, Exel Logistics two and Hay Distribution one. Cross-comparisons of performance of these centres and the subcontractors enable 'league tables' to be drawn up of performance.

The composite centres are linked by computer to head office to allow the passing of data and the imposition of monitoring and control. For all products handled by the composite centres, forecasts of demand are produced and transmitted to suppliers. The aim of the system is to allow suppliers to have a basis for preparing products. This is particularly important for short-life products where the aim is to operate a just-in-time system from the factory through the composite centre to the store. To meet such targets on delivery etc. each supplier needs information on predicted replenishment schedules.

This sharing of information is part of a wider introduction of electronic trading to Tesco. In particular, Tesco has built an electronic data interchange (EDI) community involving direct to store and distribution centre suppliers. Tesco claims that this community of over 1200 suppliers (1993) is the largest in European food retailing. Improvements to scanning in stores and the introduction of sales based ordering have enabled Tesco better to understand and manage ordering and replenishment. Sales based ordering automatically calculates store replenishment requirements based on item sales and generates orders for delivery to stores within 24 to 48 hours.

Composite distribution provides a number of benefits. Some derive from the process of centralization, of which composites are an extension. Others are more directly attributable to the nature of composites. First, the movement to daily deliveries of composite product groups to all stores in 'waves' provides an opportunity to reduce the levels of stock held at the stores and indeed to reduce or obviate the need for storage facilities at store level. In aggregate terms, the distribution stock position in the company has improved continuously. Over the 1980s, the changes have succeeded in halving the stock days in the system. Indeed, Tesco is acknowledged to be the industry leader in terms of stock turns per annum.

The second benefit of composites is an improvement to quality with consequent reduction in wastage. Products reach the stores in a more desirable condition. Better forecasting systems minimize lost sales due to out-of-stocks. The introduction of sales based ordering produces more accurate store orders and the more rigorous application of code control results in longer shelf life on delivery, which in turn enables a reduction in wastage. This is of crucial importance to shoppers, who are requiring better quality and fresher products. In addition however, the tight control over the chain enables Tesco to satisfy and exceed the new legislative requirements on food safety.

Third, the introduction of composite distribution has provided an added benefit in productivity terms. The economies of scale and enhanced use of equipment provide greater efficiency and an improved distribution service. Composite distribution means that one vehicle can be used instead of the five needed in the old network. The result is reduced capital costs and less congestion at the store. Within the composites changes such as in-bound scanning and radio linked computers on fork lift trucks further enhance productivity. In essence, throughout the system there is an emphasis on maximizing productivity and efficiency of the operations.

One of the major changes to occur in the move to composite distribution was the shift away from the traditional, 40-hour week plus overtime system for depot employees to a system of annual hours. On average, each composite handles 670,000 cases per week, rising to 880,000 at Christmas. In addition to seasonal peaks, volumes vary markedly by day of the week and by hour of the day. In labour terms, it was important to match manning levels to workload requirements. The scheme of annual hours was first introduced into Tesco's own account depots at Hinckley and Harlow prior to being implemented at other sites. The scheme involves a new contract of employment based upon a quota of hours over the year. A level of guaranteed overtime and premium payments for weekend working was built into the regular salary. Employees are grouped into a six-crew, six-week repeating cycle, which not only allows Tesco flexibility to cover crisis periods but also encourages team building within crews. This approach has been rewarded through better performance, higher morale and greater mutual loyalty to fellow employees.

The Future

The mid-1990s has presented Tesco's distribution management with a new set of challenges to overcome. Some of these challenges have arisen owing to the success of the company in vying with Sainsbury's for the position of UK top grocery retailer. Indeed, in early 1995, the trade press have the two protagonists running neck and neck in terms of market share. Tesco's successful launch of its Clubcard with five million customers, in addition to its value lines to combat the discount threat, has resulted in increased volume and number of lines going through the distribution network, especially in the composite sites. Furthermore, Tesco's success in moving to just-in-time distribution has meant that more space is required for pick by line items which require minimal or no stockholding, rather than the conventional pick by store items which traditionally were held in a regional distribution centre (RDC) for around two weeks. As lead times reduce on all items, there is less need for reserve picking slots.

In recent years some fine tuning of the distribution network has taken place. Wines and spirits have been centralized to one site at Northampton, a new RDC was opened at Magor in South Wales to

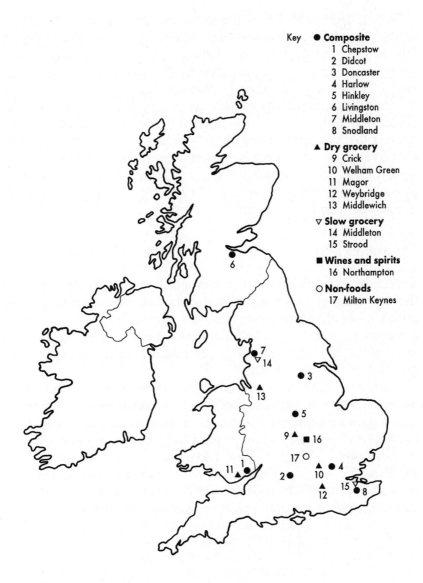

Key ● **Composite**
   1 Chepstow
   2 Didcot
   3 Doncaster
   4 Harlow
   5 Hinkley
   6 Livingston
   7 Middleton
   8 Snodland

▲ **Dry grocery**
   9 Crick
   10 Welham Green
   11 Magor
   12 Weybridge
   13 Middlewich

▽ **Slow grocery**
   14 Middleton
   15 Strood

■ **Wines and spirits**
   16 Northampton

○ **Non-foods**
   17 Milton Keynes

Figure 10.2 Tesco plc depot locations.
Source: IGD Research Services, 1995.

replace the Westbury RDC and a new composite is due to open in Southampton to deliver to the South of England (see figure 10.2 for locations of Tesco depots).

During 1994 and 1995, the government's negative attitude to further out of town store development forced Tesco to reconsider its UK strategy, which had been based on the construction of new superstores. If superstore saturation was being reached, albeit in the view of Tesco through negative planning controls, a refocusing of strategy was required. Instead of organic growth, Tesco opted for an acquisition and, after a battle with Sainsbury's succeeded in purchasing the Scottish grocery chain Wm Low for £247 million. The shift to a positive approach by government to foster regeneration of town centres has encouraged Tesco to develop its smaller, High Street metro format. By the end of 1995, 29 of these stores will be in operation, with the potential of opening another 50 stores.

Operational Issues

The move to composite distribution has had a major impact upon the manning of these regional distribution centres through the introduction of annual hours. The takeover of Wm Low has created a series of additional operational problems pertaining to the network of stores and distribution centres which needed to be integrated into the Tesco network.

In order to gain an appreciation of the current situation, some background on the evolution of Wm Low's distribution network is necessary. The company had began to move away from its Scottish base in 1985 with the acquisition of Laws Stores in the north-east of England. By 1987, Wm Low had stores from Dingwall in the Highland Region of Scotland to Goole in Humberside. Furthermore, the company intended to move further south into the midlands. At that time Low's branch profile was as follows:

Over 20,000 square feet	9
10,000–20,000 square feet	17
4000–9999 square feet	32
Under 4000 square feet	8

The policy for future store development was to develop either 'in-fill sites' or purpose built 'powerhouses'. The latter were conventional superstores in the region of 30,000–40,000 square feet; the former were off-centre developments or stores of 15,000–20,000 square feet in suburban towns with limited local competition from other multiples.

To provide logistical support to this mixed store profile, Wm Low undertook an in depth strategy study in 1987. Prior to the takeover of Laws, Wm Low had an own account operation which supplied ambient products from Dundee and frozen food from a small depot at Whitburn in West Lothian. Produce was delivered direct to stores by a contractor based at Bellshill, near Glasgow. In 1985, Wm Low inherited an own account depot at Gateshead to supply Laws Stores; however, the transport was contracted out to BRS. The distribution director, Brian Findlay, had several options open to him. He could start from scratch and assume that a new network would be introduced. He could go down the third party distribution route, one that was being favoured by other leading multiples at this time. Alternatively, he could adapt and build upon the existing network. Findlay favoured the own account option and proposed to the Wm Low board that a £15 million investment should be made on a new multi-temperature controlled distribution depot at Livingston, while the depots at Gateshead and Dundee were upgraded to handle ambient products. The site at Whitburn was closed, with staff being transferred to Livingston, and the produce contract was terminated. Table 10.1 and figure 10.3 show the new depot locations. Wm Low retained the BRS transport contract to supply stores from Gateshead. Although Wm Low moved to larger 13.3 metre trailers, it had some smaller trailers and rigid vehicles to supply stores with accessibility problems.

This network was in operation at the time of the takeover, although a rationalization of the store network had taken place. Wm Low had 57 stores, 12 of which were in England. In terms of size, only 16 were over 20,000 square feet and 30 over 15,000 square feet. As can be seen from figure 10.2 and table 10.2, Tesco's distribution network was stretched to supply its 17 Scottish stores. Livingston, its Scottish composite, was one of its oldest RDCs and its smallest composite. This site had been enlarged twice and had limited room for expansion compared with the newly constructed Wm Low depot. As a result, just under 50 per cent of all products supplied to Tesco's Scottish stores were transhipped through Livingston.

In the aftermath of the takeover, all depot managers involved in the integration of the two networks were asked to submit proposals on the way ahead for the rest of the decade. In addition to the question of integration, Tesco had opened three metro outlets in Scotland with the prospect of further developments. These sites had

Table 10.1 Characteristics of Wm Low's depots and vehicle fleet

Location	Size (square feet)	Products handled	UK regions served	Operator	Number of staff	Vehicle fleet size	Type of vehicle
Dundee	220,000	Groceries, wines and spirits, cigarettes, non-foods, branch use goods, e.g. bags	Scotland, North	Wm Low	143	18 tractors 38 Trailers	ERF, roadtrain
Gateshead	120,000	Groceries, wines and spirits, cigarettes	Southern Scotland, North Yorkshire, Humberside	Wm Low	65	–	Roadtrain
Livingston (opened Oct. 90)	140,000	Frozen, chilled produce	Scotland, North East, Yorks and Humberside	Wm Low	140	24 Tractors 35 Trailers	ERF

Source: IGD Research Services.

Figure 10.3 Wm Low and Company plc depot locations.
Source: IGD Research Services, December 1992.

already posed problems for distribution managers in terms of constraints on vehicle size and delivery times (usually 6 p.m. to 8 a.m.). In 1995, the whole distribution operation was under review by senior management and these proposals would form a major component of the review.

Table 10.2 Characteristics of Tesco's depots in Scotland and northern England

Location	Size (square feet)	Products handled	Composite	UK regions served	Operator	Number of staff	Vehicle capacity
Doncaster	300,000	1,2,3,4,6	Yes	East Midlands, South West, Greater London	Wincanton Distribution	550	60 tractor
Livingston	170,000	1,2,3,4	Yes	Scotland	Wincanton Distribution	200	30 tractor
Middleton	250,000	1,2,3,4,6	Yes	North West North Wales West Midlands	Wincanton Distribution	450	50 tractor
Middleton	160,000	5	No	North North West	Wincanton Distribution	198	21 tractor
Middlewich	330,000	4, 7	No	Wales North West Midlands Yorks and Humberside	Tesco	350	40 tractor

Key to products handled: 1, chilled; 2, ambient; 3, frozen; 4, fast moving grocery; 5, slow moving grocery; 6, produce; 7, beers.
Source: IGD Research Services.

Further Reading

Fernie, J. (1990) Third party versus own account – trends in retail distribution. In J. Fernie (ed.), *Retail Distribution Management*. London: Kogan Page, chapter 5.

Fernie, J. (1994) Retail logistics. In J. Cooper (ed.), *Logistics and Distribution Planning*. London: Kogan Page, chapter 18.

McMeekin, J. (1995) Why Tesco's new composite distribution needed annual hours. *International Journal of Retail and Distribution Management*, 23(9), 36–8.

Powell, D. (1991) *Counter Revolution: the Tesco Story*. London: Grafton Books.

Smith, D.L.G. and Sparks, L. (1993) The transformation of physical distribution in retailing: the example of Tesco Stores. *International Review of Retail, Distribution and Consumer Research*, 3 (1), 35–64.

Warner, B. (1995) *Making the Right Choice: a Guide to Distribution Solutions*. London: Institute of Logistics.

PART III

Operations and Customer Service

11

Health Care Provision at Boots the Chemists

Stuart A. West

Oxford Brookes University

Context

In August 1994, Boots the Chemists (BTC) announced its intention to open a further 200 stores: many would be of an area less than 6000 square feet and some would be re-openings in small towns, abandoned as recently as ten years ago.

Press coverage of the announcement at that time suggested that changes in the market place, particularly focusing on changing customer needs and patterns, had made such a strategy possible. BTC had already extensively reviewed its own brand provision and rationalized its product range prior to the announcement. Indications of the thinking behind the revised retail strategy may be gleaned from pronouncements at that time attributed to Gordon Hourston of BTC (then Managing Director). While acknowledging price sensitivity in some aspects of the product mix, he suggested: 'Price alone is not what customers demand.'

This case has been developed to provide the basis for class discussion of the impact of change upon a highly regulated service and product sector. Interviews with personnel from Boots the Chemists, pharmaceutical organizations and other health service professionals have been used alongside desk research to develop the content. All views expressed and analysis provided are solely those of the author, and do not represent the corporate view of Boots the Chemists, its employees or any other pharmaceutical or health service organization.

This case seeks to identify some of the changes taking place both within the environment and internally that led Gordon Hourston to this assessment. In particular, it will seek to address the impact of changes and the development of BTC's retail strategy upon the provision of healthcare products and services. It should be remembered that at this time the retail sector was pervaded by companies seeking discounting or price promotion solutions to their woes. BTC itself faced competition across much of its range from established discounters Superdrug (Kingfisher) and Supersave (Lloyds Chemist), alongside a myriad of local copycat operators and national grocery chains. Readers of the case will need to identify those distinguishing characteristics that determine appropriate responses for providers of healthcare products; these include appreciation of the legal and regulatory framework constraining such provision.

Political and economic pressure has combined with changing consumer expectation to force a reappraisal of the pharmacist's role in the delivery of health care. Increasingly the profession talks about 'community pharmacists emphasizing the range of services provided that go beyond compounding and dispensing medicines'. Change produces for BTC both opportunities and threats. It can be expected that the impact will be at both strategic and operational levels.

Readers are asked to analyse this case and the changes it outlines in the context of the necessary operational changes they will stimulate. It is necessary to differentiate between the retail strategies available to BTC and those which are available to a highly regulated business such as healthcare. Differentiation of this sort raises in itself a number of pertinent questions regarding the flexibility that is desirable and deliverable at branch and district level. Readers will need to identify the barriers and constraints that restrict local decision making, and distinguish between those which may be internally imposed and those which are a necessary function of a retailer offering professional services. It is in this context that comparison with other national retail organizations becomes problematic. While BTC's retail offer means that competition is drawn from many varied retail companies, few have to operate within such a tight legislative framework in key product areas. Attempts by Asda to discount vitamins, minerals and supplements in October 1995 help to emphasize the point. Sale of such products is conditioned by price maintenance of over the counter (OTC) medicines and discounting is not allowed. Within days Asda was forced to return prices to those recommended by the manufacturer. Asda repeated the attempt in June 1996, with similar results.

Boots the Chemists

BTC has in excess of 1100 stores (compared with approximately 300 for Marks and Spencer and 400 each for Tesco and Sainsbury's), making it one of the most widely dispersed UK retailers. The extent of its penetration of UK retailing is immense: 90 per cent of UK consumers have shopped in a Boots at one time or other; 70 per cent of women shop in one once a week. It is a little appreciated fact that BTC is the largest user of EPoS in Europe. Sales for the group to April 1994 showed an increase of 5.2 per cent to £4.17 billion, with a profit of £415.9 million before tax. Chemist chain profits rose 13.3 per cent to £322.9 million on sales 5.4 per cent ahead at £2.8 billion.

The sale in November 1994 of pharmaceutical business units for £850 million to BASF has provided a cash pile (despite a share buy back scheme) and allowed the group to focus on developing its retail and generic drugs business in Britain and on the continent.

Company profits to April 1995 were subsequently up at £849 million (including profit on disposals of £324 million). BTC profits increased by 8 per cent to £349 million, although the company suggested that High Street trading remained tough. The group's retail arm encompassed BTC, Halfords, Do It All (with W. H. Smith, but wholly owned from June 1996), Boots Opticians, Children's World and A. G. Stanley.

Healthcare Business Centre

The pharmacy services department provides a support and facilitating service for other functions within BTC. Headed by a business general manager, pharmacy services is divided into three separate functional areas. The pharmacy office is responsible for managing professional and legal issues and activities. It provides both information and advice to operations, maintains compliance with professional standards and lobbies and represents BTC interests in the wider environment. Dispensing marketing manages the marketing function of pharmacy counter sales, producing promotional materials and initiatives for BTC pharmacy operations and the products sold within it, e.g. Medilink cards (see Current Initiatives, below). Marketing is also responsible, along with dispensing operations, for monitoring consumer trends, expectations and satisfaction. Dispensing operations is a service function that offers expertise in layout, process and capacity management. Project management teams drawn from the operations function liaise with store, district and area management to pilot process management changes and improvements to individual store performance.

Stores are classified by size and locality. Large store operations are controlled separately and split into ten areas, each having an area manager with up to 20 stores. Small stores, because of their greater number, are split into eight areas (each with an area manager) and each is further divided into ten districts. Typically a district manager will be responsible for 15 to 20 stores. Each store chain is headed by a controller based at BTC head office in Nottingham.

The Superintendent Pharmacist

Any company which runs chemist shops (pharmacies) must appoint a superintendent pharmacist to manage all the professional activities of the company. The superintendent must make sure that:

- BTC pharmacies and pharmacists are all registered with the Royal Pharmaceutical Society of Great Britain (RPSGB);
- BTC obeys the law about healthcare services, medicines and poisons;
- BTC always complies with professional standards for pharmacists – the Code of Ethics.

The superintendent pharmacist can be held personally responsible for any failure in adherence to professional and legal standards. The superintendent, individual BTC pharmacists and the company face a variety of punishments for such failures, including prosecutions, being 'struck off', closure and disqualification from running pharmacies.

The responsibilities of the superintendent pharmacist require that the incumbent discharge their duties independently of the commer-

Exhibit 11.1 The professional responsibilities of the pharmacy superintendent

- healthcare equipment;
- healthcare advice and education;
- health checks such as pregnancy and cholesterol kits;
- household chemicals;
- babycare medicines and equipment;
- food supplements;
- some beauty and personal care products, e.g. sun care;
- dietary foods, e.g. gluten-free;
- products to aid dieting or slimming;
- appliances such as stockings, trusses, aids for the disabled;
- first aid products;
- all pharmacy services;
- approaches to healthcare professionals, e.g. doctors, nurses, midwives.

Source: BTC internal literature.

cial interests of the company. Reporting at board level, the super-intendent maintains the integrity of BTC's commercial activities by advising and counselling colleagues, monitoring standards and if necessary vetoing decisions that threaten professional pharmaceutical standards (see exhibit 11.1).

The Changing Environment

Government policy as it affects the NHS has had a major impact upon pharmacists and pharmacies. The nature of the sales transaction, the type of product sold and how it is classified have all been affected. Government has sought to achieve efficiency gains and cost savings by influencing the process by which people obtain medicines and the individual cost of those medicines.

Rising prescription charges (up 61 per cent between 1985 and 1992) have been accompanied by the desire to encourage people to

Exhibit 11.2 Drug categories

Medicines are classified into three distinct categories:

- Prescription only medicines (POM) may only be supplied by a pharmacist with a written order from a doctor.

- Pharmacy medicines (P) do not need a prescription but can only be sold in a pharmacy under the supervision of a pharmacist.

- General sales list medicines (GSL) can normally be sold anywhere, without prescription and without the supervision of a pharmacist.

Some medicines are referred to as 'over-the-counter' medicines (OTC). These are generally preparations, remedies and medicines in P or GSL categories that are not available for 'self-select' but kept on or behind the pharmacy counter. Security, control, sensitivity or merchandising policy determine medicines categorized in this way.

buy directly from the pharmacist medicines for minor ailments, saving the NHS both the cost of the medicine and the GP's time. Barriers to such a strategy have been both institutional (see exhibit 11.2) and based upon customer/patient preferences, knowledge and skills.

Changes regarding the nature of the sales transaction have had a profound effect upon all pharmacies. BTC as the largest individual dispenser of prescriptions in the UK (estimated to account for 15 per cent of all prescriptions dispensed) cannot be exempted. With the changing requirements of both government and consumers has come the need for changes in the knowledge, skills and administration possessed and conducted by the healthcare staff.

The Product Range and Service

An increasing number of medicines are being reclassified from POM (prescription only medicine) to P (pharmacy medicine) categories to facilitate change (e.g. Pepcid, Tagamet). Medicines with a proven record of safety and with which people can usually treat themselves without recourse to a doctor are now generally listed in the P category. However, the same medicine can be listed in several categories depending upon the symptoms it is used to treat, the dosage to be taken, the length of time of the treatment and the characteristics of the patient (adult or child etc.). This creates for the pharmacist a responsibility in matching product, person and ailment.

Pharmacists are required by law to supervise the sale to avoid any mismatch of the above, but beyond this, new demands are being made of all counter staff. Implications regarding training, retraining and recruitment exist at all levels within BTC. While changes in the conventions for dispensing POM and P products have produced more responsibility at operating level, this has not necessarily meant more flexibility. The need to ensure compliance with dispensing regulations and to promote a distinct corporate image has determined clear operating procedures for staff at all levels. To meet RPSGB requirements, BTC staff are told to use the acronym WWHAM to ensure that all relevant questions are asked when dealing with POM, P or OTC purchases.

- Who is it for?

- What are the symptoms?

- How long have you had the ailment?

- Any other action taken so far?

- Medication already being taken (for this, or other conditions)?

Changes in dispensing procedures have stimulated press attention, and BTC as the largest dispensing chemist has been included in such scrutiny.

Reports from the consumer affairs media, such as the BBC programme *Watchdog* and *Which?* magazine, suggest that pharmacies have frequently failed to discharge effectively their responsibilities, with some BTC branches (along with the others) being the subject of criticism. While the RPSGB talks of individual pharmacists' responsibility in complying with the Code of Practice, much of the subsequent adverse publicity has been levelled at companies and not individuals. To ensure that the safety controls are adhered to and are practical to implement, the RPSGB implemented changes to the Sale of Medicines Protocol from 1 January 1995, with healthcare assistants who have been on an approved training course being qualified to ask the relevant questions and sanction the sale (pharmacists must still be present but need not be notified). The BTC healthcare assistant training course carries National Vocational

Qualifcation (NVQ) accreditation and meets the qualifying criteria.

Furthermore, there is increasing evidence of changing attitudes among the general public to the advice giving role of the pharmacist. More than ever before, professional journals such as *The Pharmaceutical Journal* carry articles concerning health education and development and the ways in which pharmacists may be of influence. Surveys conducted to measure consumer perceptions conclude that pharmacists will be required to give more advice and counselling and that there are currently many pharmacies that fail to meet these criteria. Once again this has both recruitment and training implications for BTC, as the nature and balance of skills required to be an effective pharmacist changes to include enhanced interpersonal and selling skill, a change moving the pharmacist from a compounder of medicines to an expert in their preparation, effects and application.

Government has also sought to decrease the cost of managing the NHS budget by using drug and therapeutic committees to promote the prescribing of generic medicines rather than branded expensive products. Although it is already widely practised in general medical practice pressure still exists for generic substitution to become the norm.

BTC is well placed to become a beneficiary of such a move. Significant percentages of consumers are known to seek the comfort and reassurance delivered from the branding of products. While a move to generic prescribing seeks to deliver to the government substantial savings funded from the lack of product promotion (and development?), it is wholly conceivable that customers will wish to substitute a retail brand name to provide perceived security of purchase. Evidence exists that BTC's image and own brand product portfolio should enable it to capitalize upon these changes. A 1995 Mintel survey suggests that BTC has the best corporate image, placing it first among consumers in terms of value for money and being in touch with its customers.

One unforeseen consequence of the changes has been the perceived discounting of prescriptions. When a medicine costs less than the prescription charge of dispensing it, the balance is usually fed into NHS coffers to subsidize the large percentage of prescriptions that are free to the elderly, unemployed etc. More than 50 per cent of prescriptions cost the NHS less than the prescription price. Doctors can write private prescriptions (at no cost to the patient) and the patient then pays the medicine cost rather than the prescription charge. Some pharmacists have chosen to convert NHS prescriptions to private prescriptions when the patient/customer benefits, effectively discounting POM products, yet in contravention of the regulations governing the contracts under which they supply prescriptions.

It has not been the practice of BTC (or any of the large dispensing chemists) to follow this process and risk the contracts they have secured for the provision of dispensed medicines, or contravene the standards required of them by professional bodies. Some independents are prepared to challenge at a local level the legality and ethicacy of the current systems and contracts; while they are gaining some popular support from consumer groups it is unlikely that they will succeed.

Finally, consumers are beginning to buy larger quantities of homeopathic medicines and alternative remedies. BTC, which recorded increases in turnover of 100 per cent in such medicines from 1991 to 1995, has launched own brands in both herbal and homeopathic ranges. In this, BTC is rediscovering its past. In 1877, Jesse Boot, a herbalist, founded the company to dispense herbal medicines.

The Pharmacy Counter

Provision at the pharmacy counter within Boots stores is typically varied, with demand, mix and resources reflecting differences in store locality, size and competition. Exhibit 11.3 shows the population characteristics of an average pharmacy.

Locality is a major influence, determining the optimum size of store and conditioned by availability of suitable premises. BTC is one of the most widely distributed retailers in the UK, trading from small market towns and district and suburban centres through to all the major cities. Even within such diverse catchment areas, the location strategy is flexible. High Street siting, while still the most common is supplemented by split site outlets, sites in health centres (e.g. Quarterjack, Wimbourne, Dorset) and operations linked with other retailers offers (e.g. Sainsbury's).

Store size is determined by the needs generated by the catchment area and the availability and cost of suitable space. The dispensary size included will reflect the projected level of dispensing business

Exhibit 11.3 Population characteristics of an average pharmacy

While there is no such thing as a 'average' pharmacy, and the characteristics of the population vary enormously from one area to another, on
average a pharmacy might expect to serve:

- 50 or so diabetics;

- 150 asthmatics;

- 15 people discharged from hospital in the last week (including day
  surgery patients);

- 8 colostomists;

- 3 with coeliac disease;

- 750 elderly people, including 30 over 70s and 20 in residential
  care;

- 20 people suffering from cancer, of whom 4 will be receiving
  terminal care;

- one person with cystic fibrosis;

- up to 500 people using anti-hypertensive medication;

- several people who are keen to stop taking tranquillizers;

- 600 carers (carers are high users of pharmacies, with a third of them
  visiting pharmacies more than once a week);

- a few hundred people with a disability;

- many who have difficulty managing their medication;

- at least two people who have AIDS or are HIV positive;

- an assortment of drug abusers;

- 300 under fives;

- 50 pregnant women;

- a handful of discharged long stay mental patients;

- hundreds who could benefit from health education or more specific
  advice on such areas as diet, alcohol intake and stopping smok-
  ing.

Source: Royal Pharmaceutical Society, March 1992.

and the size of the pharmacy counter will vary according to size of dispensing business, store size and sales of non-dispensed health-care products. Frequently, in smaller stores the pharmacist will be responsible for both dispensing and managing the store.

All pharmacy counters will deal with a variety of products and subsequent customer purchases, ranging from those stored in the dispensary and those displayed behind the counter (but not on open access) to those products that are available on both the counter and adjacent shelving for self-select.

As previously outlined, products are classified as prescription only medicines (POM), pharmacy only medicines (P) and general sales list (GSL) products. The balance of demand in each of these categories will vary by store location and type (e.g. health centre located stores usually have a greater proportional demand for prescribed products), day of the week and time of the day. Not all BTC stores have contracts with the NHS to dispense prescriptions, and those that do not are therefore restricted in the products they can supply. Seasonal factors can influence both overall demand and the mix of product type supplied (e.g. hay fever preventatives/remedies).

BTC transactions vary enormously, ranging from the simple self-selection of a product and payment for it, to more interactive exchanges such as advice seeking and giving, counselling, respond-ing to symptoms and occasionally treatment of minor accidents and ailments. All transactions need to be conducted in compliance with the RSPGB code of ethics.

Nor is product type necessarily an indicator of either the length or the complexity of the transaction. Prescribed medicines will often require instruction and information regarding dosage, frequency, side-effects etc. Pharmacy only medicines should be checked with the patient to ensure suitability etc. Occasionally, self-select and OTC products will require consultations that are longer or as long as the aforementioned.

Advice required by BTC customers regarding P or GSL products means that the suitability criterion is often reversed, with the customer seeking information regarding the suitability of the pro-duct rather than the pharmacist reassuring himself or herself of the suitability of the patient. Information thus given may be viewed as satisfying either the physical needs of the patient through applica-tion and appropriate process or the psycho-social needs. Typically, more patients want advice than would request it if not offered

Exhibit 11.4 Staff classification and responsibilities

Pharmacy counter staff can usually be categorized within the following classifications:

Pharmacist/consultant pharmacist

- Function: to supervise and provide effective, efficient and professional pharmaceutical service at all times, in dispensing and OTC sales in the pharmacy area, within company policy and professional standards.

- Responsible to: the reporting relationship and responsibility of the pharmacist/consultant pharmacists will vary according to situation and circumstance.

- Principle responsibilities: can be categorized as professional, customer/patient and public relations, stock management, clerical and administrative, legal compliance, staff and self-development.

Dispenser

- Function: to assist in providing an efficient dispensing service according to company policy by dispensing prescriptions and undertaking general dispensary duties and prescription reception.

- Responsible to: the pharmacist responsible for the dispensing activities.

- Principle responsibilities: these can be classified as professional (compliance with regulations and company conventions), operational, including adherence to the labour management system (LMS), stock management, customer liaison, housekeeping/health and safety.

Pharmacy assistant

- Someone who has completed all healthcare assistant training and development and taken supplementary training covering some of the skills required of a dispenser.

- Responsibilities and reporting lines will vary but will usually include customer liaison, some medicine preparation and all those associated with a healthcare assistant.

Healthcare assistant

- Function: to maximize sales, provide a courteous customer sales service and through the use of company methods, make sure that stock is available for sale is attractive and merchandised in the working area.

- Responsible to: either supervisor or senior assistant (small stores).

- Principle responsibilities: can be categorized as sales, customer service (including referral to pharmacist when appropriate), stock control, housekeeping and health and safety, security.

Source: BTC Personnel Department.

(i.e. not asking for advice cannot be equated with not expecting it). Research shows that pharmacy counters where staff feel most comfortable taking on an enhanced role (that includes counselling and education rather than solely dispensing and selling) generate more demand for these services, and greater customer satisfaction.

The pharmaceutical profession has sought to develop and promote the enhanced role through the use of campaigns such as 'Ask your pharmacist'. BTC's status and image as a 'mixed goods' retailer benefits if the necessary provision of additional service required of its healthcare products is perceived as bestowing improved skills and service in transactions involving other products.

In addition to the pharmacist(s), who must always be in attendance, counter staff will variously consist of dispensing assistants, pharmacy assistants and health care assistants (see exhibit 11.4 for details). To comply with requirements of the Sale of Medicines Protocol, many BTC stores have provided separate advice and payment points located away from the pharmacy counter and staffed at busy times by either pharmacy or healthcare assistants, allowing GSL medicines to be available on self-selection. Frequently, advice points become additional payment stations for most store products, thus reducing queuing at central till points.

Layout, including till points, dispensary and customer queuing/waiting area, varies (figure 11.1 shows a counter layout in a large store). Layout planning and merchandising procedures are determined at head office. Both layout and merchandise presentation are derived from best practice (benchmarking) techniques, product

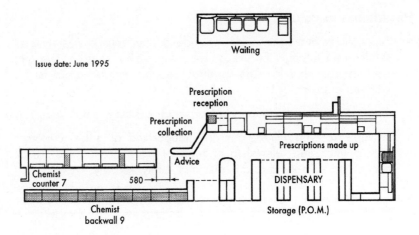

Issue date: June 1995

Figure 11.1 Pharmacy counter layout.

sales market information and operational imperatives. While layouts frequently need to be configured to satisfy specific store characteristics, little responsibility for this resides at store or district level. Restrictions based upon the Sale of Medicines Protocol and the need to present a consistent corporate image are both cited as determining the need for centralized control.

Current Initiatives

BTC's pharmacy services are involved in a number of initiatives at both national and local levels. Broadly, all can be categorized as being designed to generate extra business (i.e. managing for income) or allocate limited resources more efficiently (managing operating costs); most seek to reconcile one with the other.

Marketing based initiatives by drug companies have included advertisements seeking to capitalize upon changes in the reclassification of some medicines previously only available by prescription. Adverts emphasized products that are 'now available over the counter at Boots'. The attitude of other members of the pharmacy profession towards commercial activity of this sort is demonstrated by the reaction at the RPSGB, which approached the Advertising Standards Authority suggesting that the adverts implied exclusivity of supply.

In 1994 the Medilink card scheme available to all customers bringing a prescription to a Boots pharmacy, was launched. Registered customers are issued a card with a unique registration number, which enables staff to access a record of prescriptions issued via Boots.

Marketing of the services has stressed that customers who 'always bring their prescriptions to Boots' will have a complete record or history of dispensed medicines and thus benefit from associated features, e.g. specific advice, error spotting, compatibility of medicines and speed of service. Other activities that have been heavily promoted include a repeat prescription collection service from local surgeries, NHS equipment measuring and fitting services and an unwanted medicine disposal service. Improved services to residential and nursing homes, particularly the introduction of a monitored dosage system, have been instrumental in improving BTC's performance within an increasingly important sector.

District managers echoing the sentiments of Gordon Hourston suggest that a strategy that 'adds value' is likely to be successful for most product categories. Many, when assessing retail performance, are quick to point out, however, that significant profit growth must continue from cost control; in this context the pharmacy counter cannot be shielded from business imperatives (the extent to which counters are able to exercise control over this is in part the subject of the case). The dilemma at operating level is how to reconcile the need to add value and service whilst effectively managing cost.

A project management team has been set up to implement pharmacy counter and dispensing refits. Using benchmarking and 'best practice' techniques, project managers (seconded from the operations division) advise on dispensary layout improvements in order to maximize efficiency in the process. Projects are instigated by district, store management or head office, and are focused upon under performing units or those identified as providing the greatest value creation. Savings are mainly attributed to process efficiency gains.

Further, savings are being found from the utilization of new technology to aid staff planning. As with most retailers, systems that more closely link demand to resource scheduling are being introduced. While much of the direction for changing processes and service levels has been driven through by head office, districts in conjunction with family health service authorities have been able to develop their own initiatives and show some flexibility in approach. In 1992, BTC's store in Eltham started to provide a room for a nurse practitioner, enhancing the skills and advice available from the branch. Other stores have arranged links with other primary care professionals.

Summary

BTC is a highly complex, extensively distributed retail organization. The provision of product and service at the pharmacy counter has had to be compatible with the overall strategy of the company and comply with externally imposed restrictions regarding its products, services, processes and resources.

Within this highly regulated sector, BTC operates a tight regime with little branch autonomy regarding layout, merchandise range and planning.

The traditional role of the pharmacist is changing. A combination of government induced initiatives and changing customer attitude has resulted in the need for the pharmacist and pharmacy counter staff to undertake an enhanced role in the provision of medicines, remedies and palliatives. Changes will continue and quicken.

This case outlines some of the changes that have taken place, illustrates them with specific examples and indicates in part the effect upon and responses by BTC. It does not attempt to provide comprehensive analysis or detail – some readers may wish to undertake some competitor analysis to provide more detail. The purpose is to encourage the reader to reflect upon the difficulties encountered by an operator of a highly defined and regulated process when customer and market expectations change. Some degree of informed speculation will be needed to answer the following questions effectively. Links will need to be drawn with other retail operations with which you are familiar, and with current management processes and theory. Good luck.

Case Questions

1   You are asked to consider the product sold by BTC at its pharmacy counters. What is it and how and why has it changed? What further changes might you envisage in the next few years?

2   As a district manager within store operations, how might you manage the operations of your district to benefit from these

changes? In your answer, distinguish between those actions and decisions that can be taken at district level and those which must be confined to head office, and identify why.

3   What are the potential barriers to change?

12

Post Office Counters

Gary Davies

Manchester Business School

'We are in business to provide a unique nationwide retail service –
which meets the needs of our customers in the community on behalf
of our clients – as the leading provider of benefits distribution,
postal services, banking and bill payment facilities.'

This is how Post Office Counters Ltd (POCL) defined its mission
statement in 1989. POCL was formed as one of a number of wholly
owned subsidiary undertakings of the British Post Office in 1986.
Its role was to manage a national network of nearly 20,000 post
office outlets. As its mission statement implied, it acted as the main distribution and collection agency for a number of government services.

Table 12.1 presents the main financial figures for the business. In
real terms total turnover was increasing slightly, but many of the
activities of POCL offered little or no scope for growth and all were
under competitive threat. Costs were dominated by labour costs
(more than half of total operating costs when the staff costs in sub
post offices were included) and labour costs tended to rise faster
than either inflation or revenue. The main issue in the financial
management of the business was to find ways of filling the inevitable
profit gap in the future caused by the lack of growth in existing
business areas, coupled with rises in real unit labour costs and
pressure to reduce costs from government and clients. The over-
riding strategic issues were to reduce the cost of existing activities
while maintaining market volumes and searching for new business
to complement existing products and services. At the same time,
levels of service to the public were to be improved, not reduced.

Table 12.1 POCL statistics

	1990/1	1992/3	1994/5
Number of post offices			
Crown	1167	917	699
Agency	19,471	19,041	18,826
Value of transactions (£ million)	98,921	117,892	127,192
Volume of transactions (million)	1322	1399	1382
	1990	1992	1995
POCL turnover (£ million)	875.1	959.2	1118
Staff Costs (£ million)	250.3	257.3	242
Profit before tax (£ million)	22	28	30

Source: Report and accounts.

Sources of Income

Table 12.2 lists the main sources of business for POCL. Sixty-nine per cent of business volume was derived from just three 'clients'. The largest client, the Benefits Agency, commissioned POCL to pay cash for old age pensions, income support, unemployment benefit and child allowances to the public. POCL accounted for most of Benefits Agency payments, the remainder being direct transfers into recipients' bank accounts. In fact, a growing proportion of benefits were being paid directly into recipients' bank accounts by automatic credit transfer, a cheaper method for the agency. POCL expected its share of the pensions and child benefit markets to decline, largely because many new recipients took up the bank option. A potentially devastating threat would be a decision by government to insist that all benefits be paid into bank accounts directly. (When this had been done by the Australian government, the decision had resulted in a substantial reduction in the number of post offices.)

The second largest client was Royal Mail, once formally part of the same organization as POCL but now responsible for mail services within the Post Office Group. POCL was the main source of postage stamps for letters, although stamps were by now widely available in hotels, petrol stations and other shops. A third arm of the Post Office Group was Parcelforce, which, as the name implied, operated what had been the parcels business of the old Post Office. The Royal Mail still held a near total monopoly over letter post, but there was a potential threat of competition from parcel and courier

Table 12.2 Sources of business volume

	Per cent
Benefits Agency (once the Department of Social Security)	30
Royal Mail Letters	23
Girobank	16
Department of National Savings	4
Driver and Vehicle Licensing Authority	6
British Telecom	6
BBC	4
Other	11

Source: POCL.

companies such as TNT if the restrictions on postal services were ever eased or even removed. POCL and its sub post office agents also benefited from charges for receiving parcels and bagged mail from businesses on behalf of the Royal Mail and Parcelforce.

Girobank had been a fourth arm of the Post Office Group until its sale to the Alliance and Leicester Building Society. Most of the transaction business of about 1.5 million Girobank personal account holders was still conducted in a post office. Many of the transactions involved cash payment of bills by households. Girobank also had many corporate users and the later opening hours of post offices, compared to those of banks, was seen as providing an opportunity for POCL in corporate banking. POCL had other strengths as a financial services business. Some 40 million postal orders were purchased each year. Post offices also sold National Savings products, Government Stock and Premium Bonds.

In addition to its major clients, POCL worked for a large number of other bodies which saw a benefit in having a single channel that reached most of the British population each week. Post offices were used to issue television licences for the BBC, as a payment point for telephone bills for British Telecom and as a source of phonecards for both Telecom and its competitor, Mercury. Over 25 million vehicle licences were issued via post offices each year and approximately two million British Visitors Passports. More than £10 million worth of National Insurance stamps were retailed by POCL each year. The launch of the National Lottery in 1995 provided POCL with another opportunity to benefit from having the largest network of retail outlets in the country.

Much of POCL's business concerned the handling of cash. Money was received for products such as a Savings Certificate or a licence and paid out for a pension or a child allowance. POCL derived its revenue from the charges it made to clients for managing these transactions. Other sources of income were from property, and a number of new ventures had been started to take advantage of the substantial customer flow into post offices, including the retailing of stationery and philately, and the installation of photobooths and electronic advertising.

The Network

The familiar red and yellow Post Office sign could be found on some 20,000 outlets country wide. The POCL network represented by far the largest retail presence in the country, outnumbering the combined networks of both banks and building societies (see table 12.3). Post offices fell into a number of categories. What tended to be the largest outlets were called Crown offices. They were under POCL ownership and direct control but had declined in number from an original 1500 to below 700 by 1995. They were located mainly in the centres of conurbations and were managed and staffed by POCL. A number of Crown offices had been converted to an agency status. Frequently the original postmaster would continue to operate the business himself or herself, but as an agent rather than an employee of POCL. All Crown offices and the new agency offices offered the public the full range of post office services.

The vast majority of outlets in the network were 'sub offices', operated by independent sub postmasters, often as part of another

Table 12.3 Comparable retail networks

	Thousands
Building society outlets	
Branches	4.4
Agencies	3.9
Banks	11.7
Post offices	
Main offices	1.0
Agency offices	19.5

Source: POCL 1991/2 Review.

business. The largest group were termed 'scale payment sub post offices'. The sub postmaster received payment based on a complex system (first instituted in 1907 and revised in 1948 and 1976) designed to reflect the number of transactions made and the work involved. The payment system was not always seen as fair or as designed to encourage a sub postmaster to increase the volume of business. (One reason for this was that any increase would come at least partly by another local post office losing volume. Sub post-masters' contracts traditionally forbade any overt attempt to attract business away from another post office.)

Over 8000 of the sub post offices could be classified as rural offices. Most cost POCL more to operate than they generated in revenue. Collectively they accounted for only 7 per cent of POCL's business. By 1991, 1500 rural offices operated as 'community' sub offices. These were open for only part of the day or week, often in the front room of a private home or in a village hall. Some 4500 of the smallest rural offices had been identified as potential community sub offices. As and when the sub postmaster of such a rural office chose to retire, and particularly when no one could be found to take on the business, the change would be effected. The community office contract differed from that for the scale payment sub offices in that it included a core payment of salary and additional payment for hours worked.

A recent innovation was the introduction of a formal franchise for selected locations. The new post office franchise scheme recognized the additional value of a post office as a traffic generator within a larger store. Existing retailers were offered a post offfice within their premises in exchange for a franchise fee. A number of such franchises were created within retailers such as Safeway, Sainsbury's and Budgen.

Opening hours varied across the network. Community offices kept limited hours but most others opened on Monday to Friday from 09.00 until 17.30 and closed on Saturday at lunchtime. Some closed for lunch and a half day during the week. In principle a post office could open for longer hours, and many did, particularly the franchised offices.

The Customers

Some 28 million visits were made to post offices each week for one or more of the 150 different products or services on offer. Ninety-five per cent of all adults visited a post office at least once a year. Most favoured one particular office. Over 50 per cent of the population visited at least weekly. People in socio-economic groups A, B and C_1 accounted for 41 per cent of customers (slightly below the national average). The overall age profile of customers tended to be below the national average of those aged 18 to 24 and above the average of those aged between 25 and 34. The customer profile at individual offices varied substantially, reflecting the location of the office. In city centres the customers would include a higher proportion of business people seeking a different portfolio of services from those in an area of high unemployment, for example.

The British people enjoyed a love/hate relationship with their Post Office. In a survey in 1991, 58 per cent of those surveyed had been against the idea of privatizing the counters business, up 13 points on a similar survey the year before. Eighty-three per cent expressed 'quite a lot' or 'a great deal' of confidence in the Post Office as a whole (see table 12.4). Dissatisfiers were often concerned with queuing.

Table 12.4 Level of public confidence

	A great deal (%)	Quite a lot (%)
The Post Office	25	58
British Gas	20	61
British Telecom	17	48
Halifax Building Society	14	40
W. H. Smith	12	51
British Coal	4	29
British Rail	4	19
Federal Express	4	22
DHL	2	13

Source: Opinion Research and Consultancy.

The most important issues for users of Crown and sub offices differed (see exhibit 12.1), but queuing time was prominent in both. Long-term tracking studies of ratings for 'gives good service' and 'gives good value' showed sustained increases, while ratings for 'cares what users think' were lower in the 1990s than in the middle of the previous decade.

Exhibit 12.1 The most important issues for post office customers

Crown Office Users
(rank order of importance)

Time waiting to be served in a queue
Number of counter positions open
Frequency of queuing
Privacy to discuss my affairs
Politeness of staff

Sub Office Users
(rank order of importance)

Privacy to discuss my affairs
Time taken to be served in a queue
Staff ability to answer questions
Politeness of staff
Number of counter positions open

Source: Specialist Units Ltd, Research International.

Sub Postmasters

The National Federation of Sub Postmasters (founded in 1897) represented 85 per cent of all sub postmasters. Their elected representatives met regularly with POCL management both regionally and nationally to protect and promote their members' interests. One of their concerns was the difference between the gross income the sub postmaster received and what was left as net income after the expenses of running a post office were paid out in staff and premises costs. On surrendering the agency upon retirement the sub postmaster might expect a substantial sum for the goodwill associated with the agency. But in many inner city areas it had become difficult to sell the business because of the low net wage and even the danger inherent in the role because of the large sums of cash being handled.

POCL also reserved the right to screen and reject any potential buyer for suitability as a sub postmaster. The new agent was given training and support from area management and the outgoing incumbent. Less support was available to help to develop any other retail business, such as a grocery or newsagency, that might form part of the same shop. Few sub postmasters could rely on their post office as their only source of income, but most should have seen it as a useful way of attracting large numbers into their premises. The range of businesses run alongside a sub post office was wide – grocery, convenience store, newsagent, travel agent, even a pub – but most tended to be retailers that shoppers might visit regularly.

Maintaining a coherent image and uniform standards within such a diverse network would never be easy. Almost all offices would display the familiar red and yellow Post Office sign. Most offices had security screens fitted separating customer and staff, a safe, scales and a security system supplied by POCL, but the design of other fixturing varied.

Service

Queuing time had been measured in Crown offices since 1988. Each manager was required to take 22 samples each week at predetermined times. The time taken by a customer from joining a queue to reaching the counter was noted. A target had been set traditionally that 95 per cent of customers would wait no longer than 5 minutes. The time taken to be served was identified as the most important service issue in Crown offices (see exhibit 12.1), although what probably mattered was the perception of that time more than the reality. Research by POCL indicated that perceived time exceeded actual queuing time by 50 per cent for shorter queuing times, but customers' estimates were more precise when the queuing time was longer. If customers were researched at home rather than in the post office, the perception of average queuing time in a post office lengthened.

The difference between actual and perceived queuing times could be altered by the environment. For example, when single queues were introduced into an office where previously customers had joined one of a number of individual queues, one for each clerk, the perception of queuing time shortened even though actual queuing time would be increased by such a change. In one outlet, located in Cosham in the south of England, an open plan system had been trialed. The actual queuing times had increased while the perceived times had reduced. A study by the Post Office Users National Committee (POUNC) in 1989 had shown that actual queuing times in post offices compared favourably with those in banks and

Table 12.5 POUNC study of relative queuing times (fastest ranked first)

Rank order	Actual queuing time	Perceived queuing time
1	Sub post offices	Sub post offices
2	Crown offices	Building societies
3	Banks	Banks
4	Building societies	Crown offices

building societies, while perceived queuing times in Crown offices were rated relatively long (see table 12.5). What to do about the queuing issue became a point of debate between senior management in POCL. One view was that 95 per cent waiting less than 5 minutes was not an acceptable standard as it was not an absolute guarantee to the customer. One hundred per cent within 5 minutes was proposed, even though this would involve higher levels of staffing at key times. Another view was that perception was more important than reality, and what mattered was for perceived queuing time to be lower than in banks and building societies.

While other, similar businesses did have queuing targets, few seemed to measure actual queuing times. Many retail businesses used data on when transactions took place in the day to schedule staff and many of those who captured sales data on EPoS did so automatically. One American bank ignored formal monitoring of waiting time but told customers to ask for $5 if they believed they had waited more than 5 minutes. The American Post Office had introduced a 'lobby director programme', where a member of staff approached people in the queue, asking them about the services they needed to ensure that they had the right forms completed and that any problems were identified in advance. There had been a dramatic reduction in complaints and an increase in compliments. Sixty-seven per cent of those questioned felt the queue moved faster with the new system.

POCL field management was organized by region and area. An area manager, the retail network manager, would have some 20–30 outlets (both Crown and sub post offices) to oversee. The responsibilities of area managers included monitoring queuing times and error rates. Sanctions for unacceptable performance in sub post offices included fines, suspension or the withdrawal of the agency. One area manager described his role as 'pastoral'. To the sub postmaster the area manager was still 'the boss'. One described the relative importance of his relationships as being 'post office first, client second and customer third'.

The Way Ahead

POCL faced a number of threats to its core business, as a government agency, from direct transfer of payments from its clients to members of the public and from direct payment by the public to its other clients. Its mission statement saw the network as its main source of competitive advantage, yet at the same time it represented a source of weakness because of its cost and the perception of service. The culture of the business was changing but still reflected its origins as part of the civil service rather than the mainstream retail sector it aspired to belong to. POCL decided to focus on customer service and on improving its reputation on key issues such as queuing times in all types of post offices.

Discussion Points

1   Should POCL address actual queuing times as the target of 100 per cent served in 5 minutes suggests? What are the implications in doing so? If you were an area manager for POCL, what actions would you consider to improve queuing times?

2   What can POCL do to improve the perception of queuing times (rather than the reality)? Is this a valid option for such an organization?

3   There are far fewer Crown offices than sub post offices. Crown offices are located in major urban centres and have different customer profiles from those in most sub post offices. Crown offices cater more for large numbers of business people. The somewhat smaller sub post offices can have a high percentage of customers claiming various kinds of social security benefits (in areas of high unemployment or in areas where many retired people live). In other areas the customer profile for a sub post office is a broader mixture of benefits claimants, families and small businesses. If you were an area manager how would you take these differences into consideration?

13

Developing a Security Strategy at Metro '99

Joshua Bamfield

Nene College, Northampton

Introduction

Metro '99 was set up in 1991 as a new retail format, with 20 stores operating in the family discount/value sector of the clothing and textile market. Its parent company was the major High Street multiple retailer, Degger and Crosland plc. The core of Metro '99 stores consisted of a number of Degger and Crosland's smaller units situated in lower income High Street locations. Metro '99 held a standard inventory of 30,000 lines, selling a wide range of products, including clothing for men, women and children, textiles (including bedding), footwear, fashion jewellery, toys, videos, music and games.

Degger and Crosland appointed two of its senior personnel to run the new chain: Malcolm Tracey, who was made the operations manager, and Elizabeth Gaukroger, the general manager. They were both in their mid-thirties and their combined service with Degger and Crosland amounted to 23 years. Malcolm had a degree in English from Sheffield University, while Elizabeth had an HND from what at the time had been Lanchester Polytechnic, Coventry.

Malcolm Tracey and Elizabeth Gaukroger carried out a survey of the 20 stores when they took over Metro '99. There were a range of strategic, marketing and operational issues facing the company.

Metro '99 Ltd and Degger and Crosland plc are not the true names of the companies discussed in this case. Certain other facts have been amended to protect the identity of the companies.

Together, the stores in the new chain were marginally profitable but had suffered comparative neglect by Degger and Crosland plc in favour of its larger units established in better locations. Partly as a result, the turnover of managers was high (20 per cent a year), with newly arrived managers soon moving on to better opportunities in Degger and Crosland, or leaving the group altogether.

Degger and Crosland delegated all authority apart from major investment decisions to the two senior executives. Elizabeth and Malcolm had worked together before and were aware of each other's management styles. They agreed that Elizabeth should concentrate on buying, marketing and relationships with Degger and Crosland, while Malcolm was to focus on store operations and logistics. They both had small offices ('a sort of cubby hole actually' according to Elizabeth) which let on to the buying office, on the first floor of the largest store. They met once a week to consider the daily and weekly figures, but otherwise operated fairly autonomously. There was a high degree of trust between them based on mutual understanding.

The survey of Metro '99 carried out by the two executives showed that high levels of crime were one of the major problems facing the new chain.

The Main Security Issues at Metro '99

There were thought to be three major security issues at Metro '99. These were:

1   *High rate of theft.* The average rate of inventory shrinkage was over 3 per cent of sales, compared to the sector average for 1993 of 1.92 per cent, and was rising. Seven of the 20 stores had a shrinkage rate of over 4 per cent and one store's shrinkage was 10 per cent of sales. 'Shrinkage' is a measure of stock loss as a result of theft, administrative error and waste. Its use as a proxy measure of theft in retailing is routine.

2   *Poor store environment.* In all stores there was a disturbing atmosphere, characterized by a significant number of aggressive customers, ostentatious shoplifting and drunken persons entering the store unchecked and creating a disturbance. In one-half of the stores, there was at least one incident of verbal aggression or actual assault every day.

3   *Violence towards staff.* The poor store environment led to repeated actual or threatened violence. In the first year, one-third of branch managers were physically attacked and beaten. Shoplifters and others would occasionally display knives. Not surprisingly, staff were reluctant to challenge suspected shop-lifters.

The two executives of the new chain felt that a failure to confront and overcome the problem of violence might undermine the viability of the chain as a whole.

Metro '99 Operations

The stores were comparatively large (average sales area was 8342 square feet), all located near the centre of High Streets in secondary shopping centres, usually in the lower income areas of large towns and cities. The stores were laid out on a *free form* basis, with two main cash and wrap points, shelving and hangers round the walls to display garments and a considerable number of different types of display units and hanging garment racks arranged at angles on the sales floor itself. The width of the store and the small number of staff created 'blind spots', making it comparatively easy for shop-lifters to conceal goods. All stores had only one entrance, consisting of up to six sets of double doors, and usually 25 to 35 feet wide.

Every branch had an average of five full-time members of staff (including the manager) and between 10 and 15 part-time or casual staff. The number of part-timers might double in periods of peak seasonal demand. The company employed a total of 121 full-time staff (including administrative staff) and around 260 part-time or casual staff, although numbers varied depending on the time of the year.

Security Policy

Previously, security in what were now Metro '99 stores had been provided by Degger and Crosland's central security department. Regional security managers worked with store managers and district store managers, using a combination of store detectives in all stores, staff and management training in security awareness and limited use of electronic article surveillance (security tags). Four Metro '99 stores had installed electronic article surveillance (EAS) systems and one store had a security system to protect clothing which used plastic tags containing blue dye (inktags). None of these systems was shown to have a significant effect upon the shrinkage levels of the outlets where they were installed, although there had been some effect in reducing the general level of hostility and violence in these stores.

The Metro '99 chain was too small to justify the employment of a specialist security manager, the operations manager being primarily responsible for security. To ensure that the security problem did not worsen, Malcolm Tracey agreed that store detectives would continue to be employed in 16 stores on a full-time basis.

Shrinkage at Metro '99

In Metro '99, as in most retail firms, stock was transferred to branches at retail selling price. The difference between *actual stocks* and *projected stocks* (based on stock deliveries and retail sales) was termed *shrinkage*. In common with most other retailers, Metro '99 and Degger and Crosland used shrinkage as a proxy measure of retail theft.

The formula used to estimate shrinkage was:

shrinkage = actual stocks (at retail) − calculated closing stock

closing stock (at retail) = opening stock (at retail) + purchases (at retail) − retail sales + agreed markdowns − agreed markups

An acceptable level of shrinkage in Metro '99 was 1.5 per cent of sales, which was the average rate for Degger and Crosland plc. However, all Metro '99 outlets had shrinkage rates exceeding 3 per cent of sales.

Administrative error and waste were thought to account for 20–25 per cent of shrinkage. Administrative error could result from goods being incorrectly priced or invoiced wrongly, delivery miscounts, credit note errors and other mistakes, which were usually relatively small. Waste could occur when goods were damaged or soiled when being handled by customers or merchandise might be taken out of packets (and could not be sold or returned) and display garments might fade and become unsaleable.

Some 2200 thieves had been apprehended by Metro '99 in 1992–3, of whom 20 had been staff. The value of the goods found on thieves represented only 2 per cent of the company's total shrinkage losses for that period. No breakdown of theft was possible between staff theft, shoplifting and theft by suppliers, but Metro '99 management's perception was that theft by customers was the main source of loss. There was little evidence of staff theft (most apprehended staff thieves were found to be stealing garments costing an average of £65.37).

The result of observing (and drawing conclusions from) the store security environment pointed to high rates of customer theft, thought to be around 70 per cent of total theft. Total losses in 1992–3 could therefore be broken down as follows:

Total shrinkage	£3.532 million
Administrative error/waste	£0.706–0.883 million
Derived theft level (total shrinkage − administrative error/waste)	£2.649–2.826 million

Electronic Article Surveillance: Metro '99's Inheritance

At its formation, there were five stores within the Metro '99 chain with tagging systems. Four stores had a radio frequency EAS system and one store had an inktag system.

EAS is based on the use of electronic tags or markers attached to items of merchandise. When the items are taken past detection devices, an alarm is sounded unless the tags have been deactivated or removed. The initial EAS system consisted of radio frequency devices (first developed around 1981) using passive tags, around 4 inches in diameter. The effect of EAS upon the Metro '99 units was not significant. Comparisons by management with stores which did not have EAS systems installed indicated that shrinkage fell by 7.5 per cent between 1990 and 1992, which was too small a fall to justify the costs of the systems. It was felt that the original EAS system suffered from several problems, including a low detection rate and high false alarm rate. The low detection rate was supported not only by a very small fall in shrinkage, but by a steady decline in the number of tags held by the store. This suggested that thieves could walk through the detector gates with tagged items without the alarm being sounded. The tags could be detuned by body fluids –

e.g. by being held in the hand or under the armpit – and some thieves were able to detach the tags, by using a magnet or a device to force the security pin out of its socket in the tag. Shop staff routinely found discarded tags on the floor or in pockets of other garments.

Despite these problems, there was no evidence that staff had lost confidence in the system or that procedures for tagging were not being followed. Staff pointed out that since the introduction of EAS there had been some fall in violence and ostentatious shoplifting (customer theft where no attempt was made to conceal the act of stealing). Staff felt that these improvements had been associated with the existence of EAS.

The Metro '99 store with inktags found that these tags were not a deterrent. There were no electronics or alarms, but if the article containing the tag was stolen, the ink would stain the garment when the tag was removed. In practice, the tags could be removed by thieves within the store or frozen in a commercial refrigerator, enabling the tags to be detached without staining the merchandise. Inktags apparently had little effect upon shrinkage in the single store with the system.

Thus the experience of EAS and inktag systems of stores within the group indicated that, for Metro '99, inktags seemed to be ineffective while EAS systems had only a marginal effect upon shrinkage but a more significant effect upon the general security environment of the store.

The EAS Decision

The levels of violence and theft from shops have already been identified as being strategically important for Metro '99. After attempting to improve the situation over 12 months by better security procedures and using shop detectives in three more stores, by 1993 the organization had decided to attempt something more radical.

The rational approach to making major investment decisions, when applied to EAS, would consist of a sequence: security audit (an analysis of current shrinkage and theft patterns); assessment of all available options; development of the design requirements of the solution (on the basis of current and future retail needs); assessment of the full costs of EAS systems, including the hidden or indirect

Exhibit 13.1 Component parts of electronic article surveillance systems

EAS systems consist of three component parts, electronic tags, radio antennae and a control unit. Electronic tags, or targets, are fixed to merchandise by security pins, lanyards or adhesives, and alarm when they come within range of the detector antennae. The means used to secure the tags is extremely important, as weaknesses here will undermine the effectiveness of the whole system. The hard tag (most common in clothing and textiles) is a large plastic wafer about 4 inches long; soft tags are the size of a credit card; paper tags are semi-flexible devices, some of which are as small as the standard grocery price ticket or a small length of fuse wire.

EAS antennae (or detector gates) placed at the checkout or at (or above) the exit transmit and receive radio signals, detecting the tag when it comes within range. Depending upon the system used, tags will be detected either because a tag will introduce a specific radio frequency (and pulse rate) into the detection field or because the presence of the tag will change the field itself. The EAS detector gates are linked to a control unit: this monitors and controls the operation of the antennae and performs certain error correction functions (newer units use microprocessors). Smaller installations will have the control unit mounted within one of the gates.

The rate of technical innovation in EAS has been relatively high in recent years. The main systems available are now based upon:

1   Radio frequency (RF) systems.
2   Microwave or ultra high frequencies (UHF).
3   Electromagnetic (EM).
4   Acoustic magnetic (AM).

Recent years have seen not only the introduction of newer technologies such as EM and acoustic magnetic, but also the use of new unique specialist alloys, precision manufacturing of tags, so that miniature tags will respond to the same signal 95 per cent of the time, and the use of multiple signals and frequency splitting to provide a series of checks for tags within the field – assisted by complex algorithms in control units to distinguish between tags and other metal objects. Taken in conjunction with microprocessor and software control of system units, these developments have enhanced the effectiveness of modern EAS systems. However, EAS systems are rarely 100 per cent effective in modern retail stores, whose electrical equipment can create several magnetic fields, proving to be a very hostile environment for EAS devices.

Inktags are tags consisting of a clear plastic tag containing one or more glass phials of ink. There are no electronics or alarms, but if the garment is stolen, when the tags are removed the ink stains the garment. The success of this system must be based upon the quality of the tag securing clip.

costs (e.g. loss of sales if part of the sales area is taken up with EAS detector gates); estimation of the likely gains and losses from EAS or other options as direct and indirect benefits; piloting of the system; assessment of results of the pilot; making of the decision to go ahead; followed by a phased implementation of the chosen system. The final decision would be made as a result of measuring the net flows of revenues (mainly cost savings for EAS) and expenses over time using one or more appraisal techniques.

Metro '99 did not follow this procedure. The company's search for options was limited to EAS. Moreover, within the EAS field, a full information search does not seem to have been carried out. It was limited to three major firms. A full shrinkage audit was not carried out.

The company's security solution was to use EAS in combination with security guards placed at the store exit. The management felt that a security guard at the front of each EAS-protected store would protect the only exit, and could approach and apprehend people who might have stolen merchandise when the EAS alarm sounded. It was felt that guards on their own were not effective in apprehending shoplifters, although they could prevent much of the bad behaviour in stores. The company also felt that an EAS system on its own would be ignored by many shoplifters. However, for the deployment of guards to be effective, the stores needed a technically efficient EAS system with a high pick rate (detecting 'virtually all' tags) and low false alarm rate. Otherwise, guards would lose confidence in the system – as would actual or potential thieves. Therefore, Metro '99 decided that the best way to drive thieves away from their stores was to use EAS to detect people trying to shoplift and guards to apprehend them.

Although the number of options the company had examined was small, the Metro '99 business operations were particularly suited to their preferred solution. Metro '99 merchandise lines were mainly soft goods (easy to tag with more efficient hard tags). Shoes, jewellery, recorded music, games and tights were much more difficult to tag. The firm's stores suffered very high levels of theft, justifying expensive systems if these could reduce losses to more normal levels. The store layout also facilitated EAS: the stores had only one exit (cheaper to guard), while the open-plan layout of the store also gave shoplifters less opportunity to take tags off merchandise. The company had good administrative procedures and was relatively good about providing training: thus the company already had the capability to ensure that goods were tagged correctly and that EAS procedures were being carried out.

Thus, in response to all these considerations, Metro '99 had every reason to believe that the organization would be well placed to make a success of EAS, as long as a high quality system could be found.

Choosing a New EAS System

Information on the best EAS system was sought by discussion with the main suppliers of EAS, followed by advice from Degger and Crosland. EAS suppliers naturally provide information on their products in the most favourable light: there is no agreed means of comparing the relative performance of EAS systems. It proved difficult to weigh up the information provided by EAS companies, making the consistent advice from Degger and Crosland about the technically 'best' system very influential. Effectively, the EAS decision was made as a result of advice from Degger and Crosland – the company which had chosen Metro '99's existing EAS system.

The advice received from Degger and Crosland was that the existing EAS system was now outdated: a new electromagnetic system from a large EAS supplier was considered to meet Metro '99 specifications most closely. It was, however, expensive. Electromagnetic systems were at one time the 'cheap and cheerful' end of EAS, with a low pick rate and high false alarms (many household metal products being detected as tags). The system chosen was based upon a proprietary tag alloy (not found in any goods apart from the company's EAS tags), which responded to an alternating magnetic field around the detection gates in a very precise way. Error checking procedures were carried out automatically by the system to ensure that changes in the magnetic field were caused only by the tag (thus minimizing false alarms).

The EAS system selected was widely used by other retailers; thus it was hoped that any initial problems with the system would already have been eliminated. The EAS system was fully compatible with current store procedures and organization. The whole system, from detector gates to individual tags, was leased (thus it was financed from revenue, requiring a lower level of authorisation than with a capital outlay), and the lease could be ended in three years – enabling Metro '99 to switch to an even better system if one emerged during that time.

Electromagnetic systems can be used with hard as well as paper tags, thus ideally protecting virtually the whole Metro '99 range, from anoraks to music cassettes. However, the detection field is relatively narrow (about 1 metre, compared to 1.5–1.95 metres with radio frequency systems), so that detection gates have to be set close together. Metro '99 decided to go ahead with piloting a new system based on electromagnetic technology.

Implementation of the New EAS System

It was felt that the new EAS system would have a much more successful outcome if the stores involved were enthusiastic. The choice of stores to receive EAS was based on the quality of 'bids' from branch managers, indicating how they intended to implement the system. Metro '99 was anxious to ensure that branch managers 'owned' their EAS system: they were made personally responsible for its results, measured in shrinkage reductions. Training and staff motivation were organized by the appropriate branch manager in conjunction with the EAS supplier, not by senior executives or a project manager.

The new electromagnetic system was piloted in four stores for six months. A line of detector gates was installed inside each shop, 1 metre from the entrance. With only one entrance, all thieves would have to leave by passing through these gates. In addition, if any shopper entered the store with tagged non-deactivated merchandise from another store or objects that might be recognized by the EAS system as a 'tag', the alarm would sound when he or she entered the store, allowing the necessary action to be taken without causing embarrassment to the customer.

Ninety per cent of all merchandise in the store was tagged, the exceptions being goods worth less than £5 and 'hard' goods such as music cassettes. Hard tags were used throughout – these worked better and were a visual deterrent. Any product line to be tagged was tagged completely.

Each EAS store had a contract security guard (hired from a security company) stationed at the entrance, instructed to close in on any person at the barrier when the EAS alarm sounded. The guard did not assume that a theft had occurred, but asked customers whether they had anything which they had forgotten to pay for. Security guards were also advised to watch out for foil-lined bags, including freezer bags, and for customers going past the gates with goods held at a certain angle from the horizontal. Foil-lined bags might interfere with the signal and the gates did not detect through 360 degrees. The security guard also provided a visual check on store violence and aggression to staff.

Results of the New EAS System

After a six-month trial, the new EAS system showed that it could reduce theft, although not all stores had benefited equally. The results (August 1993 to January 1994 against the same period ending in January 1993) were as shown in table 13.1. This shows that a sales weighted average fall of 28.3 per cent was achieved in the four stores (compared with the same period in the previous year), while a control store, store Z, suffered a slight worsening in shrinkage. Store Z was very similar in location, size and turnover to store B.

While two EAS stores achieved reductions in shrinkage of 40 per cent or more, store C's reduction was only 22 per cent, and store D's shrinkage had actually increased. The managers of stores A and B were among the two best in the company, judged in terms of meeting their performance objectives for a range of criteria from profitability to merchandising. Significantly, stores A and B were known to be particularly effective in training their staff. At a later date, four of store D's staff were arrested for complicity in organized theft from Metro '99. Sales in A and B had increased by 0.4 per cent more than the group as a whole.

The general level of violence and aggression in the four stores fell considerably. Thieves and 'misfits' gave every evidence of having

Table 13.1 EAS-linked reduction in store shrinkage, six months 1993/4

	Shrinkage rate (percentage change)
Store A	−44
Store B	−40
Store C	−22
Store D	+5
Weighted average	−28.3
Store Z (control)	+3.6

moved away, although this was not completely true, as Metro '99 experience with paper tags showed. The reason for the reduction in violence and aggression is most probably a combination of the success of EAS in diverting many shoplifters elsewhere and the existence of security guards. Further benefits from the new policy came when the company discontinued the use of store detectives in EAS stores.

Data on shoplifter arrests had not been kept, but after an initial increase in the EAS stores caused by shoplifter ignorance or attempts to test out the system, shoplifter apprehensions had fallen to an average of one per week in each EAS store, compared to six per week in store Z. A comparison of EPoS data (recording actual sales) against inventory deliveries to stores indicated a strong displacement effect, as theft of non-tagged merchandise such as socks increased to an average of 15 per cent of inventory at retail prices in stores with EAS.

The costs of tagging goods proved to be much more than originally predicted and used the equivalent of a full-time member of staff for 52 weeks. It was difficult to tag goods on the sales floor itself (staff would be called away); hence it was decided to tag merchandise in the stock room. One apparent result of this was that many goods were tagged at the bottom of sleeves or at the bottom of the garment (the most easily accessible region when searching through a box of goods) rather than in the middle of the product. This was not recommended because it could make theft a little easier.

Unlike its original system, the Metro '99 electromagnetic system was able to detect tags hidden in briefcases or concealed under armpits, and could detect through metal baskets. On the evidence that Metro '99 had, thieves found it difficult to attack or tamper with the tags – very few discarded tags were found around the store.

Like many retailers, Metro '99 sold recorded music from empty sleeves and cassette cases, the contents of which were only given to the customer in exchange for payment. The use of EAS paper tags has been advocated for this style of merchandising, and Metro '99 ran an experiment in one store after three months of using only hard tags. It would allow cassettes and CDs to be openly displayed for sale and save time and increase staff productivity. However, the experiment was a fiasco. Metro '99 tried merchandising EAS tagged cassettes and CDs and cassettes displayed in special EAS holders for one day only. It found that thieves used a variety of instruments, including ballpoint pens and screwdrivers, to force open the special holders and to tear off the EAS tags. No further use of paper tags was attempted.

Some preliminary calculations of the financial effectiveness of the system can be seen in table 13.2. For the group of stores as a whole, the financial savings (by cost reduction) from EAS comfortably exceeded the costs for the four stores taken together. This is, unfortunately, only based on the first six months of the system, although the period should be long enough to compensate for any 'halo' effect (the initial period in which shrinkage can fall rapidly until thieves have learned how to circumvent the system – usually less than three months). Across the four stores an annual return on costs of 52.1 per cent has been achieved. This return covers the annual costs of the new EAS system as well as the contract security guards.

Table 13.2 Financial costs and benefits of EAS in four stores

Costs		
Equipment costs: cost of detector devices tags and other equipment		Lease £50,500 p.a.
Tagging costs: cost of 4 full-time equivalent staff (including on-costs)		£48,000 p.a.
Detagging costs: employment of extra staff during peak periods		£2,700 p.a.
Guarding costs (52 weeks)		£75,000 p.a.
Savings		
Fall in shrinkage (compared with previous year)	£206,024	
Reduced store detective costs	£32,000	
Reduced handling costs (fewer goods need to be put on shopfloor to produce £X sales)	£30,000	
	£268,024	£176,200

Net surplus of benefits over costs

Savings	£268,024	
Costs	–£176,200	
Surplus	£91,824	52.1 per cent p.a. on cost

Malcolm Tracey prepared a report on the early months of the EAS system. He felt that there was no evidence that these figures were an accident or caused by other factors. No stores in the group had recorded such falls in shrinkage before, not even the stores run by the same managers. However, it may be true that the results might measure the effects in these four EAS stores of an enhanced awareness and concern about shrinkage and theft shared by managers and staff as well as the effects of EAS and the security guards. Changes in layout and merchandising to inhibit theft had occurred in *all* stores and were therefore unlikely to have had a particularly strong effect upon EAS stores only. The introduction of EAS and guards seemed to be the most satisfactory explanation.

Operational Issues

In his report, Malcolm commented on the presence in Metro '99 of both good and bad EAS systems, as follows.

1 *Technical.* The performance of EAS systems may vary depending on supplier and on the generation of system. The fact that EAS systems tend to look the same may conceal major improvements in operational standards achieved by one system compared to another five years older. In addition, one system may be more suited to an individual location or style of retail operation than another.

2 *Managerial.* A clear strategy for the use of EAS is needed and this strategy must be implemented effectively. In Metro '99 one explanation of the different results gained by stores with the new EAS system was, simply, the quality of management.

Metro '99's previous experience of EPoS and EAS had led it to conclude that the motivation for the new system to succeed would be much greater if branch managers felt a sense of ownership of the system. The best managers gained the highest shrinkage reductions. The task for Metro '99 senior management would be to develop expertise to support branch managers, enabling high performance to be produced wherever EAS is installed.

A similar point can be made about paper tags. Paper tags are obviously not as securely attached to products as hard tags, and, in that company's environment, success with paper tags would need to be based on rethinking the layout, staffing and methods of operation for recorded music to reduce the vulnerability of tag.

Some EAS systems are discreet, with the gates either hidden completely or blending in with the store's decor. This had not been the Metro '99 approach. The company wished to communicate in order to deter potential thieves. The narrow detector gates at the entrance, the presence of the security guard at the front of the store, large EAS tags hanging off all garments and notices on the walls about EAS were all attempts to advertise the system to shoplifters and so change the behaviour of thieves. There were about four so-called 'false alarms' each day, resulting from shoppers going to the front of the store to examine a shade in daylight, or turning around from a rack and inadvertently setting off the alarm. These false alarms also reminded customers that there was an EAS system, kept the security guard alert and demonstrated that action would be taken when the alarm sounded. There was very little evidence of crime displacement to other stores in the group, and no one knew whether the rate of shop theft suffered by surrounding stores had increased. There was clear evidence, however, of increased theft of non-tagged items, suggesting either that these should be tagged or that displays should be changed to reduce the likelihood of theft.

The EAS decision had been based on the presumption that customer theft was Metro '99's key problem. However, the company found that store D's losses were also affected by staff theft. It was only when the deviant results of store D against other EAS stores were investigated that evidence of heavy staff theft came to light. When an EAS system performs poorly, this is usually taken as the fault of the system. However, with Metro '99, poorly performing EAS systems were the symptom of bad management or a different form of security issue or both factors. In either case a proper security audit ought to be the forerunner of security policy.

Management learning has to occur for EAS to be effective, but the choice of EAS is made easier because of its compatibility with existing retail systems. The next generation of tags may require a more radical approach from retailers, involving intelligent tags which can be traced or tracked, tags applied at source which can be switched on and off as the products move down the logistics channel and ever more complex standard EAS tags. In the future, improved control over the movement of goods through the distribution system, the need to switch tags on and off and the ability to read and write data in the tags may have as profound an effect upon the operations of retail businesses as did EPoS in the 1980s and early 1990s, enabling time-based competition to intensify. There are already several projects in the USA and Europe designed to bring this change into effect.

Whether retail firms with expertise in the use of current EAS and information systems will have an advantage over other companies in the exploitation of these newer systems remains to be seen.

Further Reading

Bamfield, J. (1992) *Beating the Thief: a Retailer's Guide to Electronic Article Surveillance*. Brighton: RMDP Ltd.

Clark, P. and Mayhew, P. (eds) (1980) *Designing out Crime*. London: HMSO.

Cornish, D.B. and Clarke, R.V.G. (eds) (1986) *The Reasoning Criminal: Rational Choice Perspectives on Offending*. New York: Springer-Verlag.

Ernst and Young (1992) The Ernst and Young/IMRA survey of retail loss prevention trends: thirteenth annual survey of loss prevention executives. *Chain Store Age*, January, section 2.

Speed, M., Burrows, J. and Bamfield, J. (1995) *Retail Crime Costs 1993/4*. London: British Retail Consortium/Nene College.

14

Electronic Customer Counting and Tracking Systems in Fashion Retailing

Malcolm Kirkup and Tim Denison

Loughborough University Business School and Independent Consultant (formerly Cranfield University)

Introduction

It was Monday morning and David Brewster was searching through his post to find the package. He was looking forward to examining the data that had been sent by Solution Products Systems, following completion of a research experiment that David had commissioned. He was also rather worried – he wasn't sure whether the experiment would prove fruitful, and he had spent weeks selling the idea of the research to his generally sceptical board of directors.

David was Research Manager for New Vision Ltd, a chain of fashion stores selling mainly ladies clothing. The company had 120 stores throughout the UK and was enjoying a period of steady sales growth. He had been in post for 12 months, and his job was a newly created position within the company. He was a graduate in business studies, and had worked for three years previously as a market analyst with a competing fashion retailer. He had been recruited to initiate and manage a programme of continuous research – regularly to monitor customer requirements and attitudes, competitor activities and market trends, and to recommend to the board how the company could improve its marketing to enhance sales and profit growth. He reported to the Retail Operations Director, who supported most of David's initiatives, although he was less convinced by David's latest research experiment.

The idea for the experiment had arisen about four months previously, when he had read an article in a trade journal which

discussed the technology available for electronically counting customers. The article had pointed out that a number of shopping
centres were using electronic counters to monitor footfall levels, and
some retail stores had begun installing customer counters at store
entrances and at other points around stores. The article suggested
that the data collected could help to monitor the effectiveness of
marketing strategies and customer service, to improve the layout
and merchandising of stores and to improve the management and
allocation of staffing resources. Of particular interest to David was
the observation that customer counts, when combined with EPoS
data, could permit the calculation of 'conversion rates', i.e. the
proportion of footfall converted into transactions.

David was interested in the concept of 'electronic' customer
counting, because he was aware that the company had on a number
of occasions tried to measure footfall using 'manual' counting
methods, i.e. using members of staff to stand at store entrances and
count customers on certain days of the week. This manual method
had, however, been abandoned for a number of reasons. Valuable
staff time was lost, and the counts could only be done periodically
because of the time involved. Furthermore, only simple entrance
counts could be managed, and not all branch managers followed the
instructions issued about the timing of the counts because of other
work pressures. In addition, the company had questioned the
accuracy of manual counting given inevitable boredom and mental
fatigue. A lack of consistency with the manual method also meant
that it was not possible to 'track' changes in customer numbers over
a period of time.

Electronic and automated customer counting seemed to offer
tremendous advantages. David wondered whether it might offer
long-term potential as an input to a management information
system – with stores polling their customer count data (along with
EPoS data) back to head office daily, to enable tracking of key
customer-related performance ratios over time.

Electronic Technology for Customer Counting and Tracking

When David initially investigated non-manual methods of customer
counting, he contacted a number of suppliers who offered relevant
equipment. He realized quickly that customer 'counting' was only

the tip of the iceberg in terms of what was possible, and that the technology provided the means to gather immense detail on customer movements all around a store. He found four possible technologies that could be used:

- *Pressure pad sensors*. These were basically floor mats incorporating counting devices triggered by a pedestrian walking on the mat. A number of pads could be placed across the entrance to a store (or aisle) to count total footfall, and by using different sizes of mat it was possible to cover different widths of entrance/aisle. David wondered whether such sensors would also be triggered by pushchairs and children, and he wondered how accurate the sensors would be with high volumes of footfall. He also felt that floor mats might represent a safety hazard.

- *Active infra-red beam sensors*. These devices projected a beam of light across an entrance/aisle to a receiver on the opposite side. Each time the beam was broken by a passing customer, a counting device was triggered. He was sceptical about beam sensors – how would they work if a doorway became obstructed, or if high volumes of footfall were entering the store in a continuous stream?

- *Passive infra-red sensors*. These sensors monitored the movement of people within a particular distance of the sensor. The sensors detected any changes in heat within the image they scanned, and the movement of people past the sensor therefore triggered a counting device. He felt that these sensors were safer, but he was concerned that most of the devices on the market required hard-wiring, i.e. laying cables around a store to connect the sensors to a central signal receiver and converter. Hard-wiring did not appear to offer a very flexible solution. Furthermore, he was not convinced that passive infra-red sensors would be accurate when trying to cope with high volumes of footfall.

- *Video cameras*. One supplier stressed the advantages of using video cameras for customer counting, i.e. positioning a number of cameras at fixed points around the store and recording movement on video film. The consultants pointed out that far more detailed information could be gleaned from visual recordings of customer behaviour on tape (the type of people entering the store, the extent to which they browse and examine particular products etc.), and such systems could be set up to record voices as well. However, David felt this type of service would involve a long time delay between filming and receiving the analysis of tapes, additional costs associated with the analysis of many hours of footage and high installation costs. He felt that this technology was more suited to short-term project work in selected stores, rather than as a basis for continuous and long-term monitoring of customer flows.

Solution Products Systems

By coincidence, at the time that David was meeting the various suppliers, he was approached by Dominic McGuinness from Solution Products Systems. This company had recently developed a battery-operated passive infra-red sensor, and Dominic argued that it solved many of the problems previously associated with electronic customer counting and tracking. The devices comprised small infra-red sensors that could be mounted at a store entrance (or anywhere around a store) to detect the movement of people. The devices incorporated an LCD to show visually the number of people walking past the sensor, as well as data-loggers which stored customer flow data on an hourly basis. The units also had radio-linking facilities, to transmit customer flow data back to a central computer in the store.

Having spoken to Dominic at length on the phone, David recognized some of the advantages of the sensors proposed. In particular, they appeared to offer portability and flexibility (without the necessity for hard-wiring). The facility for collecting and transmitting data on an hourly basis offered the scope to combine customer count data with the company's EPoS data (which recorded numbers of transactions and value of transactions by hour).

David was impressed with the flexibility of the whole service offered by Solution Products Systems. He could either rent or buy the equipment, and he could either process the data himself or ask Solution Products Systems to conduct the analysis and provide a regular reporting service. This flexibility provided a major advantage over other suppliers in the market, who seemed more concerned with selling large volumes of basic counting sensors, and leaving retailers to sink or swim in terms of analysing and interpreting the data.

The Experiment

With David being new to the area of customer counting (and given the general lack of enthusiasm evident among his board directors), he decided to conduct a limited experiment. The equipment was not cheap to rent or buy, and he needed to be convinced that passive infra-red technology would be accurate and reliable for customer counting. He also felt that a limited experiment would give him the opportunity to test the services and support available from Solution Products Systems.

He designed the trial around two phases. First, he wanted to assess the accuracy of the sensors. He proposed mounting one sensor in a store entrance for a period of three months to collect regular customer counts, so that its performance could be monitored. He selected an average sized store (2500 square feet), located in a large enclosed shopping centre within a major city (store A). The store was located in a relatively poor position in the centre, but annual consumer expenditure on ladies clothing in the town was substantial, at £20 million. The store was underperforming anyway, so David figured that by using this branch for the experiment he might also understand more about the reasons for poor performance. He asked the company's security manager to set up a video camera in the store, designed to capture on film the same image that would be detected by the sensor. He then recruited a consultant from a local business school to analyse video footage over the course of a number of days' trading. Essentially, he wanted to know whether the sensor was as accurate as video-recording in terms of counting footfall. He deliberately chose Fridays and Saturdays to conduct the recording to ensure the sensor was being subjected to the highest volumes of footfall into stores. He asked Solution Products Systems to mount the sensor at different heights above the ground during the period of the experiment, so that the accuracy at different levels could be tested. Daily customer counts were also collected and compared with daily EPoS data, to assess the consistency of the sensor over a period of time and to investigate battery life.

The second phase of the research experiment, which was only to proceed if the system proved reliable, sought to collect very detailed customer counts by hour of each day. David wanted to link the count data with hourly EPoS data. For this part of the experiment he decided to add another New Vision store for comparative purposes. He chose a larger store (3500 square feet) located in a large out of town regional shopping centre (store B), with annual market expenditure of around £10 million on ladies clothing. This store was one of the company's best performers, and had recently been totally refurbished, with a new fascia, a new internal merchandising layout and new visual displays. The manager of this store was also considered to be one of the best in the company, and David was curious to see how the manager might make use of the count data.

The first phase of the research proceeded without a hitch, and David was impressed by the performance and consistency of the sensor. The sensor was repositioned a number of times during the experiment, and in its final position (2 m above floor level, secured at the store entrance and looking horizontally across the face of the doorway) it proved extremely accurate.

During this first phase he was on a steep learning curve, and the experiment showed immediately that the sensor counted 'movement' rather than individual people. David noted that if two or more people walked past the sensor at the same time, the counter only recorded 'one' movement. Dominic McGuinness argued that this actually provided a significant advantage of his sensor compared to competitor systems. He argued that many people shop together as couples or families, and, if they walk into a store very close together, each 'shopper group' will only trigger the sensor once. These groups are only likely to represent 'one selling opportunity' and so a count of 'one' is more appropriate. Dominic maintained that counts of 'shopper groups' rather than 'individuals' therefore offered more realistic information for retailers.

The video experiment proved that the sensor was extremely accurate at counting the number of shopper groups entering the store – detecting between 95 and 100 per cent of shopper groups (when compared with counts taken from the video recording). As a count of individual people, the sensors detected around 71 per cent. During the experiment the performance of the sensor did not appear to be affected by 'volume' of footfall. The maximum number of shopper groups passing the sensor per hour was 226 (one Saturday lunch-time), during which time it recorded 99 per cent of groups.

Having tested the sensor system, David decided to progress to the second phase of the research experiment, which was to be conducted over a two-week period. Sensors were installed in the

Exhibit 14.1 ECCaT, EPoS and staff data for store A

No. of Shopper Groups	Mon	Tues	Wed	Thurs	Fri	Sat	Mon	Tues	Wed	Thurs	Fri	Sat
09.00–10.00 am	14	11	12	17	19	23	16	14	9	23	16	37
10.00–11.00 am	29	29	30	16	50	57	34	37	22	25	29	76
11.00–12.00 pm	33	29	26	28	44	78	50	38	29	34	45	67
12.00–13.00 pm	45	48	22	45	47	101	51	37	53	34	62	159
13.00–14.00 pm	47	39	45	29	74	123	72	46	54	51	62	132
14.00–15.00 pm	44	42	30	33	59	130	54	54	46	42	44	174
15.00–16.00 pm	39	36	39	38	56	134	48	29	53	42	58	176
16.00–17.00 pm	38	29	48	26	50	98	25	30	34	34	67	114
17.00–18.00 pm	12	2	14	5	16	44	6	2	22	12	10	47
18.00–19.00 pm			14						14			
19.00–20.00 pm			18						16			

No. of Transactions	Mon	Tues	Wed	Thurs	Fri	Sat	Mon	Tues	Wed	Thurs	Fri	Sat
09.00–10.00 am	0	0	0	2	0	4	0	0	0	0	0	2
10.00–11.00 am	4	10	4	0	4	8	2	4	2	2	6	13
11.00–12.00 pm	5	2	2	2	4	11	4	2	5	2	9	5
12.00–13.00 pm	4	4	2	5	2	15	5	5	6	4	11	17
13.00–14.00 pm	2	6	4	2	11	22	6	4	9	2	6	13
14.00–15.00 pm	6	6	4	5	8	13	4	2	6	10	13	30
15.00–16.00 pm	9	8	4	4	5	13	2	5	8	6	2	21
16.00–17.00 pm	2	4	6	2	8	17	0	0	2	9	9	27
17.00–18.00 pm	2	0	4	2	6	5	2	0	2	4	5	6
18.00–19.00 pm			0						0			
19.00–20.00 pm			2						0			

Value of Transactions £	Mon	Tues	Wed	Thurs	Fri	Sat	Mon	Tues	Wed	Thurs	Fri	Sat
09.00–10.00 am	0	0	0	11	0	113	0	0	0	0	0	38
10.00–11.00 am	111	291	70	0	122	152	26	102	74	51	169	387
11.00–12.00 pm	184	32	13	74	118	314	70	128	182	26	308	130
12.00–13.00 pm	173	102	102	326	79	389	73	156	234	90	330	434
13.00–14.00 pm	41	92	73	22	201	451	207	64	235	66	173	374
14.00–15.00 pm	156	124	96	201	202	278	83	43	315	314	493	781
15.00–16.00 pm	228	134	98	70	105	317	22	103	122	143	22	546
16.00–17.00 pm	54	139	130	77	180	433	0	0	47	158	258	713
17.00–18.00 pm	32	0	105	13	154	92	58	0	90	98	114	110
18.00–19.00 pm			0						0			
19.00–20.00 pm			83						0			

Staff Cover Data	Mon	Tues	Wed	Thurs	Fri	Sat	Mon	Tues	Wed	Thurs	Fri	Sat
Staff Hours	34.0	26.5	28.5	22.5	30.0	43.5	22.5	26.5	32.5	19.0	21.5	35.5
Full-Timer Hours	22.5	15.0	17.5	15.0	22.5	22.5	15.0	15.0	10.0	15.0	7.5	15.0
Part-Timer Hours	11.5	11.5	11.0	7.5	7.5	21.0	7.5	11.5	22.5	4.0	14.0	20.5
09.00–10.00 am	3F/1P	2F/1P	2F	2F/1P	3F/1P	3F/1P	2F/1P	2F/1P	1F/1P	2F	1F/1P	2F/1P
10.00–11.00 am	3F/2P	2F/2P	2F	2F/1P	3F/1P	3F/2P	2F/1P	2F/2P	1F/2P	2F/1P	1F/2P	2F/2P
11.00–12.00 pm	3F/2P	2F/2P	2F	2F/1P	3F/1P	3F/3P	2F/1P	2F/2P	1F/2P	2F/1P	1F/2P	2F/3P
12.00–13.00 pm	3F/2P	2F/2P	2F/1P	2F/1P	3F/1P	3F/3P	2F/1P	2F/2P	1F/3P	2F/1P	1F/2P	2F/3P
13.00–14.00 pm	3F/2P	2F/2P	2F/1P	2F/1P	3F/1P	3F/3P	2F/1P	2F/2P	1F/3P	2F/1P	1F/2P	2F/3P
14.00–15.00 pm	3F/1P	2F/1P	2F/1P	2F/1P	3F/1P	3F/3P	2F/1P	2F/1P	1F/2P	2F	1F/1P	2F/3P
15.00–16.00 pm	3F/1P	2F/1P	2F/2P	2F/1P	3F/1P	3F/3P	2F/1P	2F/1P	1F/3P	2F	1F/2P	2F/3P
16.00–17.00 pm	3F/1P	2F/1P	2F/2P	2F/1P	3F/1P	3F/3P	2F/1P	2F/1P	1F/3P	2F	1F/2P	2F/3P
17.00–18.00 pm	3F/1P	2F/1P	2F/2P	2F/1P	3F/1P	3F/3P	2F/1P	2F/1P	1F/2P	2F	1F/2P	2F/3P
18.00–19.00 pm			1F/2P						1F/2P			
19.00–20.00 pm			1F/2P						1F/2P			

F = Full-Time Staff   P = Part-Time Staff

Exhibit 14.2 ECCaT, EPoS and staff data for store B

No. of Shopper Groups	Mon	Tues	Wed	Thurs	Fri	Sat	Sun	Mon	Tues	Wed	Thurs	Fri	Sat	Sun
09.00–10.00 am	11	11	11	19	16	37		17	20	31	25	31	59	
10.00–11.00 am	45	40	33	38	62	119		41	73	81	46	62	112	
11.00–12.00 pm	55	54	55	59	62	139	72	95	170	115	83	123	154	83
12.00–13.00 pm	74	75	70	75	96	184	98	96	207	186	130	145	206	127
13.00–14.00 pm	86	66	62	85	101	197	96	96	143	237	133	151	222	146
14.00–15.00 pm	90	68	66	59	98	205	105	113	186	176	122	160	247	119
15.00–16.00 pm	87	54	48	48	58	230	97	93	118	186	266	146	215	135
16.00–17.00 pm	72	68	34	70	78	157	53	62	132	129	119	134	205	78
17.00–18.00 pm	59	34	22	67	85	92		29	57	84	73	85	106	
18.00–19.00 pm				75	89						82	94		
19.00–20.00 pm				42	76						68	57		

No. of Transactions	Mon	Tues	Wed	Thurs	Fri	Sat	Sun	Mon	Tues	Wed	Thurs	Fri	Sat	Sun
09.00–10.00 am	0	2	0	2	2	6		2	2	2	2	0	9	
10.00–11.00 am	14	11	2	6	14	17		2	8	9	4	9	11	
11.00–12.00 pm	8	5	13	11	18	28	13	11	17	17	14	24	32	18
12.00–13.00 pm	5	6	15	9	18	38	13	18	21	25	23	27	55	30
13.00–14.00 pm	21	17	5	15	17	40	13	22	21	36	25	27	43	27
14.00–15.00 pm	11	9	9	11	17	34	17	14	24	26	24	41	52	24
15.00–16.00 pm	28	5	8	13	27	47	23	19	21	15	23	26	54	23
16.00–17.00 pm	11	10	8	11	8	23	9	11	21	17	14	36	62	14
17.00–18.00 pm	18	11	6	14	19	17		4	8	5	15	14	38	
18.00–19.00 pm				15	23						15	22		
19.00–20.00 pm				10	13						21	14		

Value of Transactions £

Transactions £	Mon	Tues	Wed	Thurs	Fri	Sat	Sun	Mon	Tues	Wed	Thurs	Fri	Sat	Sun
09.00–10.00 am	0	47	0	46	56	158		26	36	47	78	0	197	
10.00–11.00 am	398	288	13	189	406	627		237	150	202	86	458	271	
11.00–12.00 pm	207	98	315	326	482	687	278	406	500	623	378	846	995	434
12.00–13.00 pm	134	181	342	166	425	802	326	711	581	726	739	837	1349	918
13.00–14.00 pm	672	353	123	490	443	988	502	436	474	909	551	824	1394	1052
14.00–15.00 pm	357	202	230	337	451	882	637	444	619	774	581	1232	1315	715
15.00–16.00 pm	796	192	178	243	626	1154	686	457	504	459	711	738	1673	783
16.00–17.00 pm	406	6	207	247	151	589	425	406	651	271	494	1026	1588	395
17.00–18.00 pm	334	269	128	357	526	474		126	206	130	562	506	1128	
18.00–19.00 pm				613	578						390	470		
19.00–20.00 pm				468	413						668	534		

Staff Cover Data

Staff Cover Data	Mon	Tues	Wed	Thurs	Fri	Sat	Sun	Mon	Tues	Wed	Thurs	Fri	Sat	Sun
Staff Hours	34.5	39.5	33.5	59.0	54.5	76.0	40.0	43.5	44.0	42.0	56.5	50.0	90.0	39.0
Full-Timer Hours	22.5	22.5	15.0	22.5	22.5	24.0	6.0	30.0	22.5	22.5	22.5	23.0	32.0	6.0
Part-Timer Hours	12.0	17.0	18.5	36.5	32.0	52.0	34.0	13.5	21.5	19.5	34.0	27.0	58.0	33.0
09.00–10.00 am	3F	3F	2F/1P	2F/2P	2F/2P	3F/5P	1F/4P	4F/1P	3F/2P	3F/1P	1.5F/1P	2F/2P	4F/5P	1F/4P
10.00–11.00 am	3F	3F	2F/1P	2F/2P	2F/2P	3F/5P	1F/6P	4F/1P	3F/2P	3F/1P	2F/3P	2F/2P	4F/5P	1F/5P
11.00–12.00 pm	3F	3F	2F/1P	2F/2P	2.5F/2P	3F/5P	1F/6P	4F/1P	3F/3P	3F/1P	2.5F/3P	3F/3P	4F/5P	1F/6P
12.00–13.00 pm	3F/2P	3F/2P	2F/3P	3F/2P	3F/3P	3F/7P	1F/6P	4F/2P	3F/3P	3F/3P	3F/4P	3F/3P	4F/8P	1F/6P
13.00–14.00 pm	3F/2P	3F/2P	2F/3P	3F/3P	3F/3P	3F/7P	1F/6P	4F/2P	3F/3P	3F/3P	3F/4P	3F/3P	4F/8P	1F/6P
14.00–15.00 pm	3F/2P	3F/2P	2F/3P	3F/3P	3F/3P	3F/7P	1F/6P	4F/2P	3F/3P	3F/3P	3F/4P	3F/3P	4F/8P	1F/6P
15.00–16.00 pm	3F/2P	3F/2P	2F/3P	3F/4P	3F/3P	3F/7P	1F/6P	4F/2P	3F/3P	3F/3P	3F/4P	3F/3P	4F/8P	1F/6P
16.00–17.00 pm	3F/2P	3F/2P	2F/3P	3F/4P	3F/3P	3F/7P	1F/6P	4F/2P	3F/3P	3F/3P	3F/4P	3F/3P	4F/8P	1F/6P
17.00–18.00 pm	3F/2P	3F/2P	2F/4P	3F/6P	2F/4P	3F/7P		4F/2P	3F/3P	3F/3P	2.5F/3P	2.5F/3P	4F/8P	
18.00–19.00 pm				1F/6P	1F/5P						1F/3P	1F/3P		
19.00–20.00 pm				1F/6P	1F/5P						1F/3P	1F/3P		

F = Full-Time Staff   P = Part-Time Staff

entrances of the two branches and the count data were recorded in two ways. First, the branch managers were asked to keep a record of the daily counts and to compare, at the end of each day, the number of shopper groups entering the store with the number of transactions achieved (from the EPoS till). He gave the managers only a limited introduction to the nature of the experiment, in the hope that they would themselves generate ideas as to how the information might be used. Second, customer count data by hour were recorded on data-loggers in the sensors. At the end of the two-week period the stored data from the sensors were removed by Solution Products Systems, transferred to a computer spreadsheet and sent to David back at head office.

When he opened the package from Solution Products Systems on the Monday morning, and loaded the spreadsheet from the disk into his *Quattro Pro* package, his immediate reaction was one of dismay. He had not appreciated that the raw count data would still require considerable analysis and interpretation to produce visual and actionable information. He immediately regretted not having asked Solution Products Systems to organize the analysis for him, a service that Dominic had in fact offered, but that David had dismissed as unnecessary. Nevertheless, he set about his task of trying to make sense of the data.

His boss had asked him to make a presentation to the board on the Friday of that week, outlining the potential applications of customer count data as a management tool at both branch and head office level (through illustrations drawn from the experiment), and recommending whether and how the company should move forward with customer counting systems. He knew that he would also have to comment on the cost-effectiveness of the system, and he was aware that the likely future cost of renting a sensor (with LCD and data-logger) for each branch, plus a weekly analysis and report from Solution Products Systems, would amount to around £2000 per branch for a counting period of three months.

He remembered that Dominic McGuinness had suggested that a useful starting point for the analysis would be to compare the customer count data (ECCaT data) with transaction data from the EPoS system and staffing data. He therefore immediately requested this information from the company's IT, finance and personnel departments (see exhibits 14.1 and 14.2).

He also telephoned the two branch managers to find out how they had made use of their daily readings. The manager of the city centre branch (store A) was excited by the data and encouraged David to let the project continue. He had calculated the average conversion rate for his branch to be 11 per cent and appeared very pleased. During the course of the experiment he had kept his staff informed of their 'performance' in terms of converting customers, and 'they were now aiming for a higher conversion of 1 in 7 customers'. David pressed the manager for other potential applications of the count data, but drew a blank. When he spoke to the manager of the out of town branch he could hardly get a word in edgeways. The manager again was enthusiastic but for different reasons – he was trying to explain why his conversion rates had declined so dramatically on one of the days, to point out the impact of school half-term on the branch's footfall for the second week and to enquire whether he could increase his staffing budget.

David put the phone down, and set to work on his presentation.

Case Questions

Main Questions:

Assume the role of David Brewster, and address the following tasks;

- Discuss the potential applications of customer-count data as a management tool at both branch and Head Office levels (through illustrations drawn from the experiment data).
- Discuss whether and how the company should move forward with customer counting systems.

Additional Discussion Points

Discuss the relative merits of the different technologies available for customer counting and tracking.

Critically appraise the whole approach adopted by David Brewster in managing the research experiment, and suggest alternative approaches.

Explore the possible wider uses of infra-red sensing technology for retailing.

15

Managing a Store Relocation Project: Marks and Spencer in Kendal

Malcolm Kirkup, Paul Walley and Daniel Ganly

Loughborough University Business School, Warwick Business School and Bournemouth University

Introduction

This case study describes the relocation in 1994 of the Marks and Spencer store within Kendal, Cumbria, UK.[1] The situation presented is a relatively unusual example of store development for the company – not just because it involves a relocation, but because it involves the acquisition and refitting of an existing supermarket.

The case begins by introducing the Marks and Spencer store development programme, and provides an overview of the objectives and broad management structure behind store development projects. The case then takes the reader back to January 1994, partway through the actual Kendal relocation project schedule. We hear from three key managers closely involved in the scheme – the technical coordinator for construction services, the store planner and the store manager – who describe in detail the reasons for the relocation, progress to date and the work still remaining. The case ends with a range of recommended tasks for students to undertake based on the information provided.

The case is based primarily on a series of personal interviews with, and information supplied by, the key managers mentioned. Supplementary information was obtained from published company information (e.g. annual reports) and from telephone interviews

The authors would like to thank Marks and Spencer for its support in developing this case study. In particular we are most grateful for the contribution provided by Paul Mellor, Mike Peterson and Katy Bull.

with representatives from other key departments and organizations involved in the project, notably Marks and Spencer's estates department (acquisitions) and external architects.

The Marks and Spencer Store Development Programme

In the financial year 1994/5, Marks and Spencer maintained its position as 'Europe's most profitable retailer' by generating a profit before tax of £924.3 million from a turnover of £6,806.5 million.[2] The company is committed to offering its customers high-quality products and an efficient service in attractive and comfortable surroundings – this requires an on-going store development programme involving expansion and modernization. In 1994/5, Marks and Spencer invested £230 million in 400,000 square feet of new selling space in the UK. In 1990, the company had 266 UK stores, totalling 9.1 million square feet of selling space. By 1995, the number of UK stores had grown to 283 on 11.0 million square feet. This rate of expansion of floorspace is set to continue for at least the next three years.[3]

Store development projects include not only the building of new stores on greenfield sites, but also modernizing and extending the footage of existing stores, and relocating others to more appropriate sites. Relocations are rare, however, as the majority of Marks and Spencer stores are already in prime retail locations. The main thrust of development for the company is focused on the High Street, but a number of highly successful stores have been opened on edge-of-town sites. The overall trend of this store development has been to increase footage in larger stores and reduce the proportion of smaller stores, and this can be seen in table 15.1.

Ultimately, any relocation project will be driven by the desire to enhance Marks and Spencer's profitability, by improving either the convenience of a store's location or the store environment, to satisfy

Table 15.1 Marks and Spencer: size distribution of stores

Size of store (square feet)	1990 (%)	1995 (%)
60,000+	14	18
40,000–60,000	19	21
Up to 40,000	67	61

Source: Marks and Spencer Annual Report and Financial Statements, 1995, p. 23.

customer needs better. To achieve a relocation in practice, a considerable amount of time, resources, research, planning and management effort will be invested. Numerous individuals and departments within the business will be involved, and many external organizations will contribute – all working to achieve the company's financial and strategic objectives. Internally, the company will call on managers with expertise in research, financial planning, construction, design, marketing, merchandising, personnel and store operations, and externally the company will receive advice and services from specialist architects, designers, quantity surveyors, planning consultants and marketing agencies. Achievement of a new store opening on time and on budget is therefore critically dependent on effective organization, coordination, cooperation, communication and teamwork.

Among this network of contributors are those focusing on construction, and those focusing on the commercial issues. The construction function ensures that the store building and infrastructure is delivered on time and on budget. Central to the construction function is the work of the store development group. Within this group, in overall charge of each new store development is a project manager, who is involved right from the early planning stages and will see the project through to opening day. The project manager's role is to get the store completed, fully operational on time, on budget and to the desired quality standards, and to provide a building that can meet the commercial requirements of the business. The project manager relies heavily, however, on a team of technical and equipment coordinators, who manage the construction and fitting-out process, an internal architect, who looks after the corporate design aspects, an estates surveyor and also a store planner, who focuses on designing the store's layout and interfaces between the commercial and construction sides of the project.

The commercial functions ensure that customer needs are satisfied through the offer made available in the new store, that sales potential is maximized and that the store is run efficiently to minimize costs. Central to the commercial success of a new store in this respect are the roles of the store manager, who has the local commercial aspects of the operation to consider, the divisional management team, which can guide and advise the store manager and store planner on issues such as staffing, merchandising and display, and the buying groups at head office, who will plan the ranges for new stores.

Other head office groups are also critical to the success of a new store. The information technology department will install the systems which connect the store to distribution centres and the computer centre. The transport department will manage the task of physically getting the stock to new stores. The corporate affairs group will help the store management team in promoting the new store opening.[4]

The Marks and Spencer Relocation Project in Kendal

The date is 10 January 1994. Marks and Spencer is six months into the schedule for a store relocation project in Kendal, Cumbria. In the text below we hear from three key managers closely involved in the scheme. Paul Mellor is the Kendal store manager, Mike Peterson is technical coordinator for construction services in the store development group and Katy Bull is store planner for the project. Their comments provide an insight into the reasons for the relocation, how the project is progressing and the tasks still to be carried out prior to the new store opening.

THE CASE FOR RELOCATION

Paul explains some of the background to the project. 'Kendal is a busy market town in Cumbria on the south-eastern edge of the Lake District National Park, which is a popular tourist area. The town is close to the M6 motorway, and about 25 miles north of Lancaster. Figure 15.1 shows our current store in Kendal at 18–20 Stricklandgate. It's a prime location in the High Street, where we are at the heart of shopping activity and we pick up a lot of passing trade. However, there are a number of problems with the site. The selling space, at 9000 square feet, is far too small to exploit the sales potential available in Kendal – the sales per square foot performances we're achieving clearly show we can support a far larger store. The narrow frontage doesn't reflect the offer behind the doors, and the long narrow shape of the store and bottleneck entrance don't help either when you're trying to create exciting merchandising. A worse problem is access to the rear of the store for deliveries – our lorries struggle to get down the narrow access roads and we pay a substantial rent for access rights across private land to get to our loading bay.

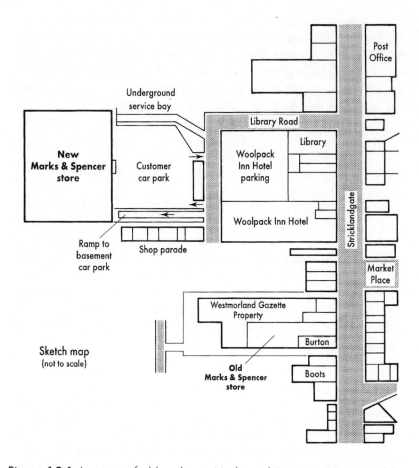

Figure 15.1 Location of old and new Marks and Spencer stores, Kendal.

'For many years the company has considered different ways to expand the old store. It was suggested at one time that we might buy the Burton site next door, but this would have cost a fortune both to buy the freehold and to integrate the buildings. We wouldn't have generated a great deal more selling space, and the sales increase wouldn't have justified the cost. We could have built a second floor and doubled the space by mirroring the ground floor footprint – but an already narrow store would be difficult to operate with extra escalators and stairs at the side. We looked at expanding to the rear, but this would have been on to land owned by the *Westmorland Gazette,* and we weren't able to agree an acceptable financial deal. We would also still have been dependent on rear-servicing for it, over private land.

'Last August the company decided it really must sort out the Kendal situation once and for all, and relocation became the only real option. A greenfield edge-of-town development was unlikely to get planning permission, but an alternative opportunity arose to acquire an existing Fine-Food supermarket in the town.[5] I alerted the business to the Fine-Food site a couple of years ago, located at the end of Library Road, off Stricklandgate. In 1993 I heard that Fine-Food were under pressure from local competition, and our acquisitions people in the estates department started seriously considering this site as an option. It is an unusual relocation choice, because we are effectively vacating a prime High Street site for a site that is off-pitch in terms of passing footfall and has to attract customers in its own right. The site isn't that visible, and existing direction signs aren't ideal. Furthermore, the Fine-Food building isn't in the best possible state, and the general area has deteriorated.

'However, the site does have a number of significant advantages. For a start, it is the ideal footage we want, with the sales area all on one floor in a very workable footprint – operating efficiencies can therefore be achieved, meaning a significantly increased turnover but with proportionately less staff and management. We'll end up with 26,000 square feet of net selling space, 5000 square feet stock area and 6000 square feet staff quarters. The large sales floor means we will be able to expand significantly our men's and ladies' clothing ranges, and offer childrenswear for the first time. We'll also be getting fitting rooms for the first time. On the food side we'll be able to double our footage. We won't actually extend the food "range" much because we've already got a good range jammed in the current store – but we can give it more space which will help customers to find what they're after more easily.

'The new site has a large car park (160 spaces, although 70 of these are underground) which is ideal for food shoppers. It will be a "pay and display" facility, but our customers will get a refund. Access for deliveries is excellent, with a dedicated entrance and purpose-built underground delivery area. Another factor in favour of the site in the beginning was the possibility of a good financial deal, and we knew we would have the opportunity to sell or lease our current site to offset the development costs. The local planners like the idea of us taking on the site – our investment will further improve the look of the building and the immediate area. With Marks and Spencer as the tenant, neighbouring traders might also see the opportunity to improve the presentation of their own businesses. By relocating nearby, of course, we can also develop larger premises without disrupting the existing store or our trade in Kendal.'

PROJECT MANAGEMENT

Mike explains his role in the project. 'The Kendal project has an overall project manager who works in the store development group, and she oversees a number of projects around the country at the same time. Because the Kendal scheme is relatively small, I have been delegated much of the project management responsibility on the construction side. My job is to ensure that all the necessary building and fitting-out work is completed on time, within the costs that have been agreed, and to the right specification. I am the interface between the commercial side of Marks and Spencer, the design team and the building contractor. I have to make sure the right people provide the right information at the right time, to ensure that the construction and fitting-out programme runs to plan and the costs are controlled. I've had an interest in the Kendal scheme from the beginning, and I will see it through until a year after opening, after which the on-going maintenance of the store is handed over to another department.'

Katy explains her role as store planner for the project. 'Store planner positions tend to be attachments and development posts within the business. Using our store management experience, we focus on ensuring that new stores are designed in a way that meets the commercial requirements of the business, maximizing sales in an attractive store environment and ensures that stores are operationally efficient to minimize costs. I liaise with all departments that have an interest in the design, building and operation of the store. I must ensure that the final layout meets the needs of the store manager, divisional management and also the buying groups – they are my clients. Effective communication is a critical requirement in my role. In Kendal the company's objective is to increase footage and sales substantially, but not to increase costs substantially. We want to build efficiencies into the design of stores – we want efficient stock handling, efficient tilling, efficient fitting rooms, efficient backstage areas and so on. My brief therefore covers a range of layout and design issues: looking at the way stock is moved around the store, positioning walkways to facilitate customer movement around the store, planning public points of access and exit, designing backstage areas (including administration quarters), positioning fixtures such as food counters, fridges, tills and displays, and deciding the width of gangways. We also work out how much space to allocate to each of the main merchandise groups (e.g. the foodhall) using our extensive databases on sales densities in existing stores. The buying groups will work with me in getting the balance right. In general the areas of each department will relate to their expected turnover, but the time of year for the store opening and the type of town will also affect the mix.

In addition to my contribution in the early stages of designing the store layout (alongside the architects, corporate designers and store manager), I will also get involved later in the project to plan the location of merchandising equipment (racks etc.). We need to know what we're doing on these things about 12 weeks before opening, because it can take that long sometimes to order some of the equipment. I'll also get involved in the last few months prior to opening, as the interior of the store takes shape, to make sure that our original plans are being delivered in practice. Sometimes you can come up against unexpected problems during the building process – particularly if you're redeveloping an older building – such as hidden columns or differences in floor levels. As these problems arise, we may need to revise the layout around them. We also need to be around when the food and general merchandise groups are checking their final layouts, in case changes are necessary.

'I work closely with the project manager whose role is to deliver the particular design of store we've all come up with, on time and within budget. The project manager has complete control of the budget, i.e. the amount of money we've been allocated by the company to build the store. I had quite a few discussions with the project manager on budget issues prior to the monies being signed off for the scheme – if I had wanted something new incorporated into the store design I might have had to make a sacrifice elsewhere, because the budget can be quite tight. In some stores we have debates over things like vinyl versus marble flooring. At the end of the day the design scheme has to be appropriate for the budget available.'

THE DEVELOPMENT PLANNING PROCESS

Paul explains, 'In the case of Kendal the whole process really got underway once the estates department had kicked off serious interest in the Fine-Food site on 9 August 1993. Right from the start the whole development planning process went without a hitch. I was involved from the beginning when we were doing the feasibility research, arguing vigorously in favour of the resite, and I remember discussing the prospects with the footage assessment unit (FAU) when they were putting together sales estimates for the site in the summer.[6] Quite a lot of research went into estimating the turnover and a host of factors were considered – existing sales performances, the proposed selling space available, the local customer profile, the size of the catchment population, local competition and so on. They also looked into how the new Kendal store might compare against other company stores with similar catchments. I fed into the FAU quite a lot of my local knowledge and views on Kendal to help in the turnover estimates.'

Mike has been closely involved in the planning activities at head office. 'At the start of September we then went through to the preparatory planning stage, during which the scheme was subjected to progressively more and more detailed examination, and had to pass through a series of project boards[7] before it could gain approval to proceed to the Capital Evaluation Committee (CEC) in early November.[8] The preparatory planning stage started with probably a month's work by a skeleton design team drawing up a broad outline of the proposed scheme. Once this had been agreed by the project board, we then studied the scheme in detail. Our architects, corporate designers and store planner produced detailed plans and layouts, even down to walkways, the food-grid and the location and size of the main sales departments. We needed detailed layouts at this stage because of the implications for costs, plant requirements, pipe runs and so on. Our quantity surveyors could then produce estimates of costs for the building and fitting-out works, and various financial evaluations could be carried out to see how the turnover estimates stacked up against the combined development and likely site acquisition costs, and what sort of return we might get. Once the final project board was happy with the scheme, the costings, the likely profitability and the outline timetable, we could then go to the CEC for ultimate approval for the funds and the go-ahead.

'After the initial feasibility research in August we then of course went into negotiations with Fine-Food, and we had to do the background planning in strict confidence. We had to be careful not to spark off any rumours of our interest in the site, which might upset the existing Fine-Food staff, until everything had been settled. This really hampered some of the early surveying, costing and planning work because we couldn't get official access to the site to examine the building in detail. Talking to the local authority about potential planning requirements was also a bit tricky – we could only hold provisional discussions while the deal with Fine-Food was under wraps. I suppose the negotiations with Fine-Food didn't take that long once the initial approach had been made. The critical stages were probably sorted by the end of October, although it took until December to conclude the exact purchase terms, sort out all the legal paperwork, agree a vacation date and so on. I remember we had a few problems with the land registry documents, which took a while to sort out. So, in effect, by the year-end Fine-Food were in a position to announce the sale.

'The project sailed through the Capital Evaluation Committee within a couple of weeks. All the research showed that the Kendal scheme would achieve the required returns, so the directors gave us the OK on the expenditure without a problem. As soon as we'd got CEC approval we went to tender on the "design and build" contract for the store. The building contractor who won the tender must have been up and running on the contract by the middle of November, beavering away on the detailed design stage with their appointed architects, quantity surveyors and various consultants, as well as talking to all the subcontractors who would be tendering to provide services and equipment for the store. We've worked closely with the building contractor of course, feeding in our views and guidance on the design and our construction requirements. We expect to hear from them any time now with the final design, detailed specifications, costings and the building timetable.'

Paul Mellor has also been involved throughout the planning process. 'I'm making sure that I have an input on the internal design of the store, because of my commercial management interest. The sales floor plan is mainly developed by store planning, who work to a successful design formula. However, given that every store has a unique configuration and customer profile, there is always room for a local commercial manager to influence the layout. Throughout the preparatory planning stages, and in conjunction with my divisional office, I fed in my views on the location and sizes of departments, and on the positioning of customer service desks, tills, telephones and so on.[9] I also felt quite strongly about the design proposals for the staff quarters and the location of the staff entrance. I want a canopy over the entrance – it rains so much in Kendal I can see staff getting soaked while they fiddle with their bags to get through the cardswipe. I've got views on how I want the car park run – ideally I want the local authority to manage it for us, and as part of the deal I'd like them to manage the greenery around the site as well. I think it is crucially important for the store manager to be involved in planning a new development – we have a valuable contribution to make and, after all, we've got to run the store once it opens.'

Paul explains the current situation on the deal with Fine-Food. 'We agreed the final terms on the purchase just before Christmas, but of course the deal was still under wraps until the official announcement of the purchase the other day. Fine-Food naturally wanted to trade over Christmas. They've given their staff a month's notice of the store closure, but they'll close at the end of the month because they'll need a week to remove their hardware and clear up.'

PLANNING THE WORK

Mike explains how the building work is likely to develop over the next few weeks, and the current position on planning approvals. 'The building contractor will have access to the site from 14 February, and within a fortnight there will be scenes of organized chaos, peppered with hoardings, huts and hard hats. The building contractor will spend two weeks or so preparing the site, and then two weeks stripping the building, removing all the unwanted fixtures, fittings and services left by Fine-Food, and putting in the new roof insulation. Then work can begin in earnest on the installation of new sprinkler, electrical and mechanical services, and the new lift.

'We'll send off for detailed planning permission for the building works in late February once Fine-Food have moved out, but we expect the dialogue with the local authority to continue for about three months before we get all the official approvals for the design, building regulations, signage and so on. It takes time to get all the necessary permissions, because some of the process requires statutory public notice periods to see if anyone has any objections. There shouldn't be any problems with the planning authority though, because our planning consultants have been sounding out the council for some time on our proposals for the store, and they seem generally happy. The main things we're seeking approval for are changes to the elevations and shop-front (moving from a sixties Swiss chalet look to a nineties rustic look, and relocating the entrances), new directional signs on Library Road and new signs on the front of the store, and of course we'll need building regulations approval.[10]

'The local planners have given us some ideas on what they want to see and what they don't want to see in the development. They've set high standards for the style and type of development work in Kendal because it is classed as a conservation area. They prefer, for example, the use of natural stone if possible, and they are very sensitive on signage. We want to use internally illuminated signs for the store, but the council may insist on exposed downlights over signs. We'll work hard to negotiate for the Library Road signage, because we want a sign that is bigger and higher than the Fine-Food one. The planners may also have views on our proposed expanse of glass in the new shop-front (which we want in order to maximize the amount of natural light on the sales floor). They may insist on mullions in the window so that we're consistent with the vertical design emphasis on other shop-fronts in the town. Our plans are to use green signs and timber trolley corrals in the car park. Timber doesn't really last long, gets smashed to smithereens and gives a real headache for maintenance, but we've decided not to use stainless steel because timber is more suited to the look we'll be trying to achieve. We'll also spend a lot of money making the car park lighting effective and making it more environmentally friendly.

'The planning approval process should be relatively straightforward for this site – fortunately the Fine-Food site already has an A1 Retail Store Use classification, so we won't have to apply for a change of use, and there aren't any restrictions on what can be sold. We'll keep in close contact with the planners throughout the development work – it's a big investment for us, so we want to make sure everything is acceptable and done properly.'

THE BUILDING AND FITTING-OUT PROCESS

'The main objective for the building contractor will be to open as soon as possible. We'll confirm the exact opening date once we've been on site a few weeks, and we'll have progress meetings every four weeks anyway to make sure things are going to plan.

'We've got a few problems with the building to sort out. We've found quite a bit of damp on the site, which hasn't been helped by the geography of the area, with water coming down from the granite and Cumbrian slate to the rear, and the expanse of wet woodland and park next to the site. The gutters have been damaged by snow, and are too small anyway. Much of the plant needs to be replaced – we'll need new refrigeration plant, a new generator and lift, and we need to service the heating under the concrete delivery ramp (which stops it freezing in winter) because it isn't working as far as we know. A lot of these problems of course were taken into account in the price we've paid for the building.

'We've got to fit out three levels of the building (see figure 15.2): the lower ground floor (underground car park, stockroom, refrigeration plant area and goods reception area), the ground floor (sales area and food hall, and backstage areas including the cold room) and the mezzanine floor (kitchen, toilets, offices and EPoS room). We won't, however, be doing a gold-leaf job on the store, because there's a limit to what we can spend, and we want to make as much use of the existing services and structure as possible.

'The ground floor fit-out will take place in three stages. It will take a week to install the high-level electrical, mechanical and sprinkler services above the sales floor and foodhall, and fix up the ceiling grid ready for the ceiling tiles to be added later. The CCTV equipment will be installed as soon as the electrical work is finished. After that we can start putting in some of the Marks and Spencer design features, like perimeter panelling, trims, skirting, coving, cornice and lighting, which will take five weeks. Once these are sorted, we can get the vinyl flooring down in the foodhall, the carpets down on the rest of the salesfloor, drop the ceiling tiles into place and put the doors on. We can then install the equipment – for the fitting rooms, the Marks and Spencer financial services desk area, the customer service desk, the wall and mid-flooring merchandising equipment, food cases and shelving, tills and phones. This flooring and equipment stage will take about five weeks. The lobby area and the automatic doors on the shop-front will be left quite late so that we can get some of the larger equipment (particularly the refrigeration plant) into the store more easily. The salesfloor needs to be handed over to the store manager two weeks before opening to give staff enough time for dressing.

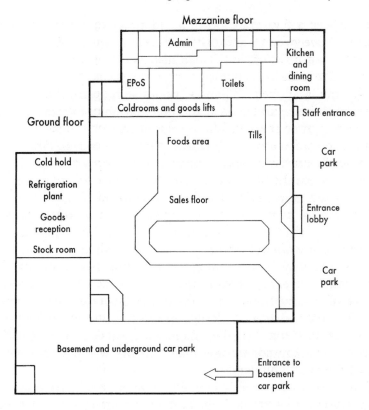

Figure 15.2 Schematic diagram: layout of new Marks and Spencer store (not to scale).

'Backstage we need to get the coldroom fully operational and wound down to temperature in time for handover four weeks before opening. Getting all the necessary partitions and services fixed up will take about four weeks; then we can install the coldroom plant over a two-week period. The final activities backstage before hand-over will be a week's work on joinery and decoration, and installing the Intrad fittings.[11]

'On the mezzanine floor we need to fit out Paul's staff areas. We'll need seven weeks to sort the basic services and joinery for the offices, kitchen and toilets, and then probably four weeks to decorate, put the vinyl flooring and carpets down, do the final clean and take in the office furniture and kitchen equipment. We should be ready to hand over the staff quarters three weeks before the opening. We're on a tighter schedule for the EPoS room, which needs to be completed and decorated in five weeks, and needs to be ready eight weeks before store opening, in time for the IT equipment (point of sale systems and distribution control) to be installed and tested by our head office IT specialists, so Paul will then be able to prepare for ordering activities.

'On the lower ground floor we've got some general improvement works in the car parking area, and preparation of the stockroom and goods reception areas (including upgrading the dock-leveller/hoist and shutters), which will probably take nine weeks. The air conditioning plant, refrigeration plant and main switch panel will be installed as part of this process. The stockroom and goods reception areas should be ready for handover four weeks before opening.

'Aside from all the fitting-out work, we've also got to get all the major equipment commissioned, of course (which is included in the time scales mentioned earlier), which means checking and testing the sprinklers, air conditioning, refrigeration plant, alarms and so on, to ensure everything works the way it should. All the IT gear will be dry run and various tests done to make sure you can communicate and that the data check out, and all the tills will be tested once they're hooked up. And then there's the outside of the building – trolley corrals, minor improvements to the layout of the car park and new white lining and signs.

'Even when the store's opened there may still be one or two snagging jobs to sort out – bits of the building or fitting-out process that we're not happy with. These will need to be completed by the building contractor as soon as he can. I can't imagine we'll have any major problems because we've got a good team of people who are very experienced in developing and opening new stores, and the building isn't particularly complicated. About six months after the opening I'll go back for a project review day, so we can all get together with the contractor to see what's worked and what hasn't. If we've tried out any new lighting or colour schemes, we'll review them and see how the plant has operated.'

THE LOCAL COMMERCIAL OPERATION

Paul is not sure yet when the new store might open. 'In the early days of considering the Fine-Food site I favoured Easter for the opening or certainly no later than the spring bank holiday at the end of May, both of which are classic times to open – particularly Easter, because not only is it a peak in itself but it is also a good opportunity then to hit the kind of merchandise that sells well between Easter and summer. The later you leave it the less window you have. Similarly, if you open in the autumn, you are set through to Christmas. For me, the most awkward time to open would be mid-season, because we would need to stock the current season's merchandise as well as prepare for the next season. One problem with opening with current stock is that the availability of the best-selling items could be limited and if we're not careful we'll be left with a lot of poorer selling lines. If necessary, I'll have to forecast what we'll need to tide us over mid-season and make sure we have stocks reserved for us. The other issue with opening dates, however, is that, while we want to open as soon as possible from a commercial trading point of view, the last thing we want to do is rush it and risk things going wrong.'

Paul explains his role and objectives in the project. 'Apart from my input on the layout of the store, my role will really come to the fore in the last 10 or 12 weeks before opening. Once we get under way, my objective will be to close the old store down successfully as well as open the new store, with minimal disruption to trade or damage to the image of Marks and Spencer in Kendal. I'll want to close the old store at the normal time on the chosen Saturday and open the new store on the following Monday morning. I'll need to maximize the standards and performance of the old store right up until it closes, and after closure I'll need to ensure it's left in an acceptable state – both operationally and visually.

'It will be my job to ensure that all the necessary preparations have been made for the new store to perform to its maximum potential from the moment it opens. I'll also have to think about the implications of some of the new equipment, ranges and facilities we'll be getting in our new store. For example, the company is currently rolling out the selling of "loose" produce (e.g. apples), so we'll be doing this in our new Kendal store for the first time. This will mean different display techniques, as well as new in-line weighing facilities at the tills. We'll also be getting the new comput-erized automated stock replenishment system (ASR) for clothing.

'I will have a keen interest in monitoring how the building works are going, and communicating any alterations I think are necessary – to help the commercial performance of the store – back to the project manager. I'm fortunate, I suppose, compared to many store managers, in that I've had some experience of working on a store development project before. I've learned a lot of best practices, and I'll be putting them into good effect on the Kendal scheme.

'One thing I must do is maintain good relations with the existing traders next to the Fine-Food car park. Once the builders move on to the site, the traders may complain that their business is affected. They shouldn't be that worried, because when we do open they will benefit significantly from the greater number of customers around. What they sell is quite complementary to what we do, and there's a super music shop and coffee bar. Actually, I also ought to have a word with the tenant on the corner who's got rather messy premises and all his gear lying around. It's right next door to where all our customers will come out, and I would like the whole area round there looking neat and tidy.

'I'll want to keep in contact with the building contractor's site manager, to keep tabs on how things are going and to learn as much as possible about what is going into my new store. I can also then keep my staff up-to-date on progress – it's important to build your staff up to the big opening day. I will also need to keep in close contact with our head office managers responsible for IT systems, buying, transport and corporate affairs, who will get more and more involved in the project as we get nearer to opening. I'll also have to maintain close and cordial relationships with various local author-ities, organizations and groups, partly to promote the scheme and keep them informed of progress, but also to make sure we're meeting the needs of the local community.

'I'll need to get involved in planning the promotional activities to publicize and support the opening. Our corporate affairs group organizes most of the promotions work for the opening of a new store, but we can influence the type of campaign and feed in our knowledge of the best local press and media to use. We've got an excellent local commercial radio station, The Bay, which covers our catchment area to a tee, so we'll definitely use them, and we'll look at the local papers, posters and other media possibilities with head office as well. The corporate affairs group has some well established promotions material to use, but we can personalize the material with my signature and change the wording if appropriate. We could do something for charge-card holders, dignitaries and staff as well to help promote the store. We can't really start working on promotions ideas or schedules until the builders are up and running – it would be dangerous to make assumptions about the definite starting date anyway until the project people have had a good look at the site. Once we start planning promotions we should have our ideas sorted within a month. As soon as we've confirmed the definite opening date we can look into the promotions schedule, which will focus on the main four weeks before launch day.

'I also want to promote the Kendal project "within" the business. We're one of half a dozen schemes being worked on at the moment, and we will be rather overshadowed by the big Gemini development at Warrington which is planned to open in mid-June. We won't want head office to forget about us in Kendal – we'll want to keep our profile up.

'I'm fortunate in that I've been allocated two extra managers for the duration of the project. To add to my existing personnel manager and finance manager, I've been allocated a deputy manager to help run the old store as well as plan the new one. I'm hoping that two months before we open I'll also have the help of an operations manager – responsible for the hardware in the buildings, deliveries, servicing, security, equipment and that kind of thing. That person will be very necessary to think about the logistics of how we are going to get all our kit on to the sales floor, plan deliveries and so on, and, crucially, he or she will have responsibility for shutting down our old store. Within a week of opening the new store, I want the old store locked up and empty. I'm determined to trade in the old store in a fit state right to the end. I'm not accepting any lowering of staffing levels or customer service standards or stock levels, just because we're shutting up.

'We'll need to recruit and train 25 new staff, and I'll organize that with my personnel manager. We'll probably need three months in total for this, with the last month on training. Training is vital in the lead-up to a new store opening, particularly training on customer service. Most of the new staff will work in operational, cleaning and catering jobs and they will work a variety of different hours. We shouldn't need any more supervisory staff than we've already got. We'll be able to operate the new store with probably only ten extra staff, yet we'll take a vastly higher turnover. This comes down to efficiency because of the layout of the new store.

'We're not strictly allowed into the store to "work" until the last fortnight, although we'll be able to pop in and out to have a look as it develops. I want to get into the new offices at least a week before opening. I want to take over the sales floor two weeks before opening so we've got plenty of time to do the dressing. We can dress the clothing up to about 90 per cent of its eventual completion, with the remaining 10 per cent being stock that we'll have in the old shop and bring over at the last minute. Food can be more of a last thing, because of the freshness consideration, but we can still dress the long-life departments in the last week, ticket it and cover it with polythene.

'There will be a process of stock-building in the distribution centre prior to the opening of the store, but this will be organized by a department at head office. This stock-build will happen gradually so that the store opening doesn't suddenly create a hole in the distribution system. For the stock-build we'll need to know exactly when we're opening, because it will affect the type of merchandise that is built up. I'll want a say in the catalogue of merchandise planned for the store, and I'll discuss this with the various merchandise groups at an appropriate stage, although I expect we'll mainly be allocated just the core lines. I think we'll possibly need more rainwear ranges and walking gear because of where we are. The stock-building process within the store itself (which is one of my main responsibilities) will happen over a two-week period, but deliveries need to be phased carefully. I'll organize this with the operations manager. On the display side, divisional office will order the frames and cardboard to arrive in time for floor dressing, and they'll send display specialists down to help get the store ready.

'The last weekend will be a real challenge with all the final preparations. I'm not sure what time we'll open on the Monday – I'll think about that nearer the time.'

Case Questions

1   Based on the information contained in this case study, assume that you are the project manager for the Kendal relocation scheme. Develop a project network for the scheme as a whole, taking into account all the early planning stages through to the main commercial aspects of the operation. You should be able to identify between 25 and 30 different activities from the case as a whole. In most cases, precedence of activities is also given directly or indirectly. Use your judgement whenever required. Identify the critical path through the network. What does this tell you about the management tasks within the project? What opening date will you be forecasting? Are you prepared to commit your professional reputation to this target date? What other problems can you foresee with the management of this project? Consider especially the resources you will need to complete the job.

2   Assume you are Paul Mellor. Develop a *detailed* plan of all activities you would be expected to organize to achieve your objectives for the new store as outlined in the case. Remember that not all possible activities have been mentioned, and some activities will need to be dovetailed with the building and fitting-out programme under way at the same time.

3   Assume you are the operations manager allocated to Kendal, and given responsibility for the shut-down of the old store at 18–20 Stricklandgate. Identify the type of activities you will need to organize, and consider the sequence of activities needed to achieve the objectives set out by Paul Mellor for this store.

Notes

1   The information in this case study, while believed to be largely accurate, is based on the memory of those involved and compiled from a variety of sources. It has also been simplified in order to focus on key learning objectives for students of management. For these reasons, the material should not be regarded as a totally factual account of events or views.

2   Marks and Spencer Company Facts, 1995.

3   Marks and Spencer Annual Report and Financial Statements, 1995.

4   Marks and Spencer, Company Information: Bricks and Mortar, 1994.

5   The name of the supermarket has been changed for the purposes of this case study.

6   The footage assessment unit is a team that identifies a requirement for additional space in a town and puts together the turnover estimates for new store development projects. This unit is part of the estates department.

7   Project boards are regular monthly meetings of heads of department, who discuss and approve progress on various projects that are running at the time. Boards would include representatives from construction, equipment, quantity surveying, planning, architecture, finance and the commercial side. A new store scheme would have to pass through three project boards before gaining approval to proceed to the CEC.

8   The Capital Evaluation Committee comprises the Deputy Chairman, joint managing directors and four executive directors, and meets monthly. It exercises a delegated authority within financial parameters set by the board. Source: Annual Report, 1995.

9   Paul Mellor, as store manager, reports to his line management at divisional offices in Edinburgh.
10 Three separate applications are needed. Planning permission is needed for changes to external elevations of the building, consent to display is required for signage, and building regulations approval is required for the standards of construction, fire protection, ventilation, safety, means of escape etc.
11 Intrad fittings are a proprietary brand of protective strips and fittings, such as buffer rails on doors and walls, designed to prevent damage in goods-movement areas.

PART IV
Human Resource Management

16

CORTCO Management Competencies for Graduate Recruits to the Retail Industry

Diane Preston and Alison Smith

Loughborough University Business School

Introduction

With a large workforce available for a decreasing number of jobs, the pressure of competition and survival means that organizations are looking closely at the requirements they have of the people they currently employ and those they may seek to employ. One of the ways in which organizations are seeking to refine their human resource policies is to define carefully, and in some detail, the competencies they require for different management levels. The ability to demonstrate that one has the required competencies at an appropriate level, and a willingness to extend those competencies as necessary, can only be of benefit to job seeking students.

This case study provides a brief history of the development of management competencies and what has become known as the competence debate. As with any theory, there are schools of thought within both industry and academia which are for and against the use of competencies in human resource management (HRM), and competence systems are by no means universally accepted. However, increasing numbers of companies are using some form of competence approach even if they do not accept the concept of a national framework. The retail industry is one sector where a competence approach is being used.

The case study outlines how competencies may be used within HRM generally and with particular reference to the retailing sector. The competencies identified by CORTCO (the Consortium of

Retailing Training Companies) for potential managers are provided in the appendix. For undergraduates who may be considering retailing as a career, this case will provide a background on the notion of competence, an understanding of the arguments for and against the competence approach and guidance on how to identify your personal competencies and demonstrate these successfully to prospective employers. A reference list for further reading is provided at the end of the case.

Competence: What Is It?

One of the problems associated with the competence movement is that competence itself is a term which has been defined with some variation by different researchers and theorists. As Preston and Smith (1993) explained, 'the aim of the competence movement is to engender management competencies as best practice across a wide range of managerial roles'. There is some confusion about whether competence refers to *personal* competence based on characteristics which an individual has and can demonstrate, or whether it refers to job competence; that is, what is necessary for a particular management role. Obviously, there is a relationship between the two and, ideally, a matching process.

A selection of definitions regarding competencies is given below:

- Competencies are 'an underlying characteristic of a person', 'a motive, trait, skill, aspect of one's self image or social role or a body of knowledge which he or she uses' (Boyatzis, 1982).

- Competencies are 'nothing more nor less than glorious human skills' (Randall, 1989).

- Competencies are 'Areas of work at which the person is competent', i.e. job related. 'Dimensions of behaviour that lie behind competent performance', i.e. person related (Woodruffe, 1991).

From the definitions it can be seen that there is considerable overlap between the personal qualities, skills and attributes which a person may bring to a management role. The competence movement, as promoted in the UK by the Management Charter Initiative (MCI), is about identifying the basic standards of performance required to undertake a management role successfully. Thus, competence is not about what you are but what you do, how you do it and whether or not you do it to the standard defined as competent.

For example, an employer who is looking to recruit by using competencies as a basis is looking for evidence which will demonstrate that the applicant has or may be capable of acquiring the competencies which have been identified by the company as essential. The word 'evidence' is key. The applicant who writes 'I was Captain of the university hockey team' will need to demonstrate how this role was performed effectively. Stating simply that you have held this particular title is not enough.

Other definitions of competence take the concept further than that of basic requirements for successful performance. A broader definition might be that a competence is a skill or a characteristic used by an individual which enables him or her to cope with a variety of situations both within and outside work in the most successful way. Thus a personal competence is multi-functional. In the same sense, it can be seen as extending beyond basic performance requirements and can be identified as a development tool.

In short, the competency approach aims to assist in developing potential by establishing and communicating standards of *superior performance*, coupled with endorsing a style of management most likely to achieve success.

Where Did It Come From?

The origins of the competence movement may be traced to the United States and the work of the McBer Consultancy, which was commissioned by the American Management Association to undertake research into managerial competence. This work was written up by Boyatzis (1982). The job competence assessment method employed sought to classify and evaluate the behaviours of a good manager. Comparing behaviours performed against a list of managerial competencies allows for individual assessment to take place and the identification of gaps. Boak (1991) describes the six stages of personal competency development based upon the work of Boyatzis:

1 Recognition of the competency.

2 Understanding the competency and how it relates to managerial effectiveness.

3   Self-assessment or feedback on the competency.

4   Demonstrating the competency (or at a higher level of effect-
    iveness).

5   Practice in using it.

6   Application in job situations and in the context of other
    characteristics.

In the UK, development of the competency approach has been largely due to the work of the MCI, which, over a period of 18 months, consulted over 3000 practising managers across the range of commercial, industrial and public sector activities. MCI has expressed competencies in terms of management tasks performed by supervisors, junior, middle and senior managers. It has sought to research and develop sets of national standards for management competence at all these levels. These have now all been piloted and published (see MCI Management Standards Directory, 1992).

The idea of a national framework arose from the Constable and McCormick (1987) and Handy (1987) reports, which concluded that the quality of management within the UK did not stand close comparison with our major European, American and Japanese competitors. The standards are intended to help to pull together the variety of management training available into a more coherent structure. The work undertaken by MCI to develop the standards involved a functional analysis of managerial work. Functional analysis is a systematic means of analysing a role in order to identify the full range of specific tasks and functions within it. Functional analysis has since been applied to a variety of tasks, including voluntary work and housework. It is argued that any task can be seen in competence terms and can therefore be assessed. This is clearly important for job seeking students whose paid work experience is limited but who can demonstrate competencies through other channels.

The Competence Debate

Critics of the competence movement have pointed out a number of problems with the development and application of competence. The arguments are briefly summarised below:

1   Holmes (1990) has argued that the value of diversity is ignored
    by the national framework and that there is a danger that the

manager is seen as a static or passive individual in an unchanging role. Others (Constable, 1990; Burgoyne,1990) have argued similarly that the approach is not developmental and that management development is being tied to a fixed agenda which may not always be appropriate. The same authors comment that flair, initiative and creativity are crucial to good management. These qualities are not easily measurable and it is probably not possible to create a universal standard for them.

2 It is argued that defining competencies concentrates too much upon 'the parts' and not enough upon 'the whole'. 'Skills are important bricks but a pile of bricks is no building' (Green, 1986). There needs to be consideration of a manager's 'fit' within the culture of the organization (Mangham, 1990). Similarly, different organizations' levels of seniority vary considerably. One company's director may be another's manager. In small and medium-sized companies many managers perform a wide variety of functions, whereas functional specialists may be employed in a large company. Competence will therefore mean different things in different contexts.

3 Cultural differences need to be acknowledged across industrial sectors, between different organizations within the same sector and, of course, national differences. The work of Hogg (1992) identified 201 significant differences between the ratings of European managers from six countries of 22 competencies. Wisher (1994) has also commented upon the difficulties of internationalizing competence. Of the original work completed by McBer, it is said that two-thirds relates only to the USA.

In practice, many organizations have bought into the concept of standards, but not necessarily the standards of MCI. It has been a useful starting point for companies that wish to use such an approach but have found the national standards not applicable to their own situation and have contextualized them to their own values and culture. The concept has thus helped to provide organizations with a system that they can use, but that does not align with the initial aim of the movement to produce a national system against which a universal set of standards and qualifications can be devised. The reality of managerial work, it is said, does not fit neatly into a national competence scheme. The CORTCO competencies are based on personal competencies which lead to standards of performance.

The work of CORTCO has concentrated upon the competencies required for managers within the retail sector. The CORTCO competencies listed in this case provide a baseline for under-graduates considering a career in retailing. CORTCO recognizes that these competencies relate to the general requirements of the industry and are a starting point. Specific roles within a retail company will require the development of more specific competencies.

Application: the Use of Management Competencies in HRM

As described above, the competency approach relies upon careful research into what good managers do consistently and focuses on the search for evidence that those competencies do exist. Now that we have defined the concept and recognized some of the related issues, it is important to reflect upon the potential applications of the concept within organizations. Basic job descriptions may provide only a vague outline of a manager's role and responsibilities within a company; a list of management competencies provides a more detailed description of what a manager will be expected to do by specifying the type of skills the manager will have to possess in order to carry out his or her role effectively.

A list of management competencies produced by a company or companies within an industry sector (like the CORTCO example considered below) is useful because it is a visible and public explanation of the job of management. Throughout their careers, managers should be able to use the list as a point of reference in order to get a better understanding of what is required of them by the organization for which they work. Inevitably, much of the personal learning about any new situation is acquired by being there, watching others who have worked there longer and assessing what appears to be the expected and accepted modes of behaviour. However, if some guidelines are provided by the employer, this process (termed organizational socialization) should be accelerated and, in theory, individuals reach optimum levels of performance in a shorter period of time. In this context, it is to the benefit of any organization to publicize its agreed list of competencies to its managers; this can be achieved through using the competency approach *throughout* the various aspects of HRM strategy.

HRM is concerned with all aspects of an individual's employment from the moment he or she enters the organization to when he or she leaves. If we consider the different activities of the HRM function throughout that time, it is clear how the concept of management competencies may be of help in areas such as:

- predicting potential;

- selecting candidates;

- appraising performance;

- succession planning;

- training and development.

One of the questions relating to this case asks the reader to consider some of the specific ways in which the concept of management competencies may help in each of these areas.

To provide one example, for job advertisements to work in terms of attracting the right people to apply for the job, much planning has to be carried out. A thorough analysis of the job itself is the first step, followed by the type of competencies which the job holder will need to possess. The advertisement should contain clear information about the competencies required; merely trying to present the job in its best light wastes time for everyone concerned, as unsuitable candidates will apply. The job advertisement should be viewed as the first step in a competency guided recruitment and selection process. Subsequent selection methods, such as application forms, interviews, assessment questionnaires and assessment centres, can be designed specifically on the basis of competencies required. The staff responsible for selecting the right person for the job will then have a very specific list of things to look for in a candidate and can, for example, ask particular questions in a recruitment interview to ascertain whether the applicant shows any evidence or promise of developing that set of competencies.

That same list of competencies could also be used as the basis of management career development, such as deciding upon who should be promoted and which individuals appear to require training in terms of meeting the competency guidelines. From the individual's point of view, the competency framework tells him or her what is or will be required in order to progress within the company. From an organizational point of view, it provides an objective basis for human resource planning, such as career succession and training and development. These plans are then geared towards creating a pool of managers who hold or will acquire the competencies which have been agreed to be the most crucial in that particular organization or sector. For example (as an aside and a question which will be raised at the end of the case), how could you as an individual provide specific evidence at a recruitment interview that you do possess some competence in something like leadership? From your understanding of the concept of competencies used by organizations and described in this case, you will realize that stating that you have undertaken a particular role would not be specific enough to provide the type of evidence for which employers may well be searching.

The CORTCO Competencies

CORTCO is a group of major British retailers who work together towards the collective aim of recruiting the most appropriate graduates into their businesses. This group of companies is Marks and Spencer, Boots, Sainsbury's, Safeway, CWS, Tesco, John Lewis Partnership and Kingfisher. Each company has its own graduate recruitment policy and process, but they also work together to fund and promote careers events aimed at careers officers and students. These are intended to increase the level of understanding regarding what goes on within the industry and what will be required of the graduates and managers who work within it (the sponsorship of this book of retailing case studies is another CORTCO initiative).

CORTCO has recently employed a management consultant to compile a list of management competencies which reflect the current thinking across the retailing sector and which can be referred to by each company. The consultant collected the current list of recruitment criteria being used by each of the retailers and, from this, compiled a generic set of management competencies which could be used by each one. Clearly, there may be slight differences in priority and wording by each individual organization (see question 4 at the end of the case study). However, this CORTCO list is extremely useful in terms of describing the overall competencies which most major retailers will be looking for in applicants for managerial positions within the industry.

The agreed CORTCO management competencies are defined in terms of the skills and qualities required of managers working in the retailing sector:

- self-confidence and personal strength;

- leadership and teamwork;

- planning and organization;

- analytical skills and problem solving;

- human relations and influencing.

A more detailed description of each of the competencies is provided in the appendix to this case study.

Summary

This case has provided an introduction to the concept of management competencies and some of the issues surrounding it. The competency approach aims to assist in developing the potential of managers by establishing and communicating standards of performance. This is of importance to those working within retailing and to potential applicants to the sector. The CORTCO list of management competencies demonstrates the high standards and multiple skills required by a retailing manager of today. Amidst the debates surrounding the concept, many major companies are using management competencies as the basis of their recruitment and other human resource strategies. Students are encouraged to reflect upon the competency approach and consider for themselves the type of skills they will need to demonstrate to potential employers and to continue to develop throughout their careers within the retailing industry.

Appendix: CORTCO Management Competencies

- Self-confidence and personal strength. (Assertiveness, Decisiveness, Flexibility, Judgement, Initiative, Stress Tolerance).

- Leadership and teamwork.

- Planning and organization.

- Analytical and problem solving.

- Human relations and influencing.

- Resilience and emotional control: calm under pressure; not easily flustered even when busy; resilient; bounces back after setbacks; not moody; has reserves of physical energy; able to work long and/or unsociable hours and maintain own performance and level of commitment.

- Confidence in themselves and their own abilities but aware not only of strengths but also of limitations.

- Self-motivated to maximize self-development opportunities. Actively attempts to influence events to achieve goals, a self-starter rather than one that passively accepts.

- Acting and communicating in a confident manner with peers and superiors. Expressing opinions which are influenced by personal convictions rather than the opinions of others, even when challenged.

- Prepared to have own opinions challenged, able to appreciate other people's perspectives, open minded and curious about new developments and ideas.

LEADERSHIP AND TEAMWORK

- Leadership: ability to guide or direct individuals (subordinates, peers, superiors) or a group towards task accomplishment without necessarily relying on authority or position.

- Displays a willingness to assume responsibility and ability to effectively perform the role needed to bring a group or individuals to accomplish a task or accept an idea.

- Communicates objectives regularly with the team; regularly reviews individual and team performance; maintains an effective team under pressure; delivers on time in line with objectives.

- Teamwork: willingness to participate as a full member of a team of which he or she is not necessarily leader; sustains an effective contribution even when the task is of no direct personal interest.

- Concerned to build atmosphere of trust and cooperation; involves others in his or her work; enjoys working with others; shares; offers help and advice; is concerned to liaise with colleagues and other professionals to achieve his or her own or shared objectives.

- Motivates a team as a group.

PLANNING AND ORGANIZATION

- Establishing an appropriate course of action for oneself and/or others to accomplish a specific goal, including the provision of resources.

- Ensures that tasks and activities are carried out in order of importance, in a logical sequence; reflects on priorities before undertaking any tasks rather than just rushing in; is not thrown off track; able to reprioritize and adjust priorities as necessary.

- Displays the skill to develop plans, set priorities and organize time and materials effectively.

ANALYTICAL AND PROBLEM SOLVING SKILLS

- Effectiveness in analysing situations and identifying issues; focusing on possible causes of problems and gathering relevant information.

- Judgement: ability to relate to data from different sources and draw logical conclusions, recognizing assumptions and discriminating between strong and weak arguments.

- Incisive analysis: able to break down information and absorb complex data rapidly; to think problems through logically and pull out the pertinent facts; to grasp the essentials of a situation quickly; does not take information at face value, has an inquiring mind; is able to see the implications of different options or courses of action.

- Weighs things up quickly; acts on the balance of probabilities. Takes account of potential threats but is prepared to back own judgement and proceed under conditions of 'acceptable risk'.

- Effectiveness in seeking out pertinent data from written/visual and oral sources. The skill to solve routine problems with timely and practical solutions, using sound judgement.

- Able to arrange and interpret numerical data. Assimilates and understands information quickly and makes proposals. Able to see an overview of situations. Prepared to take action and see things through to their completion.

HUMAN RELATIONS AND INFLUENCING SKILLS

- Taking actions which indicate a recognition of one's own impact on other people within the immediate work environment and which take account of the feelings and needs of others.

- Tactfully and diplomatically brings people around to a different point of view; is persistent but level headed when arguing a case.

- Outgoing: puts people at their ease, makes them feel comfortable/confident; is approachable and sensitive to others' needs; neither seeks out nor avoids conflict but deals with it sensibly and rationally when it occurs.

- Oral communication is clear and succinct in formal, informal and face-to-face situations; uses simple jargon-free language and is able to check others' understand without appearing condescending or talking down to them.

- Listening skills: attends carefully to what people have to say; asks probing questions; checks their understanding of what people want. Listens to what is being said and the manner in which it is said; is able to read the situation and gauge the motives behind the words.

- Effectively to utilize appropriate human relations techniques; that is, sensitivity, empathy, active listening in dealing with other people.

- Oral communication and presentation skills: ease of expression and precision in explaining views. Includes correct use of English, vocabulary, vocal clarity, tonal quality, body language etc.

- Written communication displays the ability to effectively convey ideas in writing, e.g. spelling, punctuation and syntax.

- Handles conflict appropriately.

- Sells ideas and gains others' commitment to them. Uses own skills to achieve goals and works through others to achieve goals.

- Demonstrates a positive approach and a professional image.

- Develops rapport with other people.

- Communicates in a clear and concise manner (both written and verbal).

- Sensitive to the needs and responses of others.

Case Questions

1 Consider and summarize the arguments for and against the use of management competencies. A useful exercise may be to peruse recent newspapers and management journals to establish which individual authors and companies appear to have been the main advocates and users of the competency approach.

2 Describe how you could use the notion of management competencies to help you design systems within the different aspects of human resource strategy described in the case.

3 Consider the list of CORTCO competencies: do you agree with it? (On what basis?) Are there any missing which you would want to add? (Which and why?)

4 Could a **generic** list of management competencies such as CORTCO's really be applied in different retailing organizations? Think about the retail companies you know about and/or have worked for: which of these competencies do you feel would be seen as most important, and why?

5 As the Human Resources Director of a retailing organization, design an assessment centre which will help you to decide whether applicants for managerial posts within your company hold the competencies on the CORTCO list given in the case. Which specific activities would you use, and why? In what way could they demonstrate promise/evidence of a particular competence in the applicants you are assessing?

6 As an undergraduate thinking of applying for a post as a management trainee with a retailing organization, what evidence (in addition to your curriculum vitae) would you need to

provide in order to demonstrate your suitability and competence? Consider ways in which you might translate simple statements of interests and achievements into evidence of effective performance. If time allows, either individually or in a small group, you could prepare an example of an initial application to a retailer.

7   Prepare for a recruitment interview for a trainee manager within a retailing organization. Choose a particular management position (store management, customer services, distribution etc.) within the retailing sector and, using the CORTCO list of competencies as a guide, reflect upon *specific* evidence you might provide to prove your competence in the specified areas. If you have time, role play the interview situation with a colleague.

References and Further Reading

Boak, G. (1991) *Developing Managerial Competencies*. London: Pitman.

Boak, G. and Thompson, D. (1992) *Using a personal competency model for development and assessment of managers*. Paper presented at Reframing Competencies Conference, Bolton Institute of Higher Education, November.

Boyatzis, R. (1982) *The Competent Manager: a Model for Effective Performance*. New York: John Wiley.

Burgoyne, J. (1990) Management education: MCI launches standards for first two levels. *Personnel Management*, November, 13.

Constable, J. (1990) The test of management. *Personnel Management*, November, 6.

Constable, J. and McCormick, R. (1987) *The Making of British Managers*. London: BIM/CBI.

Handy, C. (1987) *The Making of Managers*. London: MDC/NEDO/BIM Department.

Hogg, B. (1992) European management competencies. Paper presented at Reframing Competencies Conference, Bolton Institute of Higher Education, November.

Holmes L. (1990) Training competencies: turning back the clock. *Training & Development*, April.

Mangham, I. (1990) Managing as a performing art. *British Journal of Management*, 1, 105–15.

MCI (1992) *The Management Standards Directory.*

Mitrani, A., Dalziel, M. and Fitt, D. (1992) *Competency Based Human Resource Management: Value Driven Strategies for Recruitment, Development and Reward*. London: Kogan Page.

Preston, D. and Smith, A.J. (1993) APL: current state of play within management education in the UK. *Journal of Management Development*, 12 (8), 27–38.

Wisher, V. (1994) Competencies: the precious seeds of growth. *Personnel Management*, July.

Woodruffe, C. (1991) Competent by any other name. *Personnel Management Journal*, September, 30–3.

17

A Tale of Two Store Managers: Performance Measurement at Sainsbury's

Cathy Hart

Loughborough University Business School

Introduction

Monitoring and controlling the performance of retail stores is critical to the success of retail organizations. There are various dimensions along which retail performance may be measured: some more easily identifiable compared with others less quantifiable. This case examines retail performance measurement on two different levels: the store manager and the retail store. It illustrates these issues in relation to the scenario of a new Sainsbury's superstore opening, and explores the factors involved in choosing a new branch manager. The case is set in 1995 and spans a four-week period prior to the opening of the new superstore.

3 October

The new Sainsbury's superstore planned for Pilchester[1] is scheduled to open in two months time. The 36,000 square feet store is nearing completion. The petrol station is operational and the external building work is finished, services are being installed, gondolas and cabinets have been delivered and are being fitted. The in-house bakery and coffee shop will be operational within eight weeks.

[1] The characters, stores and figures depicted in this case are fictitious and any resemblance to existing stores or staff is purely coincidental.

District personnel has appointed department managers and the weekly full-time staff are being interviewed at the local job centre. Everything appears to be on schedule.

10 October

David Thomson, an experienced branch manager of ten years, had been offered the post as the new manager for the Pilchester store, but has now refused the position on personal grounds. This causes a major dilemma for the Sainsbury's management. The recent store openings programme and manager transfers have resulted in a shortage of available branch managers. It is vital that a new manager is identified and in place as soon as possible to get the management team working together ready for the handover period. Area personnel identifies two further possible candidates: Paul Mason and John Goodwin. They have differing qualities, but both are capable of managing the new store. Unfortunately, unlike the first candidate, neither has previously managed the opening of a new store, or had to develop a newly appointed management team. Another consideration is the location of the new store. It is an unusual site for Sainsbury: on the edge of town, and set in the heart of a socio-economic group C2DE area, which may create problems in attracting sufficient target customers and the right calibre of staff. Sainsbury's typical customer profile consists of a higher than average proportion of customers in the socio-economic group ABC1. However, this site was identified by the company as a crucial area, having a high competitive presence with no Sainsbury's stores within a 12 mile radius.

24 October

The countdown to store occupation has begun. News on local competitive developments reports that Sainsbury's arch rival Westwood Stores has announced the closure of its five year old superstore, just two miles away from the new Pilchester store. Local press quotes a Westwood spokesman: 'the recent recession, combined with rising unemployment in this region, has decreased local food expenditure. As a result we can no longer maintain an unprofitable store.' Other sources revealed that the underlying causes were poor operational standards, combined with labour and social related problems leading to exceptionally high staff turnover and severe pilferage. This latest news further complicates the situation. Sainsbury's is committed to opening the Pilchester store as scheduled, but must ensure that the most effective branch manager is in position to head up a team of nearly 400 full-time equivalent staff. The area management team prepares for a difficult decision, with major implications if the wrong decision is made. A brief career history and profile for each manager, together with his or her current store performance record for the past year, are assembled and circulated in preparation for a final meeting to decide who should get the post.

The following are the outline profiles of the two managers to be considered.

MANAGER A PROFILE: PAUL MASON, AGE 30

Paul joined Sainsbury's seven years ago after graduating with a 2:1 degree in business studies. He spent one year on the graduate training scheme, becoming department manager for the produce section. Within two years he was promoted to deputy manager of the same store. A year later he was given his own store. His current store is 28,000 square feet in area and located on the edge of town. It has a petrol station, delicatessen, in-store bakery and fresh fish counter. The current full-time equivalent staff are 240. His store's stock holding is consistently below the company average. The store maintains full product availability, but suffers above average reductions.

Comments. Since taking over this store, Paul has achieved a remarkable sales growth. Unfortunately, the store has a higher than average staff turnover, and morale is not as good as it could be. Fortunately, the store is situated in a position where recruitment of labour is not a problem. His staff view Paul as very efficient but unapproachable. He ensures that all staff are in his weekly management meetings and communicates the necessary information to achieve the targeted sales. Paul feels that the 'firm but fair' line is important with his team, particularly as staff quality could be better. Paul personally checks all ordering to ensure that stock is kept to a minimum and the shelf fill level is high. Although shrinkage is below company average, they do suffer high instances of internal and external pilfering. He achieves good productivity in spite of the staff turnover, mainly through some clever manipulation of schedules. (See table 17.1.)

Table 17.1 Profit and loss report, supermarket A: manager Paul Mason

Cost heading	Actual		Budget	
	£	%	£	%
Sales	26,040,000	100.00	24,500,000	100.00
Gross profit	7,291,200	28.00	6,737,500	27.50
Stock results made up of:				
Reductions	(161,448)	−0.62	(122,500)	−0.50
Stock loss	(104,160)	−0.40	(122,500)	−0.50
Trading gross profit	7,025,592	26.98	6,492,500	26.50
Distribution	963,480	3.70	911,400	3.72
Electricity	156,000	0.60	147,000	0.60
Utilities (water etc.)	13,020	0.05	12,250	0.05
Maintenance	156,240	0.60	134,750	0.55
Wrapping materials	171,864	0.66	149,450	0.61
Contract cleaning	78,120	0.30	78,120	0.32
Other contracts	5,208	0.02	5,208	0.02
Uniforms/consumables	57,560	0.22	52,000	0.21
Equipment (e.g. trolleys)	7,812	0.03	7,820	0.03
Restaurant	(28,750)	−0.11	(29,400)	−0.12
Telephone	10,416	0.04	6,500	0.03
Advertising	50,000	0.19	50,000	0.20
Cash office and till loss	2,340	0.01	500	0.00
Bank charges	26,040	0.10	22,050	0.09
Branch occupancy charges				
Rent	781,200	3.00	781,200	3.19
Rates	260,400	1.00	260,400	1.06
Depreciation	260,400	1.00	260,400	1.06
Labour cost				
Cost of hours worked	1,687,392	6.48	1,592,500	6.50
Sick pay	117,180	0.45	73,500	0.30
Holiday pay	317,688	1.22	306,250	1.25
Training costs	12,350	0.05	6,000	0.02
Discount scheme	12,000	0.05	12,750	0.05
Xmas gift	12,850	0.05	12,750	0.05
Net profit	1,894,782	7.28	1,639,102	6.69

MANAGER B PROFILE: JOHN GOODWIN, AGE 31

John has been with Sainsbury for 15 years. He joined Sainsbury's at the age of 16 after GCSEs and then entered the management training scheme at 18. After four years he became a trainee grocery manager. Over the following two years he managed two other departments before being promoted to deputy. He was given his own store two years ago. His current store is of 24,000 square feet, located in a town centre and employing 200 full-time equivalent staff. In addition to the standard Sainsbury's format, it has an in-store bakery, delicatessen and fresh fish counter. On average over the past year this store has carried excessive stockholding. Weekends usually result in many stock-outs in the store, but he experiences few losses through low reductions. The store is on an enhanced product range, which has gradually developed over the past year as new lines were being offered. Shrinkage is currently running at 50 per cent above the company average.

Comments. John's sales growth appears to be limited in the fresh foods department and he struggles to achieve growth on last year. His cautiousness may be the cause but the quality of his work is always to a high standard. He encourages his managers to be entrepreneurs in their ordering and listens to their suggestions, which has resulted in the current range situation and high over-stocks. John is well respected by staff, he has a lot of inspirational qualities in leading people, he creates a good atmosphere, good morale and teamwork. Overall, he is a good team leader. The town centre store traditionally had difficult staff recruitment, whereas now the staff turnover is 70 per cent lower compared to that with his predecessor. See table 17.2.

Company Structure

The Sainsbury's company structure may also influence the decision process, owing to the reporting structure and levels of responsibility devolved to the branch managers.

There are approximately 365 Sainsbury's stores all managed according to common operational and trading standards. They are divided on a geographical basis into six areas, each managed from an area office. Each area is subdivided into five or six districts (10–15 stores) under the operational control of a district manager. Each branch manager reports to a district manager. The management structure of a typical Sainsbury's superstore is illustrated in the organization chart in figure 17.1.

Table 17.2 Profit and loss report, supermarket B: manager John Goodwin

Cost heading	Actual		Budget	
	£	%	£	%
Sales	23,220,000	100.00	23,800,000	100.00
Gross profit	6,617,700	28.50	6,902,000	29.00
Stock results made up of				
Reductions	(23,220)	−0.10	(119,000)	−0.50
Stock loss	(185,760)	−0.80	(119,000)	−0.50
Trading gross profit	6,408,720	27.60	6,664,000	28.00
Distribution	866,106	3.73	885,360	3.72
Electricity	136,998	0.59	142,800	0.60
Utilities (water etc.)	11,610	0.05	11,900	0.05
Maintenance	125,388	0.54	130,900	0.55
Wrapping materials	127,710	0.55	145,180	0.61
Contract cleaning	75,200	0.32	75,200	0.32
Other contracts	3,000	0.01	3,000	0.01
Uniforms/consumables	45,000	0.19	50,000	0.21
Equipment (e.g. Trolleys)	7,000	0.03	7,250	0.03
Restaurant	(32,508)	−0.14	(28,560)	−0.12
Telephone	4,644	0.02	6,000	0.03
Advertising	40,000	0.17	40,000	0.17
Cash office and till loss	370	0.00	500	0.00
Bank charges	19,737	0.09	21,420	0.09
Branch occupancy charges				
Rent	722,000	3.11	722,000	3.03
Rates	300,000	1.29	300,000	1.26
Depreciation	245,000	1.06	245,000	1.03
Labour cost				
Cost of hours worked	1,504,656	6.48	1,547,000	6.50
Sick pay	51,084	0.22	71,400	0.30
Holiday pay	285,606	1.23	290,360	1.22
Training costs	3,875	0.02	5,500	0.02
Discount scheme	12,000	0.05	12,000	0.05
Xmas gift	12,400	0.05	12,200	0.05
Net profit	1,841,844	7.93	1,967,590	8.27

Accountabilities

In their evaluation of these two candidates, area managers must
ensure that the Sainsbury's ethos or objectives of a store manager is

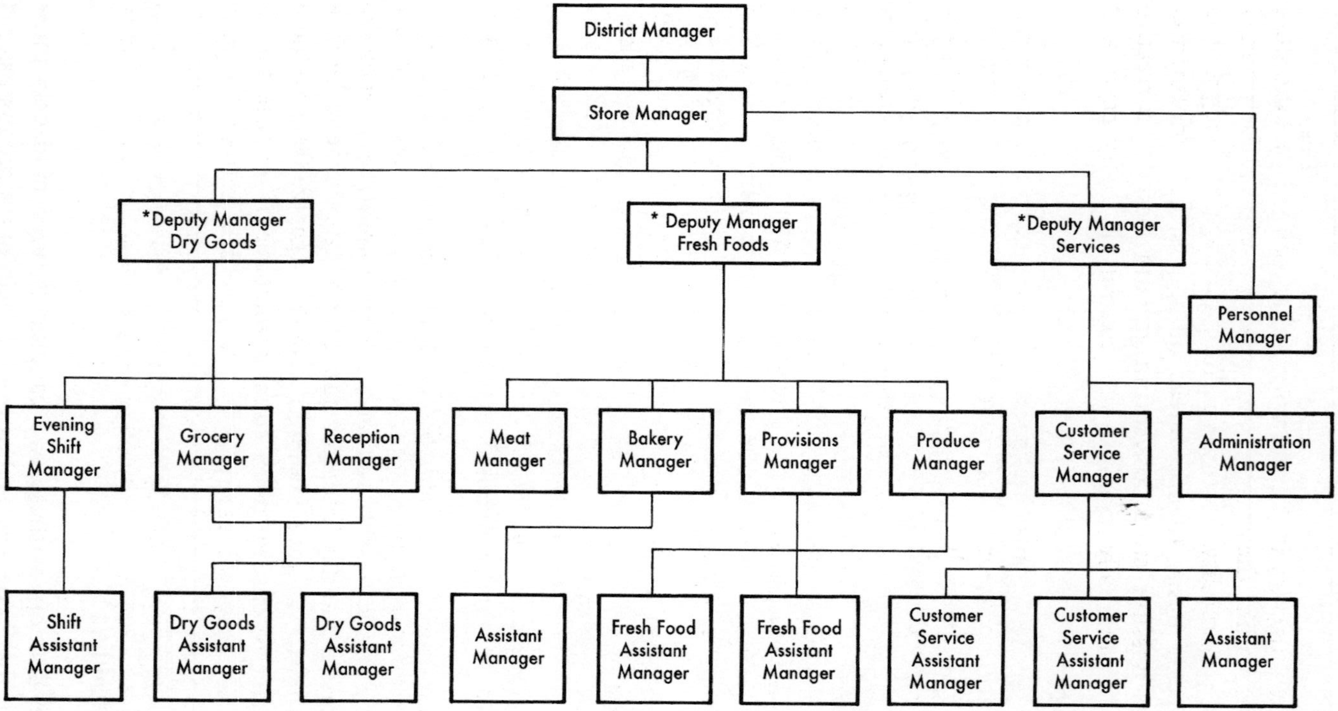

Figure 17.1 Branch management structure in a typical Sainsbury's store.

also maintained. The most recent accountabilities for a Sainsbury's branch manager have to be considered in the evaluation:

1   Prepare budgetary targets for approval and ensure that the store operates within these targets in order to achieve the planned level of profitability. Monitor performance against budget on a four-weekly basis. Identify areas of poor store performance, such as possible stock loss/shrinkage, and instigate corrective action. Continually monitor and control all utility costs and labour costs.

2   Through the deputy managers, ensure that all departments operate in accordance with company policy and procedures, in order to achieve the required operating and trading standards and expected levels of customer service throughout the store. Ensure that managers are working within company parameters in respect of ordering, stock control and control of hours of work in order to maximize the efficiency of the department. The store manager sets adequate controls, targets improvements and regularly reviews trading performance by ongoing monitoring of the quality of service, availability and display of products.

3   React to local trading conditions and maintain an awareness of local competitors' activity, i.e. changes to trading hours, promotions, intended new store openings. Exercise judgement to take initiatives in response which will increase sales, by adjusting ordering, employing temporary staff or changing staff hours to compensate for the expected increase/decrease in trade levels.

4   Organize, control and monitor management and non-management human resources throughout the store to ensure that the correct operational and trading standards are achieved throughout the day. Monitor and action improvements to productivity to achieve required levels. Organize management schedules to ensure that a suitable member of management is available during all trading hours. Ensure that staff are allocated to the correct departments at the appropriate time, and that staff skills level and ability are sufficient to ensure correct trading standards. Continually monitor and amend the store scheduling system.

5   Ensure that the premises, fixtures, fittings and contents are safely and securely maintained in accordance with company

policies and procedures in order to retain the operational viability of the store. Check that store opening and locking up procedures are implemented and that all other aspects of security are followed (e.g. key control, checks on staff shopping, alarm control, control of cash collection from checkouts, storage of reduction labels).

6   Ensure that instructions from head office departments are actioned and that effective communication is maintained with internal departments and external bodies to maximize business efficiency. Report to senior management results of trading, staffing levels, staff training needs, stock and supply data and customer information, and inform of any problems or difficulties which could impact on the smooth running of the business. Provides information on request to visiting Trading Standards Inspectorate, environmental health officers etc., correctly representing the company's trading policy/practices.

7   Ensure that company hygiene and safety regulations are fully communicated, understood and actioned in all departments and that all statutory requirements are adhered to. Examine standards of training and work practices, monitor accident rates and ensure that legal requirements to notify the local authority of accidents are met. Ensure that all equipment and staff comply fully with company and statutory requirements and that the regulations of the Food Safety Act (including training of food handlers) are enforced.

31 October

The final meeting takes place to decide which of the two managers will be offered the position of branch manager. Five people are present. The district manager for the new store, Tony Hill, is also John Goodwin's current district manager. Tony has known John Goodwin for about a year and strongly believes that John is the right man for the job. Another district manager, Steven Burton, has been responsible for Paul Mason's development during the past seven years, and is there to fight for Paul's promotion. Additionally, the operations director from head office, Graham Dunn, has developed a keen interest in the new store. His main concern is that, if not controlled properly, the situation could potentially delay the opening and subsequent performance of the new store. He was responsible for fighting for this unusual site and is not prepared to let anything impair its future success. The district personnel manager and the area personnel manager are also present to ensure that a fair decision is made and that no details are overlooked. The committee members have the store trading figures for the two managers before them and they prepare themselves for a lengthy session and debate.

Case Questions

Using material from the case, prepare answers to the following questions:

1   Identify the different measures of performance used in the case. List the specific criteria required to measure the performance of a Sainsbury's branch manager.

2   What are the implications of having the incorrect manager in place?

3   In your opinion, which of the two illustrated stores is performing better and why?

4   You are Graham Dunn, operations director. What questions would you want to ask the two candidates to enable you to make a decision?

5   Evaluate the strengths and weaknesses of each manager, and his qualities in relation to running the proposed new store. Suggest which manager would be most suitable for the position and justify your reasoning.

6   What additional tools or support would you suggest to help the new manager in his position?

18

The Public Relations Side of Recruitment and Selection

Diane Preston

Loughborough University Business School

Introduction

Recruitment and selection is one of a number of activities within human resource management (HRM) which increasingly is being devolved to line managers within an organization. It is sensible that the manager who will be responsible for the effectiveness and development of his or her staff team should be involved in selecting the right candidate for that team. It may be that line managers are not involved in every part of the recruitment and selection process but need to understand the wider implications.

Rather than just being the first stage of an individual's employment with the company, the process of recruitment and selection has to be considered in a wider context. Decisions by the company at this stage have to be made on the basis of the employee's potential, needs for training and development and suitability for career progression; that is, not just on the person's current abilities. From the company point of view, recruitment and selection represents a substantial investment in an individual and it is important that the right impression is given of the company both through the recruitment and selection process and in the early weeks of employment, so that the employee feels that he or she wants to stay with the company. The recruitment process is often presented as a one-way process with the employer choosing the lucky applicant but, more realistically (and particularly in an area where there is a shortage of labour), it is a reciprocal process in which potential employees decide which company appears to offer the most attractive package. The individual's decision will be based upon his or her assumptions about the prospective employer, influenced to some extent by participation in the recruitment and selection process. This case takes the specific example of a graduate recruitment department within a major retailing company, J. Sainsbury plc.

Background

Almost all elements of HRM can be seen from the perspective of providing an opportunity to tell individuals within or external to a company something about what that company stands for. In a performance appraisal interview, for example, the criteria against which employees are appraised can be used to set out what is expected of them. The content and design of a training programme can demonstrate to participants desired ways of working; for example, achieving team based objectives.

Recruitment and Selection

Personnel management textbooks tend to offer fairly prescriptive models of recruitment and selection, where the requirements of an individual job within an company are carefully analysed and a systematic search process is initiated on the basis of this information. Recruitment and selection has been defined as 'searching for and obtaining potential job candidates in sufficient numbers and quality so that the company can select the most appropriate people to fill its job needs' (Dowling and Schuler, 1990). The early stages of recruitment would probably follow a pattern similar to the one below.

- *Authorization*: getting permission to create or fill a post within the company is important; recruitment and selection involves time and resources.

- *Job analysis*: a thorough analysis of the job must be carried out in order to understand exactly what is required and who would be the best type of person to fill the post. It is important to recognize that the job is unlikely to be exactly the same as it was when the previous person started. Information for the job analysis could be obtained from personnel records, other people who have done the job in the past or have some involvement in it and the person leaving the company.

- *Terms and conditions agreed*: a job description and terms of employment will probably be the next stage which is likely to be carried out by personnel specialists within the company.

- *Decide target groups*: when a clear understanding of the job itself has been gained, it is then possible to know the type of people you hope will apply. This could be individuals already with the company (in-house recruitment) and/or external to it.

- *Decide appropriate recruitment methods*: the appropriateness will clearly depend on the type of job being recruited.

- *Design a job advertisement*: this may be carried out by the personnel department or an external agency. The key features should be an unambiguous statement of the key facts about the job, the type of person likely to be suitable and clear instructions as to where to apply and in what form (c.v.'s, application forms etc.)

Recruitment and selection, like every other part of the personnel or HRM process, has to form part of the company's overall manpower plan. This is basically an overview of the people requirements of the company now and in the future, and is obtained by assessing the numbers of people in the company, where they are, what skills they have now and those which they, individually and collectively, will need to acquire. From the manpower plan, current and future HRM plans can be drawn up. All this has to be completed in the context of the strategic, future plans of the company; for example, are there plans to expand certain departments, open new sites, replace old machinery or technology? The company manpower plan has to ensure that the right numbers of people (or human resources) are, or will be, available with the right sorts of skills to enable such strategic plans to be executed. This is important to understand when one is thinking about recruitment and selection and is often the basis of criticism levelled at prescriptive models, which tend to assume that the recruitment and selection process takes place in the current, static environment. Certainly, the different stages have to be planned carefully, with all eventualities considered, but it also has to be carried out in this wider context.

In a similar way, the recruitment and selection process can send messages to applicants about the company and what it might be like to work there. Whoever is involved in the process is, in effect, a representative of the company and what it stands for. This could be the individual line manager who gets involved in recruiting a new member of his or her team or an individual within the HRM department whose responsibilities include recruiting new employees into the organization. Recruitment and selection is perhaps one of the most crucial stages of HRM in that it is the point at which prior and/or initial expectations are formed or broken.

> Our department has in effect a marketing role for the company . . . an awful lot of what we do is just company marketing. (Graduate Recruitment Manager, Sainsbury's)

The Case

STAGES OF RECRUITMENT AND SELECTION AT SAINSBURY'S

Like most other good employers, Sainsbury's invests a lot of time and money in the recruitment process. This is very necessary in a retailing company of this size, where there are hundreds of stores to be staffed with individuals often working under different forms of employment, such as part-time, shift and evening work. Clearly, for each type and level of employee within the company there are likely to be slightly different recruitment and selection processes, which will be based on the identification of different characteristics and skills in the applicants considered. This case focuses upon the recruitment of graduates into the company as trainee managers.

The stages of the graduate recruitment process at Sainsburys are as follows:

- *Advertising.* Advertising of the company management training scheme through appropriate sources, such as the graduate publications GO, GET, Hobsons Casebook and Student Pages, graduate careers fairs, press advertisements. Careful thought has to be given to questions such as which sources should be used and what type of advertisements will attract graduates to apply. What words, colours, symbols will make the company attractive as an employer, yet say something about the job on offer? (See activity idea at the end of the case study.)

- *Processing of completed application forms.* The application forms are carefully designed by the company to ensure that all the information needed about each candidate is covered by the different questions asked. Sainsbury's has compiled a list of key skills (sometimes termed management competencies) which form the basis of what the company is looking for in potential trainee managers. Through the answers given and key words used on the application form, it is possible to ascertain whether each applicant shows experience or evidence of potential in these areas. Applicants are selected on a points systems, where the candidate's qualifications, elected positions of responsibility, previous work experience and so on are allocated different numbers of points. Applicants scoring high on the points system are sent a letter inviting them to attend for an interview.

- *Invitation for first interviews offered to suitable candidates.* These interviews used to be carried out by staff from the graduate recruitment department but are now held in store by managers (with all arrangements being made by the department before-hand). The intention of this is to allow graduates to see a store in action and to get a more realistic impression of the job they are applying for.

- *Assessment centre.* Successful applicants are invited to attend an assessment centre, which comprises a series of activities for the candidate, including psychometric tests and group and problem solving exercises. These have been designed by the members of the graduate training department based upon the management competencies required for the role of a retailing manager within the company.

All of the above stages are considered by the company to be important in helping to provide a positive image or advertisement for the company. They are keen that not only are graduates attracted to the company, but that they get a realistic picture of what it would be like to work there and what the role of a trainee manager within a Sainsbury's store entails. As mentioned above, interviews for the job are now carried out by store managers within a store rather than at head office level. The assessment centre has been carefully redesigned on the basis of identified management competencies both to get a better idea of how the applicant would cope with the job and to give some indication to participants of the types of roles they would have to perform and the skills required.

USING THE RECRUITMENT PROCESS AS A PR EXERCISE

The belief within the graduate recruitment department at Sainsburys is that an extremely important part of their role is to attempt to market the company to graduates and external institutions in the most effective way possible. This is not only in terms of wanting to encourage graduates to think about embarking upon a career in retailing or to apply to the company specifically, but in a much broader sense by communicating positive images of the company. A good deal of the departmental budget is allocated to these marketing purposes, which includes sponsorship of retailing degrees (like the retail management degree at Loughborough University Business School), allocation of grants to projects aimed at increasing the understanding of the retailing sector and the giving of talks and presentations at university career fairs or perhaps as part of institutional teaching sessions.

> The indirect marketing effect ranges from everything, from the shopping experience and the uniforms – if people come and see you in brown crimplene suits they don't want to come and work for you – through to their experiences at school and on work experience, through to our image when we go out on careers fairs and how they're dealt with in the recruitment process. This is apart from what happens to them when they start. (Graduate Recruitment Manager, Sainsbury's)

SUMMARY AND CONCLUSION

Using an actual example of a graduate recruitment process, this case study highlights the key considerations for a manager involved in the recruitment and selection process and also encourages students to think about the activities involved from an alternative perspective. The process of recruitment has two main aims; first, to attract and retain the interest of suitable applicants; second, to project a positive image of the company to those applicants who come into contact with it. In order to achieve both aims, careful planning is required at all the different stages of the recruitment and selection process. Sainsbury's uses a typical series of stages through which graduate trainee managers are selected, but the company has clearly thought about the effect each stage has on the people who participate. Too often, recruitment and selection is thought of as a

fairly simple process – someone leaves the company, and a replace-
ment is needed – but companies operate in an ever changing
environment and the requirements for the job, and even the job
itself, may have altered considerably since the previous incumbent
started. Even if an applicant does not get the job, recruitment and
selection offers a company the opportunity to present itself in a
good light. It is the first, and perhaps only, contact that person will
have with the company; this case suggests that it can be utilized to
good effect in helping to promote a positive impression for customers of the future.

Activity Ideas

1   Imagine that you are a HRM manager or a manager seconded to
    the HRM department. How could you ensure that the messages
    you intend to promote about your company will be understood
    by the graduates at a recruitment fair? To enable you to consider
    this problem: (a) choose a particular job within the retailing
    sector; (b) draw up a list of things you feel it would be important
    for graduates to know about it; (c) from this extended list,
    identify what you feel are the key words which you would need
    and want to get across to applicants in order to portray a
    positive picture of the company as an employer.

2   Suggested additional group activity: design two or three posters
    using pictures or images which portray the company and which
    would be suitable to use at graduate careers fairs.

3   Think through the different stages of the recruitment and
    selection process (identified in the case) and their potential
    impact on individuals in a marketing or PR sense. What could
    you do differently to encourage certain types of graduates to
    apply to your company for a career in retailing? To take two
    examples, what would you do differently at each or any stage to
    increase the number of male graduates who apply to the com-
    pany or to increase the number of applicants from a particular
    ethnic group?

4   Create an advertisement using the words, colours and pictures
    which you feel would market the company to a particular group
    of the population in the most effective and positive way. Each
    group could prepare two or more mock-up advertisements, with

a plenary vote at the end to decide the best one. In the choice of the 'winner', consideration would have to be given to *where* the advertisement would be placed, to whom (if anyone in particular) the advert would be targeted and so on.

5   Design an assessment centre of one to two days in length which includes different types of exercises and will help you to assess different management competences in individual applicants. Be prepared to present the outline of the assessment centre to the rest of the group and to be able to explain and justify your choice of activities.

Reference

Dowling, P.J. and Schuler, R.S. (1990) *International Dimensions of HRM.* Boston, PWS-Kent.

Index